THE HARTFORD OF HARTFORD

An Insurance Company's
Part in a Century and a Half
of American History

The Home Office of the Hartford Fire Insurance Company Group
in Hartford, Connecticut, from 1930 etching by Louis Orr.

THE HARTFORD

OF HARTFORD

*An Insurance Company's
Part in a Century and a Half
of American History*

HAWTHORNE DANIEL

RANDOM HOUSE • New York

INTRODUCTION

A HUNDRED AND FIFTY YEARS is no inconsiderable period of time. Even in the history of nations no century and a half has ever passed without having left its mark, and when, as now and again occurs, some business enterprise has been active and successful for so long, it is not to be doubted that it has contributed something of value to the field of which it is a part. In fact, it may have done far more than that for, having itself succeeded, it will also have had some influence even outside its own particular field, and the more far-ranging and beneficial its activities have been the more it will have contributed to the good of all.

No business enterprise of whatsoever kind can exist entirely to itself. Even the most self-centered haggler in the market place must deal with others as he buys or sells. But success—and especially success throughout any considerable period of time—requires an understanding of the fact that with each purchase, the seller should include something that the purchaser may not consciously have come to buy. Quality, value, and usefulness the customer may properly expect, but if, in addition, the seller adds real and sympathetic understanding of the buyer's needs, he will have contributed importantly to his client's satisfaction and, as a result, to his own success.

In the pages that follow, Hawthorne Daniel has told in some detail the story of the Hartford Fire Insurance Company which, as of June 27, 1960, had been in active and continuous existence for one hundred and fifty years. But this company's activities have been intimately connected with the growth and development of the United States and Canada, and, from time to time, other nations have also benefited from what it has been privileged to do. Many times in its long history the Company has played a useful and even a dramatic part when major and minor tragedies have struck in many lands.

Thus the account that follows is something more than merely the history of the Company. Its growth and development would have been impossible without the corresponding growth and development of the nations in which it has principally operated and which it mirrors. The Company justifiably prides itself on the fact that its history, as the following pages show, has been intimately a part of the greater history of these nations.

President and Chairman of Finance Committee

TABLE OF CONTENTS

CONTENTS

THE HARTFORD OF HARTFORD

CHAPTER 1

THE UNITED STATES

BEFORE 1810

WITHIN a generation of the signing of the Declaration of Independence surprising changes had taken place in the new United States. In 1775 hardly more than three million people made up the population of the thirteen colonies, and only a handful had as yet crossed the mountains to the little known lands that lay farther to the west. But by 1810 the population of the new republic had grown beyond the seven million mark, and the western frontier, which had been established at the Mississippi River when the Revolutionary War ended, had been pushed enormously farther toward the distant Pacific Coast by Thomas Jefferson's purchase of the Louisiana Territory.

Growth and development were evident almost everywhere. Four new states had been added to the federated union, and though the older and more heavily settled region along the Atlantic Coast still dominated the nation, more than a million energetic people had already found their way to the newer lands of the interior, and eager streams of others were following by every route that led into the West.

Despite this great migration, the coastal areas were also growing. In twenty years the population of Pennsylvania had almost doubled. New York State had tripled its population in two decades and a half, and in 1810 stood second only to Virginia which, within another year or two, it was due to pass. During these same years population increases were evident in every other state as well, although New England's growth, largely because the West attracted so many of its people, was sharply less than that of any other portion of the country. In Connecticut, in fact, where the rate of growth was lowest, the population had increased only four per cent in the decade prior to 1810.

For a score of years Europe had been continuously troubled by revolution and by war. During much of this time trade and commerce had been restricted, and such emigration to America as might otherwise have developed had largely been cut off. Thus the growth of the American population throughout this period had been due primarily to the high birth rate of the youthful nation and to economic causes that were not widely understood at the time.

The fact is that the industrial revolution had long been under way. In America, it is true, the people as a whole were little conscious of it, for it was in England that the most important developments in this field were taking place. But industrial developments were apparent even in America, primarily agricultural though the nation was. In Connecticut, for example, small products made of iron—nails, chain, hinges, and the like—had been manufactured in slowly increasing quantities since long before the Revolutionary War. The Hartford County village of Berlin had begun the manufacture of tinware in 1740, and tinware peddlers from Connecticut, selling small articles made of iron and steel as well, were to continue their activities throughout most of rural America for a century or more. Clockmakers, too, had long been busy in Connecticut, and even as early as 1732 hatters in London were uncomfortably aware of their Connecticut competitors.

Throughout the eighteenth century American industries were invariably small, but once the Revolutionary War had ended they began to increase both in number and in size. Even during the Revolution the fabrication of metal products had increased, and in both Norwich and East Hartford paper continued to be made, as well. In 1778 the first New England woolen mill began operations in Hartford. Two years later, in Pawtucket, Rhode Island, Samuel Slater, an immigrant from England, erected the first American cotton mill, and in 1793, when Eli Whitney, a graduate of Yale, invented the cotton gin, he not only assured the widespread development of cotton plantations in the South, but also played a vital part in the expansion of cotton manufacturing in both England and New England.

Meanwhile, shipping was rapidly expanding, aiding as well as being aided by the vigorous development of American trade and commerce.

Even in pre-Revolutionary days, when troublesome trade restrictions had been imposed on all their colonies by England, France, and Spain, New England traders, who were often willing to engage in more or less smuggling on the way, had regularly sent their ships to the West Indies. Among these islands they had profitably exchanged such New England products as salt fish and barrel staves for sugar, molasses, and rum; and this trade now continued. In fact, American ships found new and more profitable opportunities in this region, for Europe's constantly recurring wars tended to drive both British and French merchant ships from these waters. Furthermore, the Revolutionary War had hardly been concluded when venturesome American shipowners also began to send their ships on extended voyages that ultimately took them all around the world.

Much of this trade was highly profitable, and this was especially the case when ships from Boston voyaged out around Cape Horn to the newly discovered fur-producing region of the Pacific Northwest, sailing on from there to China, and returning, finally, by way of the Cape of Good Hope. In this colorful three-way trade certain Boston families began the accumulation of wealth on a scale that was unprecedented so far as America was concerned. And, with such an example before them, other shipowners—in Salem and New York especially but elsewhere as well—worked out new and profitable trading methods of their own.

Though New England and New York had built and operated ships since very early in their history, Maryland and Virginia had always led their sister colonies in exports, and they continued to do so even after independence had been won. This was owing primarily to their production of tobacco, the European demand for which had steadily increased during the better part of two centuries. During the final decade of the eighteenth century, however, new developments in America's foreign trade began to change the economic balance of the nation.

In 1790 tobacco still retained its lead among the nation's exports, but soon thereafter Eli Whitney's newly invented cotton gin brought about so great an increase in the shipment of cotton to the cotton mills of Great Britain and New England as rapidly to increase the wealth and economic importance of the deeper South. During these very years the rapid developments that were taking place in the field of shipping began to bring about an even greater and more rapid increase of wealth in New England and New York.

Europe, it should be remembered, was being greatly troubled by the recurrent wars of these unsettled days. Conditions were so far from normal on the continent that trade and commerce—and merchant shipping especially—were greatly handicapped. Throughout this period, however, the United States succeeded in remaining on the whole neutral, and increasing numbers of American ships consequently found themselves engaged in carrying cargoes that normally would have been transported under other flags. The opportunities were so great, in fact, that the demand for American ships grew enormously, and shipyards were busy all the way from Maryland to Maine. The more advantageously placed American seaports grew, as well. Exports increased, and re-exports increased even more. Where, in 1790, the two combined had been valued at little more than twenty million dollars, with such goods as had been brought to this country for re-export amounting to less than three per cent of the total, by 1799 their combined value was almost eighty million, and more than half of this still growing total was accounted for by products that came to American ports from abroad for transshipment and re-export.

Increasing numbers of American ships, in other words, were profitably carrying the products of far corners of the world to many ports in Europe, and other products were being sent back in exchange. Not infrequently, venturesome American captains deliberately ran Napoleon's paper blockade or Great Britain's real ones with such cargoes, but more often and, in the long run, more profitably, risks were minimized and cargoes were carried first to American ports where, having been transshipped, they were moved somewhat more safely to their final destinations. And this trade, highly profitable as it was, not only played an important part in the expansion of American shipping, but also contributed greatly, in the years immediately ahead, to the widespread industrialization, and the consequent economic leadership, of New England.

In the whole of the new United States, cities of any really great size were few. New York, which far surpassed the others, had tripled its population in twenty years and, by 1810, claimed 96,000 residents. Philadelphia had hardly more than half that number, Boston little more than a third, and no others approached the size of any of these three. However, certain smaller communities that were well located and fortunate in the character and ability of their people, had gained positions of importance that were sometimes disproportionate to their size.

One of these was Hartford, Connecticut. Founded in 1635, this community on the Connecticut River had been made capital of Connecticut in 1662, and by 1810, despite the fact that its population had barely reached 6,000, the town had come to be a community of much more than ordinary consequence. Measured either by its size or commerce it was of minor importance as compared with Boston or New York, nor has it ever approached these two in all the years since then. But for reasons that no one can satisfactorily explain Hartford, despite its modest size and no-more-than-moderate commercial importance, had already shown itself to be intellectually more alert than either of the larger cities. Up to the outbreak of the American Revolution, Boston had been an important center of intellectual activity, and the city had played a wonderfully constructive part in the evolution of the philosophy upon which the Revolution itself had been so largely based. But—and again for reasons that are difficult to trace or understand—Massachusetts produced little that was intellectually important in the three decades that followed the Revolution; and despite the rapid growth of New York, much the same was true there throughout that period. During these years, however, Hartford came to be intellectually so alert and active as almost to stand alone. Noah Webster, for example, was born in West Hartford and, though he spent much of his life elsewhere, it was in Hartford that he did most of his early writing; it was there, too, as well as in New Haven at the same time, that his first dictionary—"A Compendious Dictionary of the English Language, by Noah Webster, Esq."—was published "for Hudson & Goodwin, Book-Sellers, Hartford, and Increase, Cooke & Co., Book-Sellers, New Haven, 1806." It was in Hartford, too, on October 1, 1792, that this same diligent and original writer and thinker offered what appears to have been the very first really thoughtful plan for workmen's compensation and unemployment insurance. It is true that the idea was not adopted, but the very fact that Webster made such a suggestion in order to "give relief to honest, industrious, and frugal people, especially mechanics and other laborers who may be suddenly reduced to want,"* demonstrates how alert one of Hartford's minds was during this period of the town's intellectual leadership. Nor was Noah Webster an isolated mental phenomenon in the little state capital. During these very years the so-called "Hartford Wits"—John Trumbull, Joel Barlow, Timothy Dwight, David Humphreys, Lemuel Hopkins, and others, with

---

* Harry R. Warfel, *Noah Webster, Schoolmaster to America*, The Macmillan Company, 1936, p. 213.

whom Webster himself was more or less closely associated—added to the sprightliness of Hartford's atmosphere; and any real understanding of human nature plainly suggests that the alertness and animation of these minds, busy, as they were, in so compact a community, not infrequently struck sparks from other, lesser minds, thus adding to the mental brightness of the whole community.

Nor should it be imagined that the Hartford of that day was concerned only with matters of the mind. The town was fully as commercial as other towns in the state, and was busily engaged in trade. Despite the fact that it lies all of thirty-eight miles up the Connecticut River from Long Island Sound, Hartford had long been a port of consequence. It traded regularly with other ports along the coast, with the West Indies, and, now and then, with Europe, Africa, and even more remote regions. Ships played an important part in its affairs, as a single quotation from the *Connecticut Courant** for January 7, 1793, will demonstrate. It was in the paper of that date that the following report appeared:

THOMAS ALLEN'S MARINE LIST

Thurs. Dec. 27. Pleasant, serene cool morning. Wind N.N.W.

Sail'd, the Beautiful Ship BETTY AND JULIA N. SCOVEL, for Cape Francois.

Brig SALLY, Wm. Waldwell, Barbados.

Brig SAMUEL, B. Bigelow, Surrinam.

Sloop RANDOLPH, T. Wilson, Jun., Port-au-Prince.

Schooner SALLY, Benj. Buel, Africa, with a number of Danish gentlemen, and passengers.

Brig POLLY, Wells, Martinico.

These ships were all small, and their cargoes were in proportion, but any community of that period that could send five ships to the West Indies and South America on a single day, as well as a sixth to Africa, was a seaport of consequence in which overseas trade played a really important part. And this fact is borne out by the many sidelights that were forever to be detected among the small advertisements that the *Connecticut Courant* then so regularly carried.

A typical advertisement—which is especially interesting because of the firm that placed it—appeared in the *Courant* for October 7, 1793. It read as follows:

* Now known as the *Hartford Courant,* it is the oldest continuously published daily in the United States.

SANFORD AND WADSWORTH

Have received by the latest arrivals from England (via New York) an assortment of FALL GOODS, which will be sold by Wholesale, on the lowest terms for Cash or short credit—

   Among which are
Scarlet Broadcloths
Blue   do.
Drab   do.
Brown   do.
Plain and twill'd Coatings
Striped   do.
Green, Crimson, and Red Baizes
White and yellow flannel
Rattinets, Shalloons
Wildbores
Camblets
Callicoes and Chintzes
They have also for sale at the York prices Teneriffe Wine of a superior quality— Malaga do. per Pipe and Quarter Cask— Rum per Hhd.—7 by 9

WINDOW GLASS

Hartford, October 7, 1793.

Two weeks later this identical advertisement reappeared, and in the *Courant* for January 13, 1794, the same firm advertised "High Proof St. Croix Rum which is for sale by the Hhd. for Cash or approved notes at 30 or 60 days." But much more interesting, in view of the subject of this volume, is an advertisement placed by this same company in the *Courant* for April 14, 1794, and repeated on April 28th, May 5th, and May 19th. It read as follows:

HARTFORD FIRE INSURANCE OFFICE

The subscribers have this day opened an Office for the purpose of insuring Houses, Household Furniture, Goods, Wares, Merchandise, &c. against Fire.

SANFORD & WADSWORTH

Hartford, 10th March, 1794.

THE BEGINNINGS

OF INSURANCE

IN AMERICA

A<small>S IF</small> to show that their new venture into the field of fire insurance in no way interfered with their former activities, Sanford and Wadsworth placed the following notice in the *Connecticut Courant* for April 7th:

> *SANFORD AND WADSWORTH*
> Have for sale, by the chest
> Hyson
> Souchong and } Teas, of a good quality
> Behen
> *Hartford, 24th March, 1794.*

During June and July of that year this firm repeatedly advertised other imported goods for sale, adding, each time their ad appeared, "Cash and the highest price paid for Pot and Pearl ashes." And then, in the *Courant* for July 21st, another notice, which was given a position immediately below a Sanford and Wadsworth advertisement that listed some new goods just imported from London, read as follows:

> *NOTICE*
> That a Company is formed under the name and Firm of The Connecticut Insurance Company
> For the purpose of
> Underwriting on Vessels, Merchandise &c.
> Any person wishing to get their property insured, will please to apply to
> John Caldwell, at Hartford.
> *June 30, 1794.*

Even without looking further through the files of the *Courant* it can be seen that insurance was a subject with which the community was reasonably familiar at this period, which was only five years after George Washington had first been inaugurated as President. And in this regard Hartford was in no sense unique. Although insurance had developed little prior to this time, the basic idea was far from new. Demosthenes, writing in the fourth century, B.C., told how the Greeks of that day advanced money on ships or cargoes, the loans to be repaid with large interest if the voyage prospered, but not to be repaid at all in case such ships were lost. In arrangements of this kind the rate of interest was high enough to pay not only for the use of the capital, but also for the risk of losing it, and loans of this nature have been common ever since. Furthermore, even the direct insurance of ships and cargoes, paid for by premiums, was well known in Flanders as early as the beginning of the fourteenth century.

Fire insurance, it is true, had a later beginning. Vague references here and there tell of its being in use in certain European cities during the sixteenth century but the methods of that day were crude and our knowledge of them is indefinite. In 1635, however, and again in 1638, certain Londoners petitioned Charles I for a patent of monopoly to insure houses at the rate of one shilling yearly for each £20 of rent, the association to rebuild or repair those structures that were burned, as well as to maintain a perpetual fire watch, and to contribute £200 annually toward the rebuilding of St. Paul's Cathedral.

This idea failed of acceptance at the time, but the Great Fire of London, which took place in 1666, brought about developments that resulted in the opening of an office "at the back of the Royal Exchange" to insure structures against fire. Other developments followed as the idea took hold. However, the eighteenth century was well advanced before insurance of any kind developed on a consequential scale in America. The first fire insurance company in America—The Philadelphia Contributorship for the Insurance of Houses from Losses by Fire—was organized in 1752 by Benjamin Franklin and some of his Philadelphia associates, and the first policy was issued on June 1st of that year. But in 1802, when Noah Webster, whose mind was active and whose interests were wide, wrote a report on the development of insurance in the United States, he was able to list nineteen companies that were then in existence, though some of his information about them was either frag-mentary or vague.

Most of the companies to which Webster referred appear to have confined themselves to marine insurance, though some were active in other fields as well. In referring to the United Insurance Company of New York, for instance, he pointed out that it was formed "at the close of 1795 or beginning of 1796," and that "the company is authorized to make insurance on vessels, freight, and goods, on buildings, goods and furniture—on lives and for ransom of persons in captivity—and in cases of money lent on bottomry and respondentia."*

Other companies among those listed by Webster operated in fields that were equally broad, though some confined themselves more nar-rowly—to "sea risks," for example, or, as was true of the Mutual Assur-ance Company of New York, to "insuring buildings against fire." The dates Webster gives for the organization of these companies range from 1794, when the Baltimore Equitable Society was organized, to 1801, when the Marine Insurance Company of New York was formed. Be-cause this report was published in 1802, it contains no information about companies that were organized later. Oddly enough, only one Connecti-cut company—the New Haven Insurance Company—is among those named. This firm had been established by a certain Elias Shipman who had earlier been associated with a partnership that had called itself the Hartford and New Haven Insurance Company. And even this company had evolved from a still earlier one—the very one, in fact, that had called itself the Hartford Fire Insurance Company when, under the sponsor-ship of the firm of Sanford & Wadsworth, it had "opened an Office for the purpose of insuring Houses, Household Furniture, Goods, Wares, Merchandise, &c. against Fire" in Hartford on March 10, 1794.

However, Webster himself realized that his report was incomplete. "In considering the extent of the business of insurance," he concluded, "it should be remembered that a very great part of it is done by indi-vidual underwriters—but what proportion of it cannot easily be known." This was true in Hartford as well as elsewhere for, as yet, underwriters—whether individuals, groups, or chartered companies—were disinclined to accept insurance risks of any kind unless they personally knew and approved the character of those who wished to be insured. On that

---

* *Respondentia*—a loan upon goods laden on a ship, to be repaid, with interest, only in the event of the safe arrival of the goods or some part of them. It differs from bottomry which is a loan on the ship itself.

account, insurance was apt to be a purely local matter, for it was unusual for the personal reputation of any applicant to be known in enough detail except in the community of which he was a part.

It has been said, though on what appears to be inadequate grounds, that underwriting in Connecticut began in the 1790's. There is no doubt that the insurance business of the state expanded in that decade, but increasing numbers of Connecticut ships had been trading with the West Indies, and even with Europe, for a century and a half. These ships were small, too, and their owners were forever conscious of the dangers of the sea. It is not to be doubted, therefore, that marine insurance which in its various forms had been familiar to seafaring people for centuries, had long played some part in these voyages. As a matter of fact, by the 1790's, marine insurance commonly covered a very wide range of risks, insurers being known, at least in some instances, to have agreed to insure ships and cargoes against "perils of seas, men of war, fires, enemies, pirates, rovers, thieves, jettisons, letters of mart (marque) and counter-mart, surprizals, takings at sea, arrests, restraints, and detainments of all kings, princes, or people of what nation, condition or quality soever; baraty (barratry) of the master (unless the assured be the owner of the vessel) and mariners, and all other losses, perils and misfortunes, that have or shall come to the hurt, detriment or damage of the said vessel or any part thereof, for which assurers are legally accountable."*

Coverage itemized in such detail bears witness to the fact that those who wrote such policies were men of experience, and that insurance of this nature was in no sense new. As a matter of fact, even fire insurance, by this time, had been developing in England for more than a century, and though the United States had as yet developed nothing that compared with the more experienced English companies, the idea was well known. When Sanford and Wadsworth opened "The Hartford Fire Insurance Office," therefore, it was not in furtherance of a new and utterly untried idea. In fact, this very company had itself sold at least two policies prior to the actual opening of the office; and it is worth noting that these policies—or at least the second of them, for the first has disappeared and has probably been destroyed—were made out on printed forms in which blank spaces were left for the insertion of such details as could not be known in advance.

This policy—Policy No. 2—which covered a house belonging to Wil-

* P. Henry Woodward, *Insurance in Connecticut*, D. H. Hurd & Co., p. 3.

liam Imlay, of Hartford, is still in existence. Bearing the date of February 8, 1794, and insuring Imlay's house for £800, it is signed by "Sanford & Wadsworth for the Hartford Fire Insurance Company."*

It would appear from this that the Hartford Fire Insurance Company with which this volume is especially concerned was in existence at this time. But such was not the case. It was not until sixteen years later that that company obtained a charter from the state and opened its office for business. At this time Sanford & Wadsworth either signed this document for themselves, which, because of the size of the policy, is unlikely, or signed for themselves and a group of others. And, whatever the arrangement may have been, we know that the Hartford Fire Insurance Company of that day was no more than a partnership. Furthermore, it was a partnership that proved to be only temporary, for on July 27, 1795, it disappeared, giving way to another partnership that was formed "for the purpose of underwriting on vessels, stock, merchandise, &c., by the firm of the Hartford and New Haven Insurance Company."†

This new company included among its backers not only the firm of Sanford & Wadsworth, but also John Caldwell, who had later announced the organization of the Connecticut Insurance Company. Included as well were Jeremiah Wadsworth and John Morgan of Hartford, and Elias Shipman of New Haven. Exactly how these partners carried on this new enterprise is not clear, but Elias Shipman and John Caldwell conducted the business of the company in New Haven and Hartford respectively. In 1798, however, the firm of Sanford & Wadsworth was dissolved and, possibly because of this, the Hartford and New Haven Insurance Company also disappeared. And now Elias Shipman organized the New Haven Insurance Company. It was to this company that Noah Webster referred in the account of insurance that he published in 1802, but it is worth noting that in Hartford no new insurance company came into existence at this time. It is possible that fire insurance policies continued to be written there by independent groups of underwriters. Certainly this was true of marine policies, the demand for which was reasonably steady. A certain Ezekiel Williams, Jr., seems to have been a leader in this field, and it was often around him that the always changing groups of underwriters formed. John Caldwell, who had long been interested in insurance, and who was not only a successful merchant but was also

---

* For the full text of this famous policy, see Appendix 1, p. 280.
† Woodward, *Insurance in Connecticut*, p. 2.

a member of the legislature and, for a time, Major of the Governor's Horse Guards, appears to have been most frequently a member of these groups. But there were many others. Such groups often numbered ten or a dozen or even more, and the shares they normally underwrote ranged from fifty dollars or thereabouts to five or six hundred dollars or even more. The methods they followed, of course, necessitated much detailed investigation and other work, and though policies continued to be written it was only natural that the time would come when, in an effort to simplify the work involved, a new partnership would be formed.

For five years such insurance as was sold in Hartford was handled by various groups of individual underwriters, but in 1803 the Hartford Insurance Company was chartered. The charter was not actually approved until October of that year, but within the next two months the first stockholders' meeting had been called and John Caldwell had been elected president. Normand Knox, cashier of the Hartford Bank, was elected secretary, and the office the Company now opened was in a building that adjoined the Hartford Bank on the south side of Pearl Street near Main. Although the Company had been incorporated as the Hartford Insurance Company, its business was exclusively marine and it was invariably known, even on its own policies, as the Hartford Marine Insurance Company.

Elsewhere in Connecticut, too,—in Norwich, Middletown, and New London—other marine insurance companies were being formed. For a time, because of the continued expansion of American shipping, they found their business profitable. Napoleon, however, was keeping Europe in constant turmoil, and Great Britain, opposing him as best she could, invoked the so-called "Rule of 1756." This held that neutral nations could not carry on in wartime any trade that was denied them in times of peace, and under it the British contended that American ships were not to carry to France any of the products of France's West Indian possessions. Even such products as were first brought to American ports and then reshipped were said to be covered by this rule, and under it British warships captured scores—even hundreds—of American ships, taking them into British ports where they were sold after their cargoes had been confiscated.

Despite attempts to settle the difficulties that arose because of these actions, all diplomatic negotiations failed, and in 1806 Great Britain's "Orders in Council" and Napoleon's "Berlin Decree" confronted Americans with a serious situation. More and more American ships were being seized and taken into British and French ports—917 fell to the British and 558 to the French in the nine-year period that preceded the outbreak of the War of 1812—and the British insistently boarded other American ships on the high seas, seizing and removing any sailors who were thought to be British.

There was far more to the problem than can be outlined here, but when, on June 22, 1807, the British frigate *Leopard* unexpectedly fired on, and then boarded and removed four men from, the American frigate *Chesapeake,* action of some kind had to be taken.

Already Congress had passed a Non-Importation Act. But now, although President Jefferson was convinced that war was likely to come eventually, he hoped to hold it off for a time by cutting off American trade with Britain. With this in mind he asked Congress to enact an Embargo Act, and this was done on December 22, 1807.

The effects of this new law were very uneven. Many American ships were able to avoid it entirely merely by staying outside American jurisdiction. The risks they ran, of course, increased materially, but their profits grew as well. Many other ships, however, tied up in American harbors at the time the Act went into effect, were unable to move at all, and their owners, in many cases, were ruined. Furthermore, the prices of those American products that were important in the nation's export trade fell enormously. It has been said that New England's exports, which exceeded $24,000,000 in 1807, dropped to about $6,000,000 in 1808, while the decrease was even greater in the Middle Atlantic states, and greater still in the South.

By 1809 opposition to the Embargo Act had grown so great that it was repealed. Another bill was passed prohibiting trade with both France and Great Britain until one or both of them rescinded their objectionable orders and decrees. In the meantime, however, much economic damage had been done, and among the concerns that had suffered most were the new and very small marine insurance companies which, a few years earlier, had shown so much promise.

For a few months the situation took on a rosier look. The British Minister in Washington, going beyond his instructions in doing so, agreed that England would withdraw the objectionable Orders in Council if the United States would reopen trade with the British Isles. London, however, repudiated the agreement and James Madison, who had succeeded Thomas Jefferson as President earlier that year, was forced to issue a Proclamation of Non-Intercourse with England, thus continuing and even aggravating the situation that had already so greatly interfered with the activities of American shipowners and traders.

American trade and commerce were so greatly harmed by the Embargo Act and the Proclamation of Non-Intercourse that followed it that the duties collected on imports at the Connecticut port of New London dropped from $201,838 in 1807 to $22,343 in 1810. Nor was it only among shipowners and traders that distress was felt. Throughout the whole country comparable effects were evident, and marine insurance in Connecticut and elsewhere was especially hard hit as foreign trade declined.

Thus 1810 opened with no great promise. And as we look back at that remote era after the passage of a hundred and fifty years it seems surprising that the foundation was about to be laid for what is now one of America's oldest and most successful enterprises.

CHAPTER 3

THE FOUNDING

OF A COMPANY

IN HARTFORD

O N Wednesday, June 6, 1810, the *Connecticut Courant* reported the adjournment, one week earlier, of "the Hon. Assembly of this State" after a session of twenty-one days, and listed, without comment, the thirteen acts that had been passed. Nine of these were mere additions to or modifications of earlier acts. A tenth aimed at preventing the removal of the bodies of deceased persons "from the place of their sepulture." Another regulated the measure of charcoal, and the remaining two were acts of incorporation. One of these authorized the incorporation of the Humphreysville Manufacturing Company, though the *Courant* gave no inkling of what the company was to manufacture, and the other was "An Act to incorporate the Hartford Fire Insurance Company."*

As passed by the Assembly this act was made up of fifteen numbered paragraphs, and these bear all the marks of having been considered very carefully before the document was submitted for Assembly action. The Assembly, however, obviously devoted very little time to the matter for the Act was passed on the very day the session was first called to order.

It is highly improbable that such speed was accidental. In fact, Walter Mitchell and Henry Terry, both of whom were lawyers, were each paid twenty-five dollars for work they performed in connection with the granting of the charter, and it may well be that their efforts played some part in the prompt action of the Assembly. Even after the act had been passed, of course, it had to be signed by Lyman Law, the Speaker

---

* For the full text of this Act, see Appendix, p. 273.

of the House of Representatives, as well as by John Treadwell, the Governor, but those who were promoting the new insurance company had known for almost a month before the *Courant* made its first fragmentary report of the matter that their plans were progressing satisfactorily.

It is difficult, after the passage of a century and a half, to know who contributed most importantly to the founding of the new company. By the terms of the final paragraph of the Act of Incorporation, Daniel Wadsworth, Daniel Buck, and David Watkinson were authorized to call the first meeting of the stockholders, and it is clear that these three were very active throughout the formative period. But the original list of stockholders numbered eighty-three, and many of Hartford's leading men of business and affairs, as well as ten of the little city's business houses, were included.* Furthermore, the character of Hartford was such that even an enterprise of this nature was based on associations of real intimacy.

By the terms of the Act of Incorporation, the capital stock of the Company was one hundred and fifty thousand dollars, this being divided into three thousand fifty-dollar shares, and no single one of the original stockholders held more than one hundred shares, though three individuals and three commercial firms each held blocks of that size. However, the holdings of certain family groups were larger. David Watkinson, for example, personally held only eighty-five shares, but three other members of the Watkinson family held forty shares each, thus bringing the total Watkinson holdings to two hundred and five. And either by coincidence or design, four members of the Terry family held the same number. For the most part, however, holdings were small, only twenty-three individuals having purchased fifty shares or more, though it is worth noting that these twenty-three controlled 1,570 shares out of the total of 3,000.

In view of the serious economic difficulties that confronted the country in 1810, it may seem surprising that so considerable a stock issue could have been successfully floated in a community so small as Hartford then was. The amount of cash that was actually required, however, was less than might at first appear. By the terms of the Act of Incorporation, purchasers of shares were required to pay only "five per centum" of the value of their stock "in thirty days after the passing of this act, and five per centum more . . . within sixty days after the passing of this

---

* For the complete list of the company's original stockholders and the size of their holdings, see Appendix, p. 276.

act; and the remainder shall be secured by mortgage on real estate, or by indorsed notes payable thirty days after demanded by the president and directors."

In other words, the actual outlay of cash involved in the purchase of each share was only $2.50, with a similar amount to be paid "within sixty days," the remainder being secured by mortgages on real estate and by notes. Thus the cash assets that were available to the Company when the new business began totaled only $7,500, though that sum was doubled in another thirty days. However, this gives a very inadequate picture of the new company's financial backing. It is true that only this limited amount of actual cash was available to it, but it is also true that those who had purchased stock in the Company were men whose industry, honesty, and financial worth were well known in the community. Such mortgages and secured notes as they were willing to sign were sure to be acceptable by those who knew them, and in case of necessity such securities were convertible into cash after little more than nominal delays. Actual cash was then at a premium almost everywhere in the young United States; but modest fortunes, such as existed in some numbers in Hartford, were not uncommon, and these were based, almost without exception, on thrift and prudent management, and hardly at all on speculation. It was on that account that the new insurance company felt confident in disposing of its stock on terms that may appear surprising to investors of the present day.

It was three weeks after the *Courant* had so casually referred to the Assembly's passage of the act incorporating the insurance company that the first meeting of the stockholders was called. Just how important this event was in the minds of the people of Hartford it is impossible to say. The stockholders themselves naturally viewed it in the light of their personal interest, but the community as a whole seems to have given it little attention. Though the firm of Hudson & Goodwin, publishers of the *Connecticut Courant*, had purchased one hundred shares of the stock of the new company, the paper had barely mentioned the passage of the act that made the Company possible. It was probably with some real understanding of the kind of news that would most interest the people of Hartford that the *Courant* had used only nine words in reporting this matter but had followed that compact statement with a noticeably longer item that was undoubtedly of much more general interest.

"One night last week," this report read, "a number of fine sheep, belonging to Mr. Barnard, were killed by dogs in the west part of this town. A rigorous enforcement of our laws relating to dogs, would go far in preventing similar depredations in the future."

But now, with the necessary preliminary work completed, the stockholders of the Hartford Fire Insurance Company were to meet at 10 o'clock on the morning of June 27, 1810, for the purpose of electing the Company's first Board of Directors.

This meeting had been called by Daniel Wadsworth, Daniel Buck, and David Watkinson in whose hands that responsibility had been placed by the Act of Incorporation, and arrangements had been made for the stockholders to assemble at Ransom's Inn which stood among its elms not far from most of the town's warehouses near the Connecticut River, and only a little way north of the Statehouse Green.

This inn, though less impressive than the dignified Statehouse, seems to have been unsurpassed by any other structure in Hartford. Originally built as a residence by John Morgan in 1794, it had been widely known as one of the finest homes in Connecticut. In the course of a comparatively few years, however, it had changed hands and by 1810, under Amos Ransom's management, it had earned a reputation as one of the best inns between Boston and New York. Furthermore, it had established itself as a favorite meeting place for the business and professional men of Hartford, and it was in its handsome third-floor ballroom that those who constituted Hartford's most select social group held their fortnightly "assemblies" during January, February, and March of each year. These assemblies, which usually began at seven o'clock in the evening, and ordinarily continued until two, were among the most important of Hartford's social events, and the large, oval mirrors that hung at each end of the ballroom reflected not only the comfortable, recessed window seats and the room's three large chandeliers, but also such impressive gatherings of Hartford's social leaders that one of the members felt justified in writing to a friend that "our Assemblies are most brilliant," adding that "at the last there were forty ladies in most superb attire."

No doubt the stockholders' meeting of June 27, 1810, was much less "brilliant" than any of these assemblies. Still, at least twenty of the stockholders of the new company, and probably more, were Assembly "subscribers," and as such were fully as much at home in one of these gatherings as in the other. We do not know, unfortunately, just how many stockholders attended this first meeting, and it is improbable that all of

them were present. However, the well-preserved pages of the Hartford
Fire Insurance Company's leather-bound and historic record book give
the essence of what took place.

An important early entry in this old book, written clearly with the
quill pen of one Walter Mitchell who evidently had been appointed
Secretary of the meeting, reads as follows:

> At a meeting of the Stockholders of *"The Hartford Fire
> Insurance Company"* at the House of Amos Ransom, Inn-
> Holder in the City of Hartford, on the twenty-seventh day of
> June, One thousand eight hundred and ten, the following
> persons were chosen Directors of said Company—viz—
>
> > Nathaniel Terry
> > Nathaniel Patten
> > David Watkinson
> > Daniel Buck
> > Thomas Glover
> > Thomas K. Brace
> > James H. Wells
> > Ward Woodbridge
> > Henry Hudson

So far as the record shows, no other action was taken at this first
meeting of the Company's stockholders, but when it adjourned, a meeting of the newly elected Directors was immediately called and the record
book reports their actions as follows:

> At a Meeting of the Directors of the Hartford Fire In-
> surance Company at the House of Amos Ransom in the City
> of Hartford on the 27th Day of June 1810—
>
> > Nathaniel Terry, Esqe., was chosen President
> > Walter Mitchell was appointed Secretary
>
> *Voted*—by the President and Directors, That the money
> received upon the first Instalment be deposited in Hartford
> Bank to the credit of "The Hartford Fire Insurance Com-
> pany" until further order.—
>
> *Voted*—That when the money of this Company is drawn
> from Bank, it shall be done by Checks signed by the Presi-
> dent & countersigned by the Secretary.—
>
> *Voted*—That the Meetings of the President and Directors
> be held for the present at the office of Walter Mitchell in
> Hartford.—

Voted—That the Secretary purchase such Books and Stationary as may be necessary for transacting the business of this Company.—

This meeting was adjourned to the 5th Day of July next at 5 o'clock P.M. to be held at the Office of said Company.—

Walter Mitchell, Secry.

Up to this point, the only accomplishment that could be credited to the Hartford Fire Insurance Company was that it had survived its birth. But, in the last analysis, that was all that was necessary at the moment, and as we look back now after the passage of a hundred and fifty busy and constructive years it is obvious that the event was greatly more important than it may have appeared at the time.

Though the principles of marine insurance were reasonably well understood in 1810, fire insurance was quite another matter. Such fire insurance companies as were in existence in the United States at that time were mutual companies for the most part, and they operated only locally. It also appears that no one had any thought that fire risks and fire insurance rates could possibly be based on anything that even approached scientific understanding. Furthermore, in opening its office, the newly organized Hartford Fire Insurance Company, like others of that day, seems to have given less thought to the idea of *selling* policies than to making it possible for those who wanted policies to buy them. And yet it is perfectly clear that the Directors and officers of the new company, and no doubt some of the other stockholders as well, were thoughtfully considering the problems that needed to be solved.

The nine men who were elected Directors of the new company made up an unusually able group. Nathaniel Terry, who was elected President, had graduated from Yale in 1786, after which he studied law, opening an office in Hartford in 1796. He was elected and repeatedly re-elected to the General Assembly, and from 1807 to 1809 was a judge of the county court. In 1802 he was commissioned as a major in the Governor's Foot Guard, and later he was to spend one term as a member of Congress, was to be a delegate to the state convention that drafted a new constitution for Connecticut, was to serve for nine years as president of the Hartford Bank, and was to be elected and re-elected mayor of the city for seven consecutive years. Six feet four inches tall and very erect, he had a manner that was authoritative, which explains why he was often called "General" despite the fact that he never attained higher military rank than major. If the stories that are told of him are true, he was quite capable, on occasion, of knocking a man down; but more commonly, as he made his way to and from his home, he was accompanied by groups of children in whose presence his sternness was little apt to show itself.

Walter Mitchell, who was appointed Secretary of the Company, was not a Director. However, he was one of Hartford's more important lawyers, and had been appointed secretary primarily on that account. His home was in the village of Wethersfield, some four miles south of where he maintained his Hartford office next door to the Hartford Bank and not far from Ransom's Inn. He was a bachelor with a sense of humor and a genial interest in good food, and his comfortable Wethersfield home was run exactly as he liked it to be by his two sisters. Not much given to energetic pastimes, he later grew somewhat corpulent, and his hair, which he wore thrown back from his forehead, was long. He was the son of former United States Senator Stephen Mix Mitchell. Born in 1777, he was only thirty-three when the Hartford Fire Insurance Company was organized.

David Watkinson was English, and had come to America in 1795. In 1800, at the age of 23, he and his brother, William, opened a small hardware business in Hartford, and in the years that followed he succeeded in amassing a fortune that was unusually large for that day. By 1810 he had come to be recognized as an able businessman, and in the years that followed, as his fortune continued to grow, he contributed large sums to the Hartford Library, the Hartford Hospital, the Wadsworth Atheneum, and other institutions.

Daniel Buck, though only 31 in 1810, was already the proprietor of a successful general store, and in later years was to join his brother in the ownership of a steamship line that operated between Hartford and New York City. Thomas Glover was a successful dry-goods merchant and importer whose business was increasing rapidly both at home and abroad. Thomas K. Brace, who had graduated from Yale in 1801, was also only 31 in 1810 but was already the successful head of the wholesale grocery firm of Thomas K. Brace & Company. Nathaniel Patton, a member of the Norwich family of that name, had a successful printing establishment and, by prudent investment, was accumulating a modest fortune. James H. Wells was a dealer in tools, and at the time the Hartford Fire Insur-

NATHANIEL TERRY
President, 1810-1835

ance Company was organized he was manufacturing what he called "patent glass paper," which was paper faced with pulverized glass and intended for use as an abrasive.

Henry Hudson, who, in later years, was to become a manufacturer of paper as well as mayor of Hartford, was the son of Barzillai Hudson, a partner in the firm of Hudson & Goodwin, publishers of the *Connecticut Courant*. And Ward Woodbridge, who was later to become president of the Hartford Bank, was one of the wealthiest men in Hartford, his fortune being based in part on a cotton mill he owned in Massachusetts, but more importantly on the very successful dry-goods and importing firm he operated in Hartford.

Though these were the men who were most directly responsible for the establishment of the new fire insurance company, there was a financial institution in Hartford without which the new company could hardly have succeeded. This was the Hartford Bank—later the Hartford National Bank—which had been originally chartered on June 18, 1792.

Banking in the United States had begun only eleven years before the Hartford Bank was founded, and even in 1802, when Noah Webster published his report on banking and insurance companies in the United States, there were only thirty-three banks in the entire country. The first of these had been the Bank of North America, a Philadelphia institution chartered only a few months after Lord Cornwallis had surrendered in 1781. Founded in an effort to provide the Continental Congress with such means as were required for the prosecution of the War of Independence, it was also helpful to merchants in providing better means of financing than earlier methods had permitted. There had long been individual moneylenders, and the governments of the various colonies had maintained loan offices at which borrowers could obtain "bills of credit" on real estate mortgages. During the Revolution, these loan offices had been taken over by the newly established states, but their activities can hardly be said to have constituted banking except in a rudimentary sense. It was not until the Bank of North America was established that a method was evolved of combining public and private resources in such a way as to provide, by way of the bank's circulating notes, a larger and better stock of money.

Writing in 1802, ten years after the Hartford Bank was founded but while Europe was deeply engaged in the Napoleonic wars, and eight years before the Hartford Fire Insurance Company was chartered, Noah Webster concluded his discussion of banks and insurance companies in the United States with the following paragraph:

"A single remark will conclude this sketch. Within twenty years, in a young country just emerged from the depression of the colonial state, we have seen thirty-three public banks organized and put in operation, with capitals amounting to more than double the sum of circulating specie in the United States at the commencement of that period. We see that specie, or paper supported by it, now actually employed to *quintuple* the amount of the sum employed in 1780. We have seen these banking institutions and the insurance companies so well conducted that their credit has remained unimpaired amidst the enormous depredations on our commerce by the belligerent powers, and the numerous bankruptcies occasioned by those depredations and the vast speculations of our citizens. These facts, while they inspire confidence in the credit of the institutions, evince a degree of ability, diligence and integrity highly honorable to the directors and to the commercial character of the United States."

These early American banks, founded as they were by merchants, devoted themselves chiefly to providing commercial credit. For the most part, their loans were for thirty days or less and contracts for the sale of readily marketable commodities commonly provided the necessary security. It is not surprising that these banks were influential in the communities they served, or that most of them were sound and profitable. The Hartford Bank, for example, was capitalized for $100,000 when it was founded in 1792, but in fifteen years its capital had been increased to $1,000,000, and its stock was selling at a premium. Furthermore, this surprisingly strong financial institution (it must be remembered that a million dollars was a gigantic sum in any American community in 1810) was concerned primarily with Hartford, as the new Hartford Fire Insurance Company also was when it began. Not unnaturally, therefore, these two institutions, and the men who controlled them, were intimately associated from the time the insurance company first came into existence.

Those who founded the new insurance company were convinced of the need of such an institution, but they appear to have given little thought to the idea that anything much in the way of profits would result. No one expected the Company to operate more than temporarily at a loss, but even the most optimistic stockholders apparently looked forward to nothing more than moderate dividends, and even these were not a prime consideration.

Though Hartford was one of Connecticut's most important communities, it was limited in size. It was fortunately located, however, and though its economy, like that of the nation as a whole, was suffering under the impact of the Napoleonic wars, it had more than an average share of wealth. But wealth in the United States in 1810 was apt to be measured in terms quite different from those with which we are familiar today. Surplus funds were rare, and such wealth as existed was most often in the form of real estate, or warehouses and ships, shops and stores and merchandise. Possessions of this nature, however, except for land, were especially susceptible to loss or damage by fire, against which, as yet, no adequate protection had been evolved.

The ever-present danger of fire that confronted the people of that day becomes a little more apparent when we remember that open flames were almost omnipresent. Heating, for the most part, was still by wood-burning fireplaces, though stoves were slowly coming into use, and lighting was still by candle and whale oil lamp. Furthermore, matches had not yet been invented, and because striking a light by the use of flint, steel, and tinder box was apt to be a difficult and long-drawn process, burning coals were commonly carried on shovels from one room—or even one house—to another when fires were to be lighted. So common was this practice, in fact, that Benjamin Franklin warned against it, pointing out that "scraps of fire might fall into crevices and make no appearance until midnight, when your stairs being in flames you might be forced to leap out the window and hazard a broken neck in order to avoid being over-roasted."

Most houses, too, were built of wood, and even buildings which had walls of brick or stone utilized wooden beams, as well as wooden floors and rafters. Furthermore, no central water supply systems were in use as yet, and such "fire engines" as existed were mere hand-operated pumps that threw thin and ineffective streams of water from nozzles that were usually mounted on small, wheeled, wooden tanks. Water for these tanks was ordinarily supplied by volunteer bucket brigades that depended on whatever stream or pump or well was nearest.

Under such conditions it is not surprising that fires were frequent, and the losses that resulted were sometimes tragically complete. Between night and morning homes and successful businesses sometimes disappeared in flames, carrying with them the wealth and security that had resulted from years of labor and successful enterprise. Every man of property had some appreciation of this danger, and those who subscribed to the stock of the Hartford Fire Insurance Company were especially conscious of the value to the community of an institution that could provide a practical method of making good such financial losses as were due to fire.

On the other hand, it seems not to have occurred to anyone connected with the Company that they had something that needed to be *sold*. It would appear that in their minds the protection they had to offer was so very desirable that once the people of the community realized that it was available there would be no need to urge prospective clients to take advantage of it. Apparently it was with this in mind that the Directors decided to introduce the new company to the people of the community in the clearest and most effective manner possible.

The *Connecticut Courant* of that day was a four-page paper that was published on Wednesdays every second week. It had been founded in 1764, and local merchants and others had long been accustomed to calling attention to their wares and services, and to listing their needs, in small, single-column advertisements and notices, scores of which filled column after column in every number of the paper. In fact, it had been in the columns of the *Courant* some sixteen years earlier—in 1794—that the firm of Sanford & Wadsworth had announced the opening of the short-lived "Hartford Fire Insurance Office" when that enterprise had begun its limited career. And because of the pre-eminent position this paper occupied, it was natural that the very first advertisement of the newly chartered Hartford Fire Insurance Company should also appear in its columns. But the imagination and originality that had played so important a part in the organization of the new company now expressed themselves in an advertisement so unusual as to establish an utterly new precedent in the somewhat solemn columns of the *Courant*.

Here again the record fails to tell who first proposed so great a departure from the accepted advertising procedures of that day. Because the firm of Hudson & Goodwin, publishers of the *Courant*, had purchased one hundred shares of stock in the new insurance company, it is obvious that they were interested in its welfare, and it may well be that the idea for the new advertisement came from them. But whatever its origin, there can be no doubt that when the *Courant* appeared on Wednesday,

August 1, 1810, no literate person into whose hands a copy of the paper fell could possibly have failed to see the advertisement of the Hartford Fire Insurance Company.

Dr. Johnson, writing in London half a century earlier, had expressed the belief that "The trade of advertising is now so near perfection that it is not easy to propose any improvement," but this new advertisement in the *Courant* was certainly an improvement on any other ads that had ever appeared in the columns of that paper. Normally even the more impressive of the *Courant's* advertisements occupied no more than three or four inches of space in a single column of the paper, but the new insurance company, having decided to call attention to its existence, did so very boldly in an advertisement twenty times that large. Spread impressively across four columns on one of the paper's five-column pages, the advertisement also ran from the very top of the page to within an inch or so at the bottom. Headed by a dramatic drawing of a three-story building being destroyed by fire, the copy read as follows:

HARTFORD FIRE INSURANCE COMPANY

PROPOSALS
FOR INSURING

HOUSES, BUILDINGS, STORES, SHIPS IN HARBOR, AND ON STOCKS, GOODS, WARES, AND MERCHANDISE FROM LOSS OR DAMAGE BY FIRE.

The Hartford Fire Insurance Company having been incorporated by the Legislature of the State of Connecticut with a capital of One Hundred and Fifty Thousand Dollars—with a power of enlarging the capital to Two Hundred and Fifty Thousand Dollars; and the Capital of One Hundred and Fifty Thousand Dollars being already paid and secured, to be paid according to law, the Directors now offer to the public the following terms upon which they propose to conduct the business of the Company.

As all classes of citizens are exposed to great calamities from fire, we presume that prudence will induce them to pay the small premium which is required for an indemnity against such accidents. The practice of procuring Insurance against losses from fire, has already become very general through this country, and the Company are confident that the extent and solidity of their funds, and the fairness, liberality and promptitude with which they shall adjust the claims of sufferers, will ensure the confidence of this, and the neighboring States.

₀ No Insured Person will be liable to make good the Losses of others; but in the case of Fire, the Sufferer will be fully indemnified to the amount insured.—The Company also make good losses on Property burnt by Lightning."*

Then followed a list of the four "Classes of Hazards," and the "Rates of Annual Premiums for Insurance against Fire." Another section gave the "Conditions of Insurance," and among these one made it clear that "All Applications for Insurance must be made at the office of the Company, in writing; and the Subject offered for Insurance accurately described." And finally the advertisement concluded with the statement that "The company will commence business on the sixth day of August next."

Oddly enough, no names of either officers or directors appeared in the ad, and except that it bore a line reading "Hartford, July 27, 1810," no reference gave any inkling of the location of the office. On the facing page, however—page two of the four-page newspaper—a small, single-column notice that was somewhat inconspicuously placed among other notices and ads, partially made up for this omission. It read as follows:

> *HARTFORD FIRE INSURANCE COMPANY*
>
> The President and Directors give notice, That their office will be open on the 6th day of August, for the purpose of insuring against fire.
> Applications may be lodged with the Secretary any day of the week, Sunday excepted.
> By order of the Board of Directors
> *Walter Mitchell, Sec'ry*
> *July 31, 1810*

Though both the large advertisement and the small notice on the facing page referred to the Company's office as if a formal place of business had actually been established, nothing of the kind had really happened. Arrangements had been made, "for the present," to hold "the Meetings of the President and Directors" in Walter Mitchell's law office which was located on State Street next door to the Hartford Bank, and those who were interested in taking out fire insurance policies were

---

* See Appendix, p. 281, for a reproduction of this entire advertisement.

obviously expected to go there in order that their applications might be "lodged with the Secretary." The Company, however, had arranged for no actual office of its own. This was entirely reasonable under the circumstances. No one imagined that there would be any vast rush of business, and the President and Directors obviously felt that they had done all that was necessary when they had authorized the Secretary to "purchase such Books and Stationary as may be necessary for transacting the business of the company" and had paid a certain Aaron Colton $21.25 for "a large table with drawers," "a book case," and some "cloth, nails, locke, etc." With such other furniture and equipment as Walter Mitchell's office already contained, this was enough to start the Hartford Fire Insurance Company on its way. Still, the Directors wanted to make certain that the new company should be as widely known as possible, so they repeated the large advertisement in the *Courant* of September 5th. And on October 3rd they not only repeated it again but also gave it added prominence by having it appear on page one. In addition, they had the same advertisement printed as a circular which they distributed widely, even apparently arranging to have it posted in banks, inns, and other public places.

The result was that within two months of the time the Connecticut Assembly approved its charter, the Hartford Fire Insurance Company began its career with a promotion campaign that widely called the attention of the public to its existence and its purposes. Unfortunately, however, so little business resulted that nineteen years were to pass before Secretary Mitchell finally decided that he required the assistance of a clerk.

CHAPTER 4

WAR, DEPRESSION, AND THE COMPANY'S GREATEST ASSET

WALTER MITCHELL's office, which also served as the office of the Hartford Fire Insurance Company for the first twenty-five years of its existence, was on the north side of State Street in a three-story structure known as the Mitchell Building. Street numbers were not in use in Hartford in 1810, but later, when they were assigned, the Mitchell office, which had its own entrance from the street, became No. 26½, and the Mitchell Building, which immediately adjoined the smaller but more formally designed structure that housed the Hartford Bank, probably had No. 26 assigned to its main entrance. Across the street lay the State-house Green and the dignified, cupola-surmounted Statehouse itself.

Little is known of the appearance of Walter Mitchell's office, but occasional references to it suggest that while it was not small it was plain and unimpressive. We know that Walter Mitchell occupied it alone, though arrangements had now been made for the Directors of the insurance company to hold their meetings there. Aside from the occasional ministrations of a charwoman, however, the newly appointed Secretary of the insurance company had no help whatever. Even the additional equipment that had been purchased amounted to very little. "A large table with drawers," and some "cloth, nails, locke, etc.," had been delivered on July 17th, and a week later, according to the itemized bill that is still in existence, a charge of 58 cents was added for removing and doing something—the word is missing—to a bookcase.

Just when this bill was paid we do not know, but someone—Walter Mitchell, presumably—seems to have been very deliberate about it, for an additional item—"To a book case, $6.00"—was added on October 19th, bringing the total to $21.83. But now a correction was made, and the 58-cent item was deducted, thus reducing the bill to $21.25. And yet, that 58 cents was paid—apparently by Walter Mitchell himself—for in faded but clearly legible handwriting near the bottom of this old statement of account the following words appear:

> *Rec'd payment from Hartford Fire*
> *Insurance Company and fifty-eight cents.*
> *Aaron Colton.*

By August 6, 1810, which was the date the new insurance company had announced it would "commence business," the books and "stationary" the Secretary had been authorized to purchase were undoubtedly on hand, and a supply of blank insurance policies had been delivered by the printer. Thus the Company was ready to accommodate any clients who might appear. It is interesting to note, however, that very few did. We know, for instance, that on Tuesday, August 21st—fifteen days after the date set for the opening of business—John Sargeant, who lived in Windsor, urged his horse over the six miles of rutted road that led south beside the river into Hartford, and made his way to Walter Mitchell's State Street office. There he asked about a fire insurance policy on his dwelling in Windsor and, before the day was over, Policy No. 3 was issued. It is not unlikely, too, that Secretary Mitchell, in preparing this document, explained that Policy No. 1 had been purchased by James Lathrop, a building contractor of Hartford, and that Policy No. 2 covered the Hartford grocery and crockery store owned by Charles Seymour. But we have no way of knowing whether or not the Secretary was favorably impressed by the fact that in the first fifteen days of the company's active existence, only three policies had been sold.

Had those who founded the new company looked to it as their only means of livelihood it seems reasonable to suppose that they would have been more impressed than they obviously were with the importance of promoting the sale of policies. As it was, however, the insurance company was secondary to other interests. All the stockholders and Directors had other holdings and sources of income, and some had many. President Terry, for example, an attorney who had frequently been elected to public office, was also a man of means and had invested in various businesses, among which was a distillery in East Windsor. And the other stockholders, too, were active in other enterprises—enterprises which took more of their time and attention than the insurance company did.

It would be easy to imagine that those who had purchased stock in the new company, and especially those who had been chosen as Directors, were fully convinced of the importance and value of insurance. But the fact is that though President Terry insured his Hartford home by purchasing Policy No. 4 a little over two weeks after the office opened, and James H. Wells, a Director, insured his Hartford hardware store by purchasing Policy No. 6 a week or so later, some of the Directors were very slow about taking out policies, and a good many of the stockholders apparently never did. Even Secretary Mitchell—though the records of those days are less than perfect and may do him an injustice—seems not to have insured his Wethersfield home until Policy No. 2089 was issued, after the passage of almost twenty years.

It should be borne in mind, of course, that in 1810 insurance was not a universally accepted, or even a universally understood, idea. People had gotten along since the beginning of time with very little in the way of insurance, and it was easy for almost anyone to question the value and practicality of such "newfangled" ideas. Everyone was convinced that fires, though frequent and sometimes very destructive, were entirely a matter of chance, and many a property owner no doubt felt that paying out good, hard-earned money so as to be reimbursed for fire losses that might never develop was a foolish and wasteful thing to do.

Others, of course, were more open-minded, though even among the enthusiasts very few had begun to suspect that any generalizations or averages or percentages could ever provide anything more than a vague and inaccurate basis upon which the business of insurance could be erected. No one understood what facts would be required, and even the most obvious ones could not as yet be compiled in sufficient detail. Those who had given the idea any thought understood that risks varied, and with that in mind the premium rates that were established varied also, but such rates as were offered were little more than hopeful guesses some of which were far too low while others were more than a little too high. It was easy to conclude that rates had to be low if clients were to be attracted, and it was not difficult to say that rates had to be high enough to pay such operating costs as were necessary and such losses as were likely to eventuate. But to transmute these generalities into actual rates that were sound and justifiable was beyond the powers of even the most competent insurance men of that day.

In issuing Policy No. 1—a "builder's risk" of $4,000 for three months— Secretary Mitchell asked and obtained a premium of $5.00. On August

24th, however, when Charles Jencks & Company applied for a $10,000 policy for one year on the company's East Windsor distillery, Policy No. 5 called for the payment of a premium of $125. Policy No. 22, on the other hand—a $20,000 Policy for one year on Charles Sigourney's Hartford hardware store—carried a $50 premium, though Policy No. 21—a policy for $10,000 on James R. Woodbridge's dry-goods store—had called for a premium of $75.

It is clear from these early examples that in determining their rates, the Directors of the Company already knew that differing risks called for different charges, though the rates that were in effect—in these four instances they were 25 cents, 50 cents, 75 cents, and $1.25 per 100 dollars per annum—were hopeful guesses rather than well-informed estimates. However, in addition to the actual premiums, there was something else that worked to the advantage of the Company, as P. Henry Woodward, writing in 1897, made clear.[*]

"The hazard," he pointed out, "was less than it seems, for the character of the insured, though unmentioned in the policy, formed one of the most important elements in the contract. Every risk was accompanied by a survey of the property, and the written representations of the owner had the force of a guaranty. Persons desiring insurance solicited it as a privilege from the officers of the company, and, being required to carry themselves a material part of the hazard, the two parties to the agreement became partners in the venture. A man of bad reputation found difficulty in obtaining a policy on any terms. At first no commission was paid to agents, their compensation coming from the survey and policy fee, which varied with the labor, and was collected from the assured.

"Then, too, the population was homogeneous and almost entirely of English parentage. The spirit of Puritanism still pervaded New England. Branded often by latter-day critics as cruel and ridiculed as narrow, it is admitted to have encouraged the growth of the rugged virtues."

In a town so small and compact as Hartford then was, the Directors, the President, and the Secretary of the Company naturally saw each other often. In all likelihood, too, Company problems and developments were frequently and informally discussed. In fact, this may go far toward explaining the lack of details in the Company's well-preserved old record book. On the other hand, it would appear that neither the President nor any of the Directors gave much time to the Company. From the very first, Secretary Mitchell attended to almost everything except as the Directors

[*] Woodward, *Insurance in Connecticut*, Boston.

occasionally assigned some task to the President or to a committee.

The Directors' meetings seem to have been both informal and irregular. So far as the record shows there was no set time at which they were to be held. In 1814, for example, only three meetings seem to have been held. Walter Mitchell, however, not infrequently recorded certain facts out of order and as if by afterthought, and it may very well be that some were never entered at all. Even an old Company checkbook that is still preserved is remarkable for what it fails to tell. Many check stubs carry no date and some fail to record even the amounts for which the checks were written. It may be that other records now lost or not rediscovered include these important details, but if not, one can only wonder how the Secretary kept the record straight or even how the Company's books were balanced.

Though it is recorded that the first meeting of the Directors "was adjourned to the 5th Day of July next at 5 o'clock P.M. to be held at the Office of said Company," we have no knowledge of any action that was taken at that time. In fact, it may be that no meeting of any great consequence was held until November 14th when the Directors instructed President Terry and Nathaniel Patten to act as a committee in obtaining, either by subscription or purchase, not more than forty shares of the stock of the Hartford Bank.

The reason for this was that fifteen thousand dollars was in the Company treasury as a result of payments made on stock that had been purchased, and the Directors were considering how to invest these funds both safely and productively. As of that day, surplus funds were a rarity in the United States, and the care of such funds was little understood. Merchants and traders were inclined to expand their businesses when profits made that possible, and farmers, when crops and prices permitted, were inclined to buy more land or, by lending money on mortgage, to help their neighbors buy it. But securities such as are so widely available today were then almost unknown. In 1789 Congress had authorized an issue of bonds for the purpose of refunding the Revolutionary War debt. Banks and insurance companies were also coming into existence, and public improvements were being started. Sound securities, however, were comparatively few, the market for them was limited, and speculators confined themselves mostly to land "deals" of various descriptions. It is no wonder that little experience had as yet been gained in the field of wise and conservative investment.

The Hartford Bank, however, had earned an excellent reputation even beyond the borders of Connecticut. It had already come to be one of New England's strongest financial institutions and it is understandable why the Directors of the Hartford Fire Insurance Company should have decided to invest in some of the bank's stock, the par value of which was $400 though it was selling at a premium of four per cent.

The forty shares of bank stock President Terry and Nathaniel Patten were authorized to purchase would have cost $16,640. Only $15,000 was available, however, and the Directors, in issuing their instructions, had added, "Also, that they obtain a loan from said bank of such an amount as they shall judge requisite to effect said purpose."

Acting on these instructions, and apparently with the idea of purchasing the full limit of forty shares, Terry and Patten arranged for a loan. But for some reason that is not clear, they borrowed only $1,224, which was $416—the price of one share—less than the proposed purchase would have required. This loan, added to the $15,000 that was already available, brought it to $16,224, but Terry and Patten seem to have been very conservative in outlook. It was not until December 13th that their final action was taken, and then—again for reasons that are not available—they bought only 14 shares, paying $5,824 for them. The remainder of the sum that had been placed to their credit was returned to the Company treasury.*

Though all the early clients of the Hartford Fire Insurance Company were expected to apply at the office of the Secretary for such policies as they might wish to purchase, it soon became apparent that the people of other localities were potential clients also. Within a couple of months policies had actually been sold to residents of East Windsor and Middletown, and the people of other communities were just as much in need of insurance though they were little likely to come to Hartford for their policies. If trustworthy representatives of the Company could be established elsewhere, however, and a system could be evolved that would make it possible for the Company to maintain control while permitting such freedom of action as able representatives would be certain to demand, it soon became apparent that the Company might find it possible to operate successfully in a wider field.

No one knows who first suggested the idea, and there is no record of how the first agent came to be chosen. We know only that on December

* From the time of this first purchase until the present, the Hartford Fire Insurance Company has continued to invest in this bank's stock. As of December 31, 1959, the insurance company's assets included 24,300 shares of stock in the Hartford National Bank and Trust Company, the value of which was $923,400.

27, 1810, when the Company had been in existence less than five months and had not yet sold its fifty-fifth policy, Jonathan George Washington Trumbull, of Norwich, a grandson of Jonathan Trumbull who had been one of George Washington's valued counsellors as well as Connecticut's Revolutionary War governor, became the first agent ever appointed by the Hartford Fire Insurance Company and the first local agent of any insurance company in the state of Connecticut. Actually he was what the Company then called a "surveying" agent, and it is probable that Policy No. 60, which insured Jabez W. Huntington's Norwich hardware store for $10,000, was prepared in the Hartford office on January 9, 1811, as a result of Agent Trumbull's first survey and report.

Other "surveying" agents were appointed at irregular intervals, but the records contain few details. Here and there the names of some of them are mentioned and a few, we know, were appointed by "note written." Such policies as they brought in were handled, as all the others were at first, by the Hartford office and nothing remains to tell us how effective any of the agents were. Before a year had passed, however, "recording agents" were being appointed and these, unlike the "surveying agents," were authorized, under rules that at first were less clear than they might have been, to issue policies. When any policy was issued, the agent who handled it merely reported it to the Hartford office, remitting such funds as had been collected.

Though this change marked an important improvement in the system, the methods that were followed were still unsystematic. The Directors appear to have had no plan. Such agents as they approved seem usually to have asked for their appointments and no specific rules governed them all. In appointing new agents the Directors sometimes placed limits on their authority, and no thought seems to have been given to the idea of developing nearby territory first or of appointing agents in the country's larger cities.

The first of the new "recording agents" was appointed, apparently by Secretary Mitchell, sometime in 1811. He was Ebenezer F. Norton, of Canandaigua, New York, but little is known of his record. Nothing remains to tell what he accomplished, and he resigned in 1813. According to the Company's old record book, a meeting of the Directors was held on June 17, 1813, and the following action was taken:

> *Voted,* That the resignation of Ebenezer F. Norton, Esqr.,
> Agent for this Company at Canandaigua, etc., be accepted
> & Elisha B. Strong, Esqr. of sd Town is hereby appointed

Agent in lieu of sd Ebzr F. Norton, Esqr. with the same
powers to countersign Policies and transact other business
relative to this Company as was vested in sd Norton.

Nathl Terry, Presdt.

Though other agents were appointed, their number increased only
slowly at first, and, so far as the record shows, few were appointed in
Connecticut for a decade or more. Even in 1835 there were only 6 in the
entire state who had produced any business; yet by that time there were
17 in New York, 5 in Massachusetts, and 2 each in New Hampshire and
Vermont. At more distant points, there were 2 in Georgia and 1 each in
Alabama, Louisiana, Tennessee, Missouri, and Illinois, though none had
yet been appointed in any of the other states.

Early in April 1811, Isaac Bull, one of the original stockholders of
the Hartford Fire Insurance Company, purchased Policy No. 100 when
he insured his Hartford home, and a few weeks later, when Secretary
Mitchell totaled the Company's income, he learned that the premiums
so far paid had amounted to $2,784.51. But in addition, $638.53 had
been received in interest and dividends, thus bringing the total income
to $3,423.04. From the time the Company's office had been opened, in
other words, to the end of April 1811, the total income from all sources
had averaged about $385 a month.

Even in 1811 this could hardly have seemed a gigantic sum. Nevertheless, when the Directors considered the Company's condition on May
31st which, they decided, marked the end of the first year, they seem
to have been reasonably well pleased. Even after they voted to pay
Secretary Mitchell $300 for his first year's work, and after they had
added another $30 for the use of his office and for firewood that had
been consumed in the company's interest, they found that the first year's
expenses had amounted to only $530.38. And, by great good fortune, no
single claim had been entered against the Company on any of the policies that had been written.

Apparently satisfied with conditions as they found them, the Directors voted the Company's first dividend—50 cents a share, a total of
$1,500—to be paid on the first of July. So far as the record shows, no
one was troubled by the fact that more than a few individual risks had
been accepted that equaled or surpassed the Company's entire cash
assets. As yet no one knew how to convert the *probability* of loss into

any reasonably accurate *expectation* of loss, and it was consequently impossible to determine the value of the risk or to know what assets were necessary to make it reasonably certain that all losses could be covered.

It would appear that the Directors, having checked Secretary Mitchell's figures, reached the conclusion that the Company showed a gain, as of May 31, 1811, of $1,168.66. No thought was given, however, to anything like a reserve to cover losses which might result from policies still in effect and on which premiums had already been paid.

Though Secretary Mitchell's figures may have given the Directors the idea that the Company's progress was satisfactory, they were competent New England businessmen who knew that economic conditions in general were far from good. Napoleon was still keeping Europe in a furor, and even the Atlantic Ocean was far too narrow to keep America from feeling the effects. Both the Berlin and the Milan decrees, which had been issued by the French Emperor in 1806 and 1807, had been enormously troublesome. Now he issued another decree which was intentionally ambiguous but which gave some people, including President Madison, the impression that the two earlier ones were to "cease to have effect." The trouble was that the new decree contained an involved and unclear provision that enabled the French to hold that this was to be the case only if the British decided to revoke their Orders in Council, or if the United States should somehow succeed in maintaining its rights upon the high seas.

The British Government, more experienced in dealing with Napoleon than President Madison was, refused to believe that the emperor had revoked anything. Unfortunately, however, no British minister was in Washington at the time, and no American minister was in France. Furthermore, William Pinkney, the American minister to London, had left Great Britain in a moment of irritation. John Quincy Adams, our minister to Russia, sent reports to the effect that Napoleon's whole system of decrees was about to collapse, and the *chargé d'affaires* in the American Legation in Paris assured the State Department that the French emperor was trying to lure us into war with Great Britain merely for his own purposes. But at the very moment when the United States and Great Britain needed them most, they both lacked the diplomatic representatives who, in all probability, would have been able to make these matters clear.

The fact is that both Great Britain and France had long been seizing American ships, though France had seized many more than the British had taken during the preceding five years. But Napoleon's new decree nevertheless succeeded in tricking President Madison and Congress into entering a war against Great Britain for which the United States was in no way prepared.

Great Britain, already strained to the limit, was willing to revoke her Orders in Council rather than add to her difficulties, but an unfortunate series of calamities delayed her action. There were riots among the poor; King George III finally went mad and a regency bill had to be passed; the Prime Minister was assassinated and when, at last, the Orders were revoked, it was too late.

By this time economic conditions in both Great Britain and France had grown so bad that the policy of economic pressure that had been originated by Thomas Jefferson and implemented in 1807 by the passage of the Embargo Act was beginning to produce the results for which Jefferson had hoped. Despite diplomatic inadequacies, war might not have come had it not been that a series of serious Indian troubles coincided with the election to Congress of a number of impatient young men from the West and South.

The shipping interests of the country and the people of New England, impressed by the improvement in foreign trade during 1811, were opposed to war, but a number of congressmen, led by Henry Clay, John C. Calhoun, and others, were urging war with the idea that Canada could readily be seized. Though Great Britain, within another month, was to rescind her Orders in Council, a Foreign Office statement which reached America in May 1812, not only gave the opposite impression but also criticized President Madison's acceptance of Napoleon's ambiguous promise.

It was at this time that President Madison was being pressed by Henry Clay and other congressmen who favored war. Refusing to admit that Napoleon had tricked him, he asked Congress to declare war, listing as reasons Great Britain's impressment of our seamen, her violation of our three-mile limit, and her refusal to rescind the Orders in Council. About this time Parliament finally got around to withdrawing the Orders in Council and, had normal diplomatic relations been in effect, it is not unlikely that war would have been avoided. As it was, however, word of this important British action had not reached America when, on June 18th, to the bitter disappointment of American shipowners, as well as most of the other people of New England, war was declared.

With the country in no way prepared for war, America's military efforts were singularly unsuccessful. Several attempts to invade Canada failed miserably and, except for a number of naval victories in which American ships defeated a number of British frigates and sloops-of-war at sea as well as two small naval forces on Lake Erie and Lake Champlain, American successes were few. By 1814 our commerce had been driven almost completely from the sea, our coast was blockaded, and a British force, entering Chesapeake Bay, marched to Bladensburg, Maryland, where a hurriedly gathered militia force was easily defeated, permitting unopposed entry to Washington. There, before burning the unfinished Capitol and the White House, a group of British officers are said to have eaten a dinner that the fleeing President had left untouched on the dining-room table in the White House.

By now many Britons and Americans were eager to end the profitless struggle, and in October 1814 the Massachusetts legislature issued a call for a convention to be held at Hartford for the purpose, it was said, of revising the Federal Constitution. The convention actually met in December, but the meetings were behind closed doors and the nation widely feared that actual secession was in the wind. In the end, secession was not proposed, but the convention went so far as to suggest that "States which have no common umpire must be their own judges, and execute their own decisions."

While this was going on in Hartford, a treaty of peace between Great Britain and the United States was signed in Ghent and, though none of the original reasons for the war were mentioned in it, it brought the struggle to an end. Before word of the treaty reached our shores, however, the Battle of New Orleans was fought and won, thus gaining for the Americans a useless but very welcome victory at the end of a conflict in which victories had been few.

Actually no one had been benefited. Even Napoleon, who, for a time, had gained by our entrance into the war, was in exile on Elba when the Treaty of Ghent was signed, and in the long run the struggle accomplished very little except to embitter Anglo-American relations.

Having opposed the war, and having also played a part in the nationally unpopular Hartford Convention, the Federalist Party, and Rufus King, its candidate, carried only Massachusetts, Connecticut, and Delaware in the election of 1816, and James Monroe was elected President. Politically, Southern leaders were still dominant. Monroe, conscious of this, nevertheless chose John Quincy Adams to be Secretary of State. Economically, however, New England was stronger than it had been. Because of Napoleon's endless wars and the naval blockades they

brought, Americans were compelled to increase their output of manufactured goods. The first successful cotton mill in America had been built
in 1790, and fifteen years later—in 1805—only some five or six thousand
spindles were operating in the whole of New England. The long period
of "non-intercourse" with Europe, however, had been climaxed by several years of increasingly stringent wartime blockade, with the result
that the nation's industries had greatly increased. By 1815 fully half
a million spindles had been installed in New England factories, and
great increases had become apparent in other industries as well.
The steamboat was now in use, also. Robert Fulton's *Clermont*, which
had first voyaged up the Hudson in 1807, had been succeeded by
many others. By 1811 a steamboat was running more or less regularly
between Pittsburgh and New Orleans on the Ohio and Mississippi rivers.
By 1815 one of these new craft—the steamboat *Fulton*—had visited Hartford, and within another four years the steamship *Savannah* actually
succeeded in crossing the Atlantic.

Land transportation was improving as well. Roads were often bad, it
is true—rutted, rough, and dusty in periods of drought; ice-encrusted and
occasionally blocked by snow in winter; always muddy during periods
of rain, and sometimes hub-deep and impassable when the spring thaws
came—but turnpikes had been increasing in number for a generation.
Between 1795 and 1815 eighteen had been chartered in Connecticut
alone. A period of canal building had come as well; and in 1817, when
New York State authorized the building of the Erie Canal in order to
link the Hudson River with the Great Lakes, the even more rapid growth
and development of the West was assured.

Shortly after the end of the War of 1812, British manufacturers,
troubled by the growth of manufacturing in the United States, began to
"dump" their products in America. Often selling their products at prices
that were lower than the American cost of manufacture, they hoped to
drive their American competitors out of business. But in this they failed,
for American manufacturers—and especially those of New England—
were usually well enough established to hold their own. Despite occasional hardships they continued to grow. By 1819, however, economic
difficulties that were at least in part a result of the war finally brought
about a financial panic that surpassed anything of the kind the nation
had previously experienced.

Many New England manufacturers, despite the headway they had
made, had been hurt by British "dumping." Land speculators throughout

the South and West had paid high prices for large holdings, and new settlers, moving into the West in large numbers, had borrowed heavily in order to make the necessary payments on the purchase of government land. Many small state banks, operated by inexperienced bankers, had made loans too readily, and when the United States Bank, which itself had not been well managed, decided in 1818 to insist on the payment of all state bank notes while refusing to renew any personal loans or to accept any notes but its own, a financial panic abruptly burst upon the country. Many state banks failed. Land values shrank enormously. Foreclosures were widespread, and economic ruin confronted many individuals and even some communities. Recovery was slow and by 1824, when Congress passed the nation's first "protective" tariff, national alignments had begun to take shape that were to lead, in another generation, to civil war and the nation's greatest tragedy.

Under conditions such as these it is not surprising that the progress of the Hartford Fire Insurance Company was slow. And yet, despite the difficulties that confronted both the country and the Company, foundations of real permanence were being laid. Between 1810, the year in which the Company had been founded, and 1820, when the third census of the United States was taken, the population of the nation had increased by a third. Industrially and agriculturally, despite the panic of 1819, the increase had been even more spectacular, and thoughtful observers of that day were already predicting even greater growth to come. The Hartford Fire Insurance Company, on the other hand, was definitely less fortunate. It showed a loss in 1819 and a slightly smaller loss in 1820. In later years there were to be much greater losses, too—losses beside which the Company's 1820 assets would appear almost ludicrously small. And yet, even in 1820 a sturdy foundation had been partly laid, and an asset was available that Walter Mitchell would never have thought to enter in the books.

Weaknesses in plenty were a part of the Hartford Fire Insurance Company in its tenth year. The men who ran it, however, despite their many faults and their frequent lack of understanding, were men of character. This was the Company's greatest asset, and on it, more than on any other thing, its future was to rest.

CHAPTER 5

PROGRESS, DIFFICULTIES,

AND A

STOCKHOLDERS' REVOLT

T HE AGENCY system of the Hartford Fire Insurance Company, though inaugurated soon after the Company was founded, expanded very slowly. In the first eight years only three policy-writing agents succeeded in transacting any business for the Company. In 1819, however, when Hooker Leavitt was appointed agent in Greenfield, Massachusetts, the President and the Directors chose a new method of compensating him. "The compensation to be allowed," the record of their action reads, "is 5 per cent on Premiums recd by him on all Policies issued by him together with the charge for the policy."

"The charge for the policy" was 50 cents, a well-established sum paid, in those days, to the agent by the person then sometimes called "the insurent." This reference to a commission, however, is the first in the Company's history, though other references were soon to follow. Within another three years, in fact, some of the more productive agents were granted a commission of 10 per cent "on all premiums received by them exceeding $1,000 in any one year." This was one of the Company's earlier attempts to encourage the sale of policies, but when more experience had demonstrated the dangers inherent in this approach, the Directors ultimately decided to eliminate volume bonuses of this nature.

Following the authorization of the first commission someone seems to have urged the Company to expand somewhat more vigorously. In 1821 agents were appointed in New Haven, Boston, New York City, and elsewhere though it must already have been obvious that the appointment of new agents did not necessarily result in selling additional policies. Strangely enough, nine years were to pass and the agent in New York was to be replaced before the Company's first policy was sold there. And, stranger still, it was not until twenty-five years had passed and the first agent had been followed by another and probably by another still that the first policy was sold in Boston. In the meantime, however, the Directors had been giving more thought to the matter of commissions. But even after raising some of them to 10 per cent other contracts permitted the collection of only five.

The net income of the Company had been $2,784.51 when Walter Mitchell made his first annual report on May 31, 1811, and the annual figure had increased modestly each year until 1816 when it reached $6,301.23. Thereafter, however, until 1820, it was noticeably less. No deficit resulted except in 1816, 1819, and 1820. The total gains for the eight years in which gains had been shown amounted to $15,233.43. There had been deficits, however, of $10,955.15 in 1816, $1,319.93 in 1819, and $1,035.97 in 1820—a total of $13,311.05. A dividend of 50 cents a share had been voted in 1811. In 1812 this had been increased to 90 cents, though the Directors also called for the payment of $5 a share on stock subscriptions. In 1814 the dividend was increased to $1.20. Economic difficulties that arose late in the year, however, forced the Directors to omit the second semiannual payment.

Secretary Mitchell was still the Company's only employee, his salary having been increased to $330 in 1813, and to $360 the following year. He was now paid semiannually and the amount paid for the use of his office and for firewood had been increased to $60. In 1815 the semiannual dividend again became 60 cents, and on January 20, 1816, Walter Mitchell's figures showed a Company surplus of $11,427.70. The result of this was that when the stockholders were called upon in April to pay $4 a share on what they still owed on their stock, the Directors immediately provided for the payment by voting a dividend of $4 a share. Two months later, however, the stockholders were informed that they were expected to pay 25 per cent of what they still owed on their stock when they next renewed their notes, and that additional payments of the same size were to be made whenever the notes were again renewed until they were paid in full. In July, however, as if to take a little of the sting out of this demand, another 60-cent dividend was declared.

Though Nathaniel Terry had been re-elected President of the Company each year since it had been founded, and was to continue in that position for many years still to come, it would appear that the time he gave to company business was growing less. In 1817 he was elected to Congress, serving a two-year term, and in 1818 he was also a delegate to the constitutional convention that drafted a new constitution for Connecticut. In 1819 he was elected president of the Hartford Bank, and he held that position until 1828 despite the fact that he also became Mayor of Hartford in 1824 and continued in that office until 1831. Under the circumstances he naturally found it impossible to attend all of the Company meetings, and Nathaniel Patten was consequently authorized by the Directors to act, in President Terry's absence, as president *pro tem*.

The Directors sometimes met at Walter Mitchell's office, but more convivial meetings were occasionally held at one or another of Hartford's better taverns. Very few details are available to explain just what was discussed and decided at these meetings, but the fact that others beside the Directors were usually present and that in addition to the suppers that were served, generous quantities of wine and other potables were consumed, suggests that such business as may have been considered was discussed in an atmosphere of great good fellowship. On January 6, 1813, for example, one of these genial gatherings was held at John Bennett's comfortable Hartford tavern, and though no record remains to tell how much company business was conducted, John Bennett's receipted bill suggests at least a little of the atmosphere of the gathering. The names of those who attended this meeting are not available, but seventeen suppers were served, so in addition to Walter Mitchell and such Directors as were present, there were at least seven guests.

John Bennett's receipted bill for what he served in connection with this meeting is as follows:

The Gentlemen Directors of the Fire Insurance
   Company—

            To John Bennett—

 1813
Jan'y 6

     To 17 Suppers & repasts $12.75
        12 Bottles Best Wine .... 18...
        3 " *Spirits* .... 3...
        3 " *Porter* 1.50
       2¾ Doz. Cigars .... .75
                  ——
                $36.00

  City of Hartford, Jan'y 16, 1813
         Rcd payment John Bennett

The record includes a number of other bills of this nature, and some of the suppers to which they refer provided even more generously for the Directors and their guests. There is even some evidence that Walter Mitchell failed to make any record whatever of a number of these suppers, just as he occasionally failed to record other activities. Now and again he noted that certain payments had been authorized by the Directors on certain specific dates even though no meetings seem to have been held on the indicated days. Undoubtedly the Secretary informally obtained such authority as he required. At the same time it seems obvious that, despite the meticulous care he often took with very small amounts, he sometimes failed to keep proper records of some of these transactions.

For a number of years the Secretary's records were very neat and legible, though even from the first they were often lacking in detail. It would appear that much of the Company's business was carried in his head and that some omissions in the written record were due to the fact that no one cared to bother with the details. Secretary Mitchell has had his defenders, but genial and willing though he apparently was, he seems to have had little inclination to devote every moment of his time to the business of the Hartford Fire Insurance Company or even to his other office duties. It was always time-consuming and often very difficult to traverse the four miles of unpaved and sometimes rutted or very muddy road between his Wethersfield home and Hartford and he not infrequently was late in reaching his office. Sometimes he left early, too, and if he came in on Saturday which, to the people of that time, was as much a work day as any other, he might be gone by noon. On occasion he is even said to have taken the Company's records to Wethersfield, keeping them there for days at a time and compelling those who wished to arrange for insurance to make the trip to his home in order to procure it.

Though the Company had agents in other communities, none was appointed in Hartford, the Secretary having expected the Company's clients to call on him from the very first. In the course of time, however, merchants and others of the community, lacking any easy method of making appointments in advance, had so often found the Secretary absent and the office closed when they had business with the Company, and had so frequently been inconvenienced and delayed, that the idea took form that a new insurance company should be organized. It *was* organized, too, being incorporated in May 1819, as the Aetna Insurance

Company. Furthermore, some of those who had been original stockholders in the Hartford Fire Insurance Company were active in its organization. Thomas K. Brace and Ward Woodbridge, for instance, both of whom had long been Directors of the Hartford, not only purchased stock in the Aetna but also sold their stock in the older company, and resigned as Directors. Furthermore, Mr. Brace was chosen to be first president of the Aetna.

A few stockholders in the new company continued to hold their stock in the Hartford though President Terry and Secretary Mitchell, as well as some of the Hartford Directors, actively opposed the new organization. Terry and Mitchell, in fact, were so active in their opposition that they argued openly before the legislature against the charter for which Aetna's organizers had applied. Still, their opposition accomplished nothing and the new company was formed. It began just as modestly as the Hartford had nine years earlier.

In 1819, despite the fact that the Hartford Fire Insurance Company's net income was approximately twice what it had been at the end of its first year, Walter Mitchell's books showed a loss of $1,319.93, and in 1820, despite a modest increase in net income, the Company's loss was almost as great. From 1821 to 1825, however, business improved each year and each annual statement showed a gain. It is not surprising that under the circumstances Walter Mitchell's salary was increased to $460 in 1824, while an additional $55 was paid to him for office rent, firewood, and even stationery which, oddly enough, he seems to have supplied. And President Terry, though no salary had been paid him before, was paid a hundred dollars for the six-month period that ended on May 31, 1823, and thereafter he was paid at the rate of $200 a year. It is interesting to note that these payments to the President and the Secretary were never authorized in advance. Instead, they were voted semiannually and were accepted as payments for work already done.

At a meeting held by the Hartford Board on June 15, 1822, an important bit of business was transacted. Unfortunately the record omits many details that it would be interesting to have. It seems not to have attracted much attention at the time, but it has now come to be accepted as a move of some historic consequence, for this was one of the first cases of reinsurance ever completed in America.

> *Voted,* the old record reads, "That this company do approve and hereby ratify the contract entered into by our agent, Roger S. Skinner, Esq., of New Haven, with

Samuel Ward, Harvey Sanford and L. E. Wales, Esq.,
a committee of the New Haven Fire Insurance Company,
dated June 13, 1822, agreeing to indemnify said New
Haven Fire Insurance Company against all loss and damage
by fire in consequence of any policy of insurance issued
by said last mentioned office."

A later record shows that the "Hartford Fire Insurance Company, in consideration of certain sums paid to them by the New Haven Insurance Company, have agreed to indemnify and save harmless said last mentioned company from all damage and loss from the unexpired policies which have been issued by said last mentioned office or company," and in doing so the Hartford Directors executed a bond "in the penal sum of One Hundred and Fifty Thousand Dollars" to assure the New Haven company, the charter of which was about to be revoked, that the Hartford would faithfully adhere to the terms of the agreement.

Despite the lack of detailed information in the Hartford's records it is apparent that this experiment in reinsurance was successful. The Company's net income for 1823 exceeded that for 1822 by a third, and in 1824 it was more than twice as great as it had been two years earlier. In fact, during the first fifteen years of its existence, the Company's luck was remarkably good. Risks equal to or greater than its entire cash assets were frequently accepted, but such losses as materialized were almost always small. There had been no losses whatever in the first year of the Company's existence, and for the next three years they totaled only $421.84. As policies in effect grew in number losses naturally increased, but any examination of Walter Mitchell's early records is certain to suggest that he felt dividends to be much more deserving of careful presentation than such losses as the Company suffered and, as luck would have it, losses continued to be minor for another eleven years.

During this period the Company regularly contributed to the support of the city's four-man "watch," and in 1815 Secretary Mitchell was authorized to contribute $300 toward the purchase of a new fire engine for the city. There were other, lesser contributions, too, and for many years it was apparently company policy to pay five dollars to whatever engine company first reached a fire with its equipment in working order. Occasionally there were other rewards as well, as the following quotation from an old record shows. This action was taken by the Directors in November 1818, and it is easy to conclude that the damaged property was covered by one of the company's policies.

Voted, That Augustus Andrews, Col. Watrous, Mr. Kennedy, and Mr. Rogers be paid fifteen dollars each & Elisha Sears Ten Dollars & B. H. Lovell Five Dollars out of funds of this company in consideration of their active, laudable & successful exertions in extinguishing the fire in this city on the evening of the 2 Novr inst. & That Mr. Bartholomew be requested to take Receipt for the same.

Such individual losses as were suffered during the Company's early years seem very small by the standards of our much later day. For example, $112.10½ was paid to Joseph Wheeler on January 21, 1812, to cover damage caused by fire in his Hartford dry-goods store; $150.75 to Charles Jencks & Company of East Windsor on April 12th of the same year for damage by fire in the company's distillery; $152 for damage to Noah Patten's house in January 1814. It is true that in 1816 there was a $2,000 loss in Middlebury, and other losses during that year increased the total to quite the largest sum so far paid out in any single year, but thereafter losses declined, and from April 1820 to November 1823 the total amounted to only $66.25. The time was coming, however, when losses were to mount and the Directors, ignorant, as they were, of the financial preparations that should have been made during the fortunate years since the Company's founding, were soon to be confronted with responsibilities they would find it difficult to meet.

The agency system had continued to grow, and the Company's net income, which had been $5,258.48 in 1820, was $19,753.93 in 1826. But losses now began to mount. In 1827 alone they totaled $37,567.67 and the Directors voted to borrow at the Hartford Bank, using the Company's Hartford Bank stock as collateral, though as yet they were not prepared to suspend the payment of dividends. In little more than another year, however, losses mounted even higher as a result of a conflagration in Augusta, Georgia. Furthermore, fires struck elsewhere, too. There was a $10,000 loss on a distillery in New York, a $12,300 loss on a woolen mill in Connecticut; and a fire in the Griswold Manufacturing Company's plant in Norwich resulted in a payment of $15,000.

Confronted by these calamities it is not surprising that Secretary Mitchell and the Directors of the Company showed their concern. Details are lacking, but it is obvious that word reaching Hartford from Augusta had suggested that the conflagration there had been incendiary in origin, and pending further information, the Company's Directors decided to suspend business in that city. In fact, they were so concerned that, with less logic, they also instructed the Company's agents in Savannah and New Orleans "not to take any more risks at present either by renewal or original policy."

The letter Secretary Mitchell wrote to the Augusta agent reads as follows:

Hartford, 21 April 1829

Joel Catlin, Esqre.

Dear Sir,

I have recd the documents in support of all the claims upon the policies mentioned in your letter of the fourth instant except the following, viz.: No. 439323 in favour of Mr. Kirkpatrick, Isaac D. Smith & E. Woods. Your letters communicating two other incendiary attempts have been recd. Our apprehensions from these attempts are at the highest pitch & under their influence the Board instruct you to take no more risks either by renewal or original policy till you receive from them other instructions. They are now deliberating upon the proper rates of premiums to be required in future and it will be necessary they should be furnished with further information on this subject before they decide. This would probably be done more satisfactorily after a conference between yourself & the agent from this place. It has been impracticable to engage an agent to leave here before next week at which time he will make all despatch possible. The Board wish you in the meantime to inquire into the value of the Buildings destroyed by the fire and generally to make such arrangements as to detain the Agent as short a time as possible. I wrote you last week which you will probably receive before this reaches you.

I remain etc.

W.M. Secy

In another letter written on the same day to S. B. Parkman, the Company's agent in Savannah, Secretary Mitchell, despite his concern over the heavy losses the Company had suffered in Augusta, expressed his confidence in the Hartford's ability to meet the demands that were being made upon it. "You may assure Mr. Haversham," he wrote, "that notwithstanding the loss this office has sustained at Augusta his will be fairly and promptly met."

Because of the Company's increasing business Secretary Mitchell had felt justified, a few months earlier, and may have felt compelled, to ask the Directors to authorize the employment of someone who could devote his full time to the Hartford office. As we have noted, from the time the Company had been founded, both President Terry and Secretary Mitchell had devoted much of their time to activities quite separate from those of the Company. In February of that unfortunate year of 1829, consequently, a young man by the name of Lewis Bliss had been appointed as the Company's first clerk. Given a desk in a corner of Secretary Mitchell's office, he had been attending to such duties as the Secretary had assigned him for only a couple of months when word of the Augusta calamity arrived.

Travel had never played any great part in President Terry's or Secretary Mitchell's company activities. The Secretary had felt it necessary on at least two occasions to go to New Haven, but such other trips as he had made had not been numerous. President Terry, having often been called upon to travel in connection with his other activities may, on occasion, have performed tasks for the Company on the way. Now and again some one of the stockholders or Directors had made short journeys on Company business, as Seth Terry had on at least three occasions. In 1821, for example, he had journeyed—on horseback, apparently—to Poughkeepsie, New York, in order to look into the possibility of authorizing a more than usually large policy on a textile mill there. Company agents, too, had sometimes been asked to make short journeys on company business. So far, however, no one had ever taken a really extensive journey for the Company though the Augusta conflagration now necessitated one. After some discussion, it was the newly hired clerk who, despite his limited experience, was chosen for the task.

New though he was in the Company's employ, Lewis Bliss was already in the confidence of the Secretary and the Directors. It was clear that the total of the Company's losses in Augusta would surpass any other it had previously suffered, but the young man was nevertheless authorized to settle all claims and to draw on the Company for such payments as he approved. Drafts drawn on the Company in this connection were to be payable within sixty days.

No search of the Company's records has yet revealed any detailed report of exactly what Lewis Bliss accomplished. He performed his difficult task to the satisfaction of the Directors, as many references show, and because he had been told that the Company intended to accept its full responsibility in connection with every claim, the adjustments he made, which totaled $59,312.79, were so satisfactory to the affected policyholders that the Company's reputation was definitely enhanced. As a result, though the Company's business in Augusta, Savannah, and New Orleans remained suspended for a time, its agents were presently authorized to begin again, though at higher rates.

Lewis Bliss, incidentally, was being paid at the rate of $500 a year when he was sent to represent the Company in Augusta, and despite his success on that mission, no increase in pay resulted. It was not until 1832 that his salary was raised to $600.

Here and there in the limited records of those days, it is possible to discern signs of discontent among the Directors of the Hartford. Even as early as 1816 or 1817 this was evident, and in 1819 the resignation of several Directors led to—or at least coincided with—the founding of the Aetna Insurance Company. From time to time in later years, too, other changes took place in the Board of Directors, and it has been suggested that dissatisfaction with the operation of the Company was apparent at least in some degree as long as President Terry and Secretary Mitchell remained in office.

By 1826 it is obvious that rumors were adrift, hinting that the Company had suffered very serious losses, and in a letter to Daniel Stebbins, the agent at Northampton, Massachusetts, who had written to ask about it, the following appears:

> Yours of the 25th Inst. is recd. The suggestion about losses by this Office is entirely a *mistake*, or what is more probable a *misrepresentation*. I do not recollect that the Hartford F. I. Compy have lost a single dollar either at home or among any of their Agencies since the loss of Mr. Nathl Patten's building, which happened in the month of March last, & this was not a very heavy loss. The Aetna & Protection offices in this city have, I believe, met with *some* losses, to what amount I do not know.

This part of the letter was signed by "W.W." who added a postscript explaining that "Mr. Mitchell is absent from Town on a journey but will be home in a day or two." Who "W.W." was we do not know, but the importance attached to his explanation is attested by the fact that

Nathaniel Terry himself must have read it for he added another post-script, which read as follows:

> P.S. The business of the H. F. In. Co. has generally been
> conducted with success—for the last three or four years
> remarkably so. They have made good dividends during that
> time & have had a surplus which has been constantly in-
> creasing & is at this time very considerable.—Our capital is
> as well secured as that of any other Compy whatever. I do
> not believe that one cent of it is at hazard.
>
> Respectfully yours etc.
>
> Nathl Terry

But that was in 1826. By the end of 1827 the situation was surpris-ingly different. In a letter written by Walter Mitchell to S. B. Parkman, the Company's agent in Savannah, the Secretary refers to "a series of losses for the last year quite unexampled for this Office."

Actually the Company's entire surplus which, a year earlier, had been about $20,000, had disappeared, though the Secretary, doing his utmost to be optimistic, put the best face he could on the matter. "Notwith-standing these losses," he explained, "we can assure you that our capital stock remains unimpaired with the exception of about 3 or 4,000 Dls. where the losses have not yet become due . . . I believe there is no office in this country that is more safe according to the amount of their capital than this as is evinced by the fact that we have paid but little short of $40,000 this year for losses sustained in that time & yet our capital is in that favorable state above mentioned."

Conditions fortunately improved somewhat in 1828, but the losses suffered in Augusta in 1829 far surpassed the "unexampled" and more scattered ones of two years before. Incidentally, the bad news from Augusta had hardly been digested when word from Savannah told of a $6,000 loss there. Shortly after having learned of this loss, Secretary Mitchell had occasion to reply as follows to a letter from Timothy Dwight of New Haven:

> Hartford, 24 April 1829
>
> *Tim'y Dwight, Esqre.*
> Dear Sir,
>
> Your letter of yesterday is recd. As the Board have not
> met since I cannot therefore at present answer but one

subject of it—that respecting the failure of this Office. We have met with a heavy loss at Augusta—not however as great as the papers represent. Another loss at Savannah of $6,ooo has occurred since. These will probably deprive the stockholders of a dividend for a year or two. But the security of the assured is not essentially impaired by the losses hitherto sustained. They will be promptly met & whenever our stock is so far impaired as to render the assured insecure it will be deemed a high moral duty of this Board to set the example of declining a compensation when an adequate consideration cannot be extended to the assured by affording him that protection which he has a right to expect. If such a crisis should occur we shall not fail to give early notice to our agents.

I remain etc.

W. Mitchell, Sec'y.

Another letter, which was written the next day to William Leffingwell, also of New Haven, was similarly confident. "We are not surprised," it said in part, "at the report of our failure after so many similar ones respecting the Phoenix Bank & Hartfd Bank. But like them I trust they will turn out to be unfounded. It certainly is not true from any losses we have heard of. Our losses may for some time affect the dividends but must be much greater to essentially impair the security of the assured."

Obviously the Secretary was doing what he could to brush aside any thought of the Company's possible collapse. He was good at expressing confidence, too, but one wonders just what his correspondents would have thought had they known that the Secretary himself, who had purchased fifty shares of stock when the Company was founded, had sold the last of it eight years earlier, perhaps because he was not overly impressed by the Company's future even then.

As he suggested in these letters, the stockholders were about to be "deprived" of dividends for a time, but this was not to be merely "for a year or two" as he had so casually indicated. Difficult though the situation appeared at the moment, even greater difficulties lay ahead, and from November 1829 to April 1842 no single dividend served to gladden the hearts of the Hartford's stockholders.

The total income of the Hartford Fire Insurance Company for the first twenty years of its existence—a period which ended, according to

Walter Mitchell's records, in April 1830—was $241,297.29. Premiums had accounted for $219,640.97 of this total, and interest had made up the rest. During these same years the Company's disbursements had amounted to $327,818.47, and as a result the Company's capital position was seriously weakened. Expenses had been $29,791.91, dividends $122,-100, and losses had amounted to $175,926.56, two thirds of which had descended upon the Company in the unfortunate years of 1827 and 1829. In 1829 alone the Company's losses had been $89,469.59, two thirds of which had been due to the conflagration in Augusta.

These figures, it should be noted, give only an inadequate idea of the Company's position. Actually they show nothing more than the total income and total outgo. No reserve had been set aside to meet future contingencies.

Though details are for the most part lacking, it would appear that the dissatisfaction that had periodically been expressed was growing greater. Prior to 1829, no difficulties had arisen such as confronted the Company now. Yet it should be pointed out that even when increasing losses culminated in the catastrophe in Augusta the Directors seem to have been impelled to handle the claims as promptly and satisfactorily as possible before insisting on such administrative changes as many of them favored.

The Company had frequently borrowed from the Hartford Bank, but prior to 1829 the loans had never been very large. Usually, too, the Company's profits had made it possible to pay them off without undue delay. When news of the Augusta conflagration reached Hartford, however, it immediately became apparent that in order to meet the demands that would shortly be made upon it, the Company would have to borrow on a much larger scale than ever before. The news arrived early in April and on May 5th, at a meeting of the Directors, the following action was taken.

> *Voted,* That the President, Eliphalet Terry & David Watkinson be and they are appointed a Committee to effect a Loan in favor of the Company for an amount not exceeding Sixty Thousand Dollars & as security for sd loan to pledge the Stock belonging to this Company in The Hartford Bank & also the Stock Notes of this Company for the third installments.

Though the committee was in this way authorized to borrow $60,000, it was necessary to obtain only $51,300 in order to pay all of the Augusta claims. When the notes covering this amount came due, however, additional losses made it necessary to renew them though the total sum still due was moderately reduced. But the Hartford Bank, probably troubled by the Company's continued losses, seems to have suggested that other arrangements be made. Nathaniel Terry, still president of the Hartford Fire Insurance Company but no longer president of the Hartford Bank, was consequently authorized to make such arrangements as were necessary with a certain Harmon Hendricks of New York.

The authorization, as passed by the Directors and recorded by Walter Mitchell, reads as follows:

> *Resolved,* That the President be authorized to Sign & the Secretary to Countersign a power to Harmon Hendricks to sell so much of the Hartford Bank Stock pledged to him as security for the payment of the notes of the Company to him, sd Hendricks, as shall be necessary to pay any & every of the notes of this Company whenever any of such notes shall be due & remain unpaid for the term of twenty days, taking all reasonable care to obtain the best price for such stock.
>
> Nathl Terry, Predt.
>
> Test. W. Mitchell, Sec'y
>
> The above resolve was passed at a meeting of the President and Directors of the Hartford Fire Insurance Company on the 27th February, 1830, and a copy sent to Mr. H. Burr to be delivered to Mr. Hendricks together with a power signed by the President & countersigned by the Sec'y in pursuance of the Resolve.

For the next five years the Company seems almost constantly to have been engaged in attempting to work its way out of debt. The problem that had now grown so great had actually been in existence since 1827 when the Company's losses had swept away its limited surplus and this prolonged era of borrowing had begun. For eight years there was an almost constant round of borrowings and note renewals. Time and again new loans served merely to pay off old ones, with the result that the total amount borrowed during this period—a figure somewhat in excess of half a million dollars—greatly exaggerates the Company's actual indebtedness at any given time. It serves, however, to dramatize the Company's difficulties, and the Directors deserve some admiration for standing firm and refusing to admit defeat. Though many details are lacking, and we know that Company-owned securities were utilized in obtaining many of these loans, we know also that some of the Directors personally assumed the responsibilities for others.

Writing in 1940, Richard M. Bissell, who at that time was President of the Hartford Fire Insurance Company, admitted that "we do not know how much the then stockholders knew of the manner in which the business of the Company was being conducted or as to its financial condition. It is hard to believe that the administration of Messrs. Terry and Mitchell would have been allowed to continue as long as it did had the great mass of stockholders known of the desperate expedients to which, during the last years of their administration, these gentlemen were put in their endeavors to keep the Company afloat. The Company was then in a very precarious condition."

It is impossible to say just when the stockholders learned that the Company's condition had come to be so bad, but it is perfectly clear that ultimately they decided to do something about it. No record remains to tell us just what they thought, and there is no way of knowing whether or not any barometer was capable of determining the state of their feelings prior to the annual meeting of stockholders that was scheduled for June 1835. The very fact, however, that abrupt and positive action was taken when they met suggests that plans had been made at least a little while in advance. Still, President Terry and Secretary Mitchell may not have been aware of it, and this may also have been true of some of the Directors. Certainly no suggestion of coming trouble is to be found in the only record we have of the preceding meeting, which reads as follows:

> At a meeting of the President & Directors of the Hartford
> Fire Insurance Company on the 26th of May 1835
>   *Voted,* that Nathaniel Terry, esq., be allowed Two
> Hundred Dollars for his Salary as President of the Company
> for the last half year
>   *Voted,* that Walter Mitchell be allowed One Hundred
> Dollars for his Salary as Secretary for the last half year
>   *Voted,* that Lewis Bliss be allowed Four Hundred Dollars
> for his Salary for the last half year
>
> > *Nathl Terry, President*

That seems calm and casual enough. No hint is to be found there that anyone was apprehensive. In fact, it is only because of the action that was taken at the stockholders' meeting nine days later that it is possible to conclude that serious opposition to President Terry, Secretary Mitchell, and their supporters at last came clearly into the open. The revolt, we know, was notably successful, but the record of the meeting at which the revolt took place is utterly lacking in colorful details. Written in a hand that had never before appeared in the record book, it read as follows:

> At a meeting of the Stockholders of the Hartford Fire Insurance Company on the first Thursday of June 1835, convened pursuant to public notice, at their office in Hartford for the choice of Directors, The following persons were chosen Directors for the year ensuing—

Eliphalet Terry	James H. Wells
S. H. Huntington	H. Huntington, Jr.
Albert Day	Samuel Williams
F. I. Huntington	Elisha Colt, and

> R. B. Ward
>
> *H. Huntington, Jr., Chairman*

> At a meeting of the Directors of the Hartford Fire Insurance Company on the First Thursday of June 1835, Eliphalet Terry was chosen President and James G. Bolles was chosen Secretary.
>
> *H. Huntington, Jr., Chairman*

For twenty-five years the Hartford Fire Insurance Company had made such progress as had been possible under the irregular and uncertain leadership of Nathaniel Terry and Walter Mitchell. By good fortune rather than good management it had weathered the difficulties of its early years only to find itself confronted by problems that some observers may well have thought to be insuperable. Luckily, too, those who were now responsible for the Company's welfare had no way of knowing that the years ahead were to develop even greater dangers. And yet, in a way, the worst was over. The revolt had succeeded and an important change had been made. Despite great difficulties still to come, the future of the Company was bright.

CHAPTER 6

"CALAMITY BY FIRE"

IN NEW YORK

The change that accompanied the election of Eliphalet Terry as President of the Hartford Fire Insurance Company marked the beginning of a new era in the Company's development. Except as difficulties had occasionally necessitated determined action, the Company's affairs had formerly been handled somewhat casually, for no one seems to have felt the Company's business to have been his primary concern. All the former members of the Board were resolute, successful men. Had they not been, the Company's mounting difficulties would have led, in all probability, to the suggestion that liquidation might be the easiest, and possibly the most sensible, way out. It is hard to believe that the idea had never entered any of their minds during the difficult years that followed the Augusta disaster. But whatever they may have thought, no such suggestion seems ever to have been proposed. Despite the lack of system that was shown in the operation of the Company, and despite occasional evidence of a lack of business judgment so far as fire insurance was concerned, nothing suggests that any of those who had formerly been actively in control of the Company were lacking in character.

In this latter respect the new administration did not differ from the old, but the revolt of the stockholders had no sooner taken effect than the casual and unsystematic methods that had prevailed for so long changed sharply for the better. The records that tell of the changes that were made are just as lacking in colorful details as any of the earlier records are, but they make it clear that a new atmosphere had been created.

On the day of the "revolt" three separate meetings had been held.

The first of these had been the meeting of the stockholders at which the new Board of Directors had been elected.*

The second, which had been called as soon as the first had adjourned, had been a meeting of this new Board at which the new President and the Secretary had been chosen. With this accomplished, the second meeting adjourned and "a meeting of the President and Directors" was called. Oddly enough, however, the newly elected President did not preside. Instead, James H. Wells, who had been a Director ever since the Company had been founded twenty-five years before, occupied the chair, and it was he who wrote and signed the following record of the meeting:

> At a meeting of the President and Directors of the Hartford Fire Insurance Company held on June 4, 1835, Mr. James H. Wells presiding, it was
>
> *Voted,* That Mr. Lewis Bliss be requested to assist in the business of the office until otherwise ordered by the Board: and that he receive such compensation as may be satisfactory to him, and may be agreed to by the Chairman of this meeting.
>
> *Voted,* That the Secretary prepare as soon as practicable, a table of the unexpired risks taken by this office, designating the different amounts taken, at different rates, and as far as practicable, the kinds of property insured.
>
> *James H. Wells, Presiding Officer.*

Simply stated though this is, it raises as many questions as it answers. Why, for instance, should a Director have occupied the chair in the presence of the newly elected President? Why should "the Chairman of this meeting," and not the new President, have been the one authorized to approve "such compensation" as Lewis Bliss was to receive? And can it be that up to this time "the unexpired risks taken by this office" had never been tabulated, or that Walter Mitchell had failed to classify "the different amounts taken, at different rates, and . . . the kinds of property insured"?

It is impossible, after the passage of a century and a quarter, to answer such questions with complete assurance. However, the presence of Mr. Wells in the chair suggests that the differences of opinion that had led to the replacement of five of the former Directors may not have been

---

* Five members of the Board were replaced at this meeting. These were Nathaniel Terry, the former president, Seth Terry, J. D. Bull, Harvey Seymour, and Fontienne Raphel.

entirely absent even insofar as this sixth one was concerned. And this is borne out by the fact that within the next ten weeks Mr. Wells disposed of the stock he held in the Company and resigned as a Director.

As to the questions raised by the instructions given at this meeting to the new Secretary, the answer is probably easier. Nothing in the Company's records or in Walter Mitchell's methods, so far as we know them, suggests that any adequate tabulation had ever been made of "the unexpired risks," "the different amounts taken, at different rates," or "the kinds of property insured." Each policy, we know, was based on certain specific information that the Company had always insisted on obtaining. In all probability, however, little or no thought had ever been given to the idea of studying these policies as a whole. They had never been classified or divided into related groups in such a way as to make it possible to draw generalized and widely applicable conclusions from them. In other words, the Company seems to have carried on its business for a quarter of a century without making any serious effort whatever to begin the compilation of the basic data upon which a thorough understanding of the business of fire insurance necessarily depends.

This lack of interest in compiling information that is now known to be of vital importance might seem astonishing. In 1835, however, the problem assumed different proportions. Insurance had still not gone so very far beyond the early stages of its development. Even those who were best informed were still no more than vaguely conscious of many fundamentals that now seem axiomatic. Walter Mitchell and others of his day are not to be blamed for failing to understand what no one else had fully grasped as yet. Instead, the newly elected Directors are to be commended for visualizing even dimly an important problem that then needed so greatly to be solved. Their instructions to the Company's newly chosen Secretary—and similar developments for which this and other insurance companies were responsible during these formative years—were far more important to the future of insurance than were apparent at the time. In a way, this and certain related developments marked the beginning of the end of an extended period of groping. Until about this time insurance companies had been able to do little more than feel their way, and even yet they were often compelled to do so. But little by little their more forward-looking officials were coming to understand the principles upon which the business of insurance should be based. Because of this, such instructions to the Secretary as were voted by the Hartford's Directors on June 4, 1835, pointed the way to an infinitely greater future for the Company—and for fire insurance generally—than any person of that day could possibly have imagined.

For the first few years of the Hartford's existence active competition with other insurance companies had presented no serious problem. Other companies existed but they were few, and none operated very effectively outside the communities in which they were established. Little by little, each of the more successful ones broadened its field of action, and new companies were formed, as well. Consequently, by 1835 Walter Mitchell's long-established method of merely waiting in his office for such prospective clients as might come, was definitely outmoded. The Hartford Fire Insurance Company's way of doing business underwent no change, however, and one can only wonder why.

Almost every number of the *Connecticut Courant* which, by 1835, had come to be a weekly paper published every Monday, carried the advertisements of a number of insurance companies. On March 9, 1835, for instance, six different companies advertised in its columns, and of the six the Hartford's ad was quite the least impressive.

It was the *Courant's* policy, apparently, to publish all related advertisements together. Because of this the six insurance ads, none of which was large, appeared one after another, on this particular day, in the second column of the newspaper's front page. Each advertisement was one column in width, and the first, which occupied about two inches of the column, advertised the Mutual Insurance Company of Hartford, a comparatively new fire insurance enterprise. Next in line, and occupying fully twice as much space in the column, was a boldly set advertisement of the New York Life Insurance and Trust Company, a firm now long since gone and in no way connected with the present New York Life Insurance Company. Immediately below this was a much smaller and less impressive ad. Set in very small type and occupying no more than three quarters of an inch in the column, it read as follows:

FIRE INSURANCE

The Hartford Fire Insurance Company will receive Proposals for insurance against loss and damage by Fire, at their office in the city of Hartford, each day of the week, Sundays excepted.

Walter Mitchell, Secretary
Hartford, Jan. 5, 1835.

Originally inserted in the *Courant* in January of that year, this unimaginative little notice had often been repeated without changing even the date of its original appearance. Sometimes it had appeared alone, though usually other insurance advertisements had been published beside it, and in this instance it was followed by a 2-inch ad of the Howard Insurance Company of New York, below which came a 4½-inch ad of The Protection Insurance Company of Hartford, and a 3-inch ad of the Aetna Insurance Company of Hartford.

Even without looking further through the files of the newspapers of that day, it is clear that by 1835 competition had entered the field of fire insurance. With the single exception of the New York Life Insurance and Trust Company, all these advertisers were fire insurance firms, and four of them were Hartford companies. A good many others were also in existence elsewhere in the United States. Walter Mitchell and his associates may have been justified, twenty-five years earlier, in expecting propective clients to apply in person for such insurance as they may have required, but that was true no longer. And yet the unimpressive little ad that appeared on March 9, 1835, and that continued to appear at irregular intervals from then until June 1st, seems to have constituted the whole of the Hartford Fire Insurance Company's "promotion campaign" during this difficult period in its existence.

It is not impossible that dissatisfaction with this method of approach played some part in bringing about the revolt of the stockholders. We know that this ad appeared again and again until June 1st, four days before the meeting at which the new Board was chosen. And we know that it never appeared thereafter. We know, too, that when the *Courant* came off the press on June 8th—four days after the new Board had been elected—the paper made no report whatever of this bit of news. Even the next week the event was similarly overlooked, though many less consequential news items found their way into the paper's columns. One of these, which appeared on June 15th, reads as follows:

NOVEL SPECTACLE. The Ogdensburg Times states that a Car is now exhibiting on the Saratoga and Schenectady Rail Road, propelled by a horse walking inside of it, so that instead of a horse travelling before the car as formerly, he now travels inside the carriage and propels the car at the rate of a mile in four minutes. This is indeed an age of wonders.

In the meantime, as can readily be imagined, the new Board and the Company's new officers had been busy. The old record book gives few details of the meetings they held, though it explains that Eliphalet Terry was authorized "to vote on the stock owned by this company in the Hartford Bank," and Levi Ward, Jr., Esq., was "reappointed agent of this company for the city of Rochester & its vicinity." Furthermore, the Directors agreed that Ward was to "receive 10 per cent commission together with the charge for the policy as a compensation for his services."

While these developments were under way, someone was busily engaged in preparing the copy for a new advertisement that appeared in the *Courant* for the first time on July 6th. Published on page 4, it occupied about four inches of column 3 and read as follows:

HARTFORD FIRE INSURANCE COMPANY

OFFICE NORTH SIDE OF STATE HOUSE SQUARE, BETWEEN THE HARTFORD AND EXCHANGE BANKS.

This institution is the oldest of the kind in the State, having been established more than twenty five years. It is incorporated with a capital of 150,000 dollars, which is invested and secured in the best possible manner. It insures Public Buildings, Churches, Dwellings, Stores, Merchandize, Furniture, and personal property generally, from loss or damage by fire, on the most favorable and satisfactory terms.

The Company will adjust and pay all its losses with liberality and promptitude, and thus endeavor to retain the confidence and patronage of the public.

Persons wishing to Insure their property, who reside in any town in the United States, where this Company has no Agent, may apply through the Post Office, directly to the Secretary; and their proposals shall receive immediate attention.

The following gentlemen are Directors of the Company:

Eliphalet Terry	Samuel Williams
James H. Wells	F. J. Huntington
S. H. Huntington	Elisha Colt
H. Huntington, Jr.	R. B. Ward
Albert Day	Eliphalet Terry, President

James G. Bolles, Secretary

June 29   *tf 75*

Unimpressive though this may appear after the passage of a century and a quarter, it nevertheless suggests a little of the broader point of view and increased energy that were now being exhibited by the management of the Hartford Fire Insurance Company. There was certainly nothing small about the field of action that was now being visualized for the Company. Business was being hopefully sought "in any town in the United States" and in the months that followed, this advertisement appeared again and again in the columns of the *Courant* without the change of a single word except on September 14th, when the name of James H. Wells was replaced in the list of Directors by that of Edwin D. Morgan.

Though details are lacking, a feeling of increasing confidence somehow appears between the lines of Secretary Bolles' neatly written script. Business was increasing, too, and a new clerk—Christopher C. Lyman—was appointed at a meeting held on July 20th "to assist the Secretary in all matters proper for a Clerk to Transact." At the same meeting the Directors also "appointed an Agent of this Company for the town of Berlin, Conn. & vicinity," and the Company's new office in Hartford—the first it ever occupied that was wholly its own—was a busier place than Walter Mitchell's office had ever been. Occupied by the Secretary and two clerks, all three of whom were full-time employees, as well as providing a place for the President, and for the Directors when they met, the office gave better and more continuous service than the Company's clients had ever known before.

New plans were in the wind, too. Secretary Bolles was making a study that was soon to bring more business to the company. Only ten weeks after the new Board of Directors had been chosen, the Secretary's newly developed plan was approved and accepted by the Board. Eliphalet Terry himself recorded what took place, as follows:

> At a meeting of the President & Directors of the Hartford Fire Insurance Company held August 19, 1835, it was
>
> *Voted,* That James G. Bolles, Secretary of this Company, be authorized to travel on the business of the Company and to pursue the route marked out in the sketch by him presented to this Board, with such deviations as in his opinion the interests of the Company may require.
>
> *Voted,* That he be authorized and empowered to insure property and issue policies on behalf of the Company during his absence, wherever and whenever, in his opinion, the interests of the Company will be promoted by his so doing.
>
> *Voted,* That he be authorized & empowered to establish

agencies, and designate Agents in such places as in his
opinion the interests of the Company may require.

(signed) *Eliphalet Terry, Pres.*

As these plans began to go into effect, the Company's income began
to grow. New agents appointed by Secretary Bolles brought in new business, and agents who were already established were encouraged to increase their efforts. As yet the Company had accomplished nothing in
the city of Boston, being unwilling, perhaps, to compete with Boston
insurance companies for business in the city, but elsewhere in Massachusetts—in Springfield and Northampton, especially, though also in a
dozen smaller communities—policies were being sold in ever larger
numbers. In New York City, the population of which had now reached
a quarter of a million, no single Hartford policy had been sold until 1830.
The city had many insurance companies of its own, of course, but now,
with its population increasing at an unprecedented rate, business of every
kind was growing, and Hartford Fire Insurance policies grew in number
with every passing month. Elsewhere in the country, too—even as far
west as Illinois and Missouri, and as far south as Louisiana—the Company's business was increasing. Furthermore, though losses had been
heavy for eight long years, now, by great good fortune, they declined.
For the first half of 1835 they amounted to less than three thousand dollars, and by November conditions had improved so sharply that it began
to be apparent that a dividend might shortly be declared for the first
time in six years.

The Company had had all too little cause for celebration at any time
in the years just passed. Within six months, however, the new Board of
Directors had seen so great a change for the better that a celebration
of some kind seemed called for. Suppers such as the Directors had formerly enjoyed had not been held for years, but now, with conditions so
much better and with a dividend about to be declared after so long a
period of financial drought, a supper was in order. Already the Directors
had passed a special vote of thanks to President Eliphalet Terry and had
approved the payment to him of $300 for his first six months in office.
And now, in mid-December, they held their supper, genially congratulating each other on the Company's brightened prospects.

Meanwhile, as sometimes happens in December, a cold wave, moving from the Great Lakes into the Hudson River Valley, spread across
Connecticut. Preceded by a heavy fall of snow, it drove the temperature
down until, even in the city of New York, thermometers registered zero,

while in Hartford on the evening after the Directors held their supper, the temperature was as low. Every Connecticut road was blanketed in snow, and fires in every stove and fireplace were burning brightly to guard against the first hard freeze of winter.

New York City, despite its rapid growth, was still confined to the lower part of Manhattan Island, and what the *New York Journal of Commerce* was soon to refer to as "the most business part of the city" lay south of Wall Street between Broadway and the East River. Here, crowded together in scores of irregularly shaped blocks which, for the most part, were separated from each other by some of New York's narrowest and most irregular streets, stood hundreds of crowded structures. In this area were many of the city's busiest and most important warehouses, wholesale merchants, and shipping firms, and their premises were crowded with great accumulations of foreign and domestic merchandise. Dry goods and hardware, wines and liquors, furniture, supplies for ships, spices from the Far East, sugar from the Caribbean, olives, dates, and raisins from Spain and the Near East—all this and more besides filled the crowded buildings that lined street after street from Trinity Church to Coenties Slip and from Wall Street to the Battery.

All day long on that cold December 16th a sharp wind had whistled across the city. Laden drays, pulled by blanketed horses, had gone about their business as usual except where ice on the cobblestones made the footing difficult. Business was not greatly hampered, and the messenger boys from the city's many offices actually made better time than usual, running their errands at unaccustomed speed with mittened hands covering their ears. Little by little the temperature dropped, and the wind, increasing in force with the setting of the sun, swung into the northwest as the city's places of business closed.

Busy though the streets had been all day, they were all but deserted as night came down. Taverns and saloons were as well lighted as usual though their patrons were few. Here and there a light shone dimly as some warehouse watchman stirred the fire that kept him warm. Aboard the ships that lay at the South Street piers an occasional conscientious mate mounted to the deck to see that the lines were still secure. But activities were entirely normal only in an occasional newspaper office or pressroom, and few reasons seemed good enough even there to cause anyone to face the cold outside.

At 131 Pearl Street, a stone's throw south of Wall Street and very near Hanover Square, stood a store that was owned by the firm of Comstock

& Andrews. Like other business houses in this quarter of the city, it had been open on that cold Wednesday in December, but unlike some of its neighbors it seems not to have had a night watchman. It is easy to imagine that by six o'clock or a little after, with the cold wind blowing stronger than it had all day, the bookkeeper and the clerks said good night to both members of the firm, and, wrapping themselves up in heavy coats and mufflers, left for home. A little later both partners probably left as well, after looking about as usual and locking the heavy door.

For the next three hours or so the Comstock & Andrews store stood as motionless and dark as its neighbors did, while the cold wind whined through the irregular streets of the neighborhood. On the north side of Wall Street a hundred yards or so away, the office of the *Morning Courier and New York Enquirer* was busy with the task of getting out the next day's paper. On Broad Street, a little farther away, the office of the *New York Journal of Commerce* was similarly engaged. For the most part, however, the whole vicinity was almost deserted, and no one knows just how the coming tragedy began. We can be reasonably certain that some-one had banked the fire in the stove that stood not far from the book-keeper's tall desk in the office of Comstock & Andrews, and it may be that a small hot coal, displaced, perhaps, by the thrust of a poker, had fallen unseen to the floor, and had disappeared into some small crack or cranny. In all probability, something of this kind had happened, and a fire, small and hidden, smoldered for hours though no one saw it until nine o'clock. By that time it had spread a little and flames were plainly visible, though still it did not seem to be especially serious. Suddenly, however, it was out of hand. Window panes, cracked by the heat, fell out, and the flames, enlivened by the wind and no longer even partially restrained, swept suddenly through the building. Even before the alarm could be given the gale, fanning great tentacles of flame from window after window, set fire to the adjoining buildings.

"The wind being fresh from the Westward," said the *New York Journal of Commerce* two days later, "half a dozen stores were in a blaze in a few minutes. Added to this, the firemen were so exhausted . . . and their hose so much frozen, that the raging element was unavoidably per-mitted to roll on unobstructed, until it had gained such tremendous power that resistance, for the time being, became entirely useless. Store after store, and block after block, was swept down with astonishing rapidity. . . . The fire commenced about 9 o'clock on Wednesday evening, and raged with unabated violence for at least eight hours; and in one or two localities they [*sic*] were not fairly got under till 12 o'clock on Thursday noon,—or fifteen hours from the time it broke out."

It was not until December 21st that the people of Hartford read of the fire through the columns of the *Courant*. Even then, in the absence of any telegraphic or other rapid means of communication, the best the *Courant* could do was to reprint the story that the *Journal of Commerce* had published three days earlier in New York.

The ruins were still smoking, however, when the first news of the tragedy reached Eliphalet Terry. A hurrying post rider apparently brought the first vague news to Hartford but other accounts followed and by the evening of the 18th, forty-eight hours after the fire had started, Eliphalet Terry, Secretary Bolles, and their associates probably knew that the Hartford's hoped-for dividend would not be paid. They could hardly have known as yet just how vast the fire had been, but they must have realized that the Hartford had suffered heavy losses—heavier ones, in all likelihood, than it had ever known before. Even with some of the early reports that were sifting into Hartford came word that many of the affected insurance companies were threatened with bankruptcy.

Perhaps the first carefully weighed report that was read by the President and the Directors of the Hartford Fire Insurance Company was one that appeared in the *New York Commercial Advertiser* on the day after the fire and that may have reached Hartford on December 19th.

"New York has been for fifteen hours in flames," this account began. "They are not yet extinguished. A large section, and that the oldest and most wealthy portion of the city, is in ruins; and whether the progress of the Destroyer is yet completely arrested, we cannot tell. Since the conflagration of Moscow, no calamity by fire, so extensive, and so dreadful, has befallen any city in the world."

In two full columns the whole progress of the fire was described, and the city's losses were estimated with surprising accuracy. Admitting that "in all cases of great public or individual calamities . . . the first . . . reports are of course greatly exaggerated," the account had added that "We take it for granted—nay, it is admitted on all hands—that the fire insurance companies are all ruined."

A few years earlier the Hartford Fire Insurance Company had itself been all but ruined, and even yet it had not fully recovered. But now it had suffered new losses that no one could estimate as yet—losses that were certain to exceed the Company's slender assets. But was that a reason for admitting failure?

Eliphalet Terry shook his head, and called a meeting of the Company's Directors. Then, having gained their backing, he went to the Hartford Bank where he listed the Company's assets and itemized all the Hartford policies that were in effect in the city of New York. And finally, pledging his personal fortune as additional security, he arranged with the bank for the Company to draw upon it to the limit of such claims as might arise as a result of the New York holocaust.

A final hurried meeting of the Directors was called and, with all the Company's plans explained and approved, President Terry and Secretary Bolles, armed with their authority and with copies of every Hartford policy that was in effect in the city of New York, ordered a sleigh and a team of horses, and started out across 108 solidly frozen, snow-covered miles for the half-ruined city of New York.

Like other cities that had faced comparable disasters, New York had its full share of hopelessly discouraged citizens. By the time President Terry and Secretary Bolles had reached Manhattan Island and made their way to Wall Street, the desolation the fire had brought and the discouragement that had resulted seemed to dominate every other aspect of the city. In large part, too, the discouragement that was apparent everywhere was less because of the fire itself than because of the widespread failure of the insurance companies upon whose promises and financial soundness so many had depended. Having paid their premiums in the belief that their policies would stand between them and such losses as fire might bring, many New Yorkers had now learned that the security they had purchased had been counterfeit—that the protection they had sought had been a mockery. Even those whose property had not been damaged—whose buildings were unharmed and whose goods had not been touched by fire—were as doubtful of the value of insurance and of the protection their policies provided as those whom the fire had ruined. The mere mention of insurance was enough, in many instances, to start a veritable tirade of abuse.

William Walker was the Hartford's New York agent, and once he had been assured of the Company's determination to pay every honest claim, he hurried to spread the news. The firm of Shipman, Corning & Company, themselves unhurt except as their clients had suffered, offered

ELIPHALET TERRY
President, 1835-1849

office space in which President Terry and Secretary Bolles could carry out their complicated task. Policyholders, directed to the office by William Walker, were assured that their policies were absolutely sound, and that their every claim would be met in full. Edwin D. Morgan, who had become a Hartford Director only three months earlier, also lent a helpful hand in the long and difficult task of checking losses and submitting claims. Wherever President Terry and his associates went they assured those with whom they talked that every Hartford claim would be met with a minimum of delay, and as soon as President Terry and Secretary Bolles were able to establish themselves in the office Shipman, Corning & Company had provided, claims began to be itemized and studied and approved.

Almost the whole of the discouraged community was quite convinced that insurance had proved itself to be no more than a snare and a delusion, but President Terry and his fellow workers shortly began to create an atmosphere of confidence wherever the holders of Hartford policies were to be found. Nor were these the only ones who carried this good word. Those who learned of this unexpected development excitedly spread the news throughout the city, and the despair that had been so widespread for a time began to give way before the confidence that emanated from the Hartford Fire Insurance Company's temporary office.

At first few found it possible to believe this unexpected news, but working constantly, and ably seconded by Secretary Bolles, Agent William Walker, and Director Edwin Morgan, President Terry quickly began to overcome the city's doubts. Tall, clean-shaven, and handsome in his black suit and neatly tied white stock—plain-spoken and considerate in dealing with the Company's worried policyholders—assured and convincing as he stated and restated his company's determination to pay every claim its policyholders could justify, he served as a focus from which renewed confidence began to spread. And little by little, as groups of policyholders began to realize that the Company this man represented was living up to every promise it had made, they and those about them came to accept the fact that these representatives of the Hartford Fire Insurance Company were in New York not only to pay all claims that had grown out of the policies the Company had written in the city, but also to write new insurance for those who needed it.

It was the better part of two months before the last of Hartford's New York policyholders had been located and aided in the settlement of his claims. President Terry had been called to Hartford in the meantime, but he had returned to New York where, working steadily in the temporary office close beside the city's burned-out area, he and his associates had at first been all but overwhelmed by the reiterated expressions of discouragement and disbelief. But as more and more claims were studied, adjusted, and paid, disbelief gave way, and discouragement came to be replaced by confidence. Where, at first, no one thought of anything but claims, assurance returned and claimants, eager though they were to have their claims adjusted, were also convinced of their need for other Hartford policies.

Total losses in the great fire of 1835 have been variously estimated. More than six hundred buildings were totally destroyed, and no accurate estimate of their value or the value of their contents has ever been compiled. The *New York Commercial Advertiser,* attempting to estimate the losses shortly after the fire, pointed out that "the mere amount of property wasted and destroyed, not by the flames but in the confusion, and hurry, and desperation of the time, is probably equal to the entire loss (by fire). It is lamentable to see . . . thousands upon thousands and tens of thousands of dollars lying wasted around, in the form of ruined merchandise."

It is no wonder that estimates of loss range all the way from fifteen to twenty-six million dollars. Much of the loss, not having been covered by insurance, was never accurately reported. Other losses, fractionally made good when bankrupt insurance companies made such payments as they could, were often inadequately reported. And in addition to the actual destruction by fire, more than a score of insurance companies went bankrupt, and others were strained to the very limit of their ability to pay. The Hartford Fire Insurance Company, however, promptly adjusted every claim and, having paid a total of $84,973.34, succeeded in turning a great calamity into a great opportunity. Though confidence had been at low ebb in New York on the day President Terry and Secretary Bolles arrived after the fire had burned itself out, it had been surprisingly regenerated by the time these two finally returned to Hartford some two months later. And the Hartford Fire Insurance Company, to the surprise and gratification of its Directors, found itself writing more new policies than it had ever written at any earlier period in its history.

For the six-month period ending in April 1835, premiums paid to the Hartford had totaled $19,260.15, but confidence had so greatly been renewed, and the Hartford's reputation had so greatly grown, that the corresponding six-month period that ended in April *following* the fire brought in insurance premiums that totaled $97,841.75. A new era in the history of the Hartford Fire Insurance Company had begun, and, as P. Henry Woodward[*] wrote sixty years later, "The day of small things had passed."

It is widely conceded that Eliphalet Terry and the Directors of the Company, in their determined acceptance of their responsibilities in the half-ruined city of New York, aided importantly in the establishment of sound fire insurance methods in the United States. An important bit of fire insurance history was made, in fact, as a result of the long and diffi-cult sleigh ride President Terry and Secretary Bolles made just before Christmas in 1835.

It has often been pointed out that even if this action of the Hartford's President and Board of Directors had been arranged in advance for noth-ing more than the commercial advantage of the Company, it would have deserved high praise. Planned as it was, however, with no apparent thought beyond those that stemmed naturally from the conscience and sense of responsibility of the individuals concerned, it occupies a unique place in the history of fire insurance in the United States. That the Directors themselves were impressed by Eliphalet Terry's work is proved by the expression of their appreciation in the Company's record book, and it is interesting to note that "The thanks of this board" was also sent to the New York firm of Shipman, Corning & Company for the use of space in their office. Furthermore, Director Morgan was "allowed" $210 "for his service for this company in N.York in the months of December, January, and February last" and William Walker, the Company's New York agent, was paid $400 in lieu of income he would have received as agent had the new business written during President Terry's visit to New York been assumed by the Company through his agency.

The New York fire, having been by far the greatest tragedy of its kind that had ever visited an American city, naturally attracted atten-tion everywhere. Because of the heavy losses that had resulted, many property owners throughout the country who had given little thought to fire insurance began to feel the need for it, though some still were doubt-ful because of the failure of the bankrupt fire insurance firms to make their policies good. But the reputation of the Hartford Fire Insurance Company had gained immensely and the increase in business that was well under way before the Company's representatives had left New

[*] *Insurance in Connecticut,* p. 16.

York, continued even after they returned to Hartford. So much new business was being written, in fact, and President Terry had to give so much time to personal affairs as well as to affairs of the Company, that within two weeks of his return it was decided by the Board that a vice-president was needed. Less than a year before, Hezekiah Huntington, Jr., had presided at the meeting of the revolting stockholders, and it was he who now became the first Vice-President in the Company's history. Exactly what the post then meant to the Directors is not clear, for no specific duties were assigned to it, and, remarkably enough, no salary was paid to the person who held it either then or at any time in the next sixty-seven years. It was not until 1903 that any Vice-President of the Hartford Fire Insurance Company ever found his name on the Company pay roll.

Meanwhile the Company's business was growing at a surprising rate. Because of its newly gained reputation its agencies were busy almost everywhere, and it was clear that many new agencies could be established advantageously. At a Directors' meeting held in May 1836, a discussion seems to have taken place in regard to the need for more travel on the part of the officers and Directors of the Company. Already, Director Samuel H. Huntington was on his way to Indiana for the purpose of appointing efficient agents in various parts of that state. Elsewhere, too, new agents were being put to work, and the Directors now decided that when any of their number were called upon to travel in the Company's interest, they were to be allowed $3 a day—a generous amount in 1836—for their expenses. At the same meeting, $200 was voted as President Terry's salary for the preceding six months, and, apparently with the work he had done in New York in mind, an additional $150 was added. The Directors also voted $500 to pay Secretary Bolles' salary, and they added an additional $150 for his work in New York, as well. Apparently because Assistant Secretary Lyman had satisfactorily carried on the Secretary's work as well as his own while the President and the Secretary had been away, $50 was even added to his pay, bringing his total income for six months to $150. And it was generously decided that whenever the Secretary was called away on business, his expenses would be met by the Company, and he would also be paid at the rate of $2 a day.

Only eleven months earlier, the stockholders of the Hartford Fire Insurance Company had been so dissatisfied that an almost wholly new Board of Directors had been elected. Other changes had been initiated, too, and conditions had improved. But then the very greatest disaster in the Company's troubled history—or so it must have seemed—had suddenly wiped out all the assets the Company still retained, and had once more forced it deeply into debt. Almost $85,000 had to be paid to policyholders in New York and, for a time, doubts as to the future of the Company must have entered some minds.

With remarkable rapidity, however, and on a greater scale than anyone could have hoped, new business was written and new premiums were paid, the Company's premium income increasing at such a rate as had never been known before. During the whole of the previous year premiums had amounted to $37,732, and a supper had been held in celebration. The celebration had been premature, it is true, but another might have been held a year later with much more justification, for when the figures could finally be compiled, it was learned that the premium income for 1836 had reached the surprising total of $124,992—a sum that exceeded all the New York losses with $40,000 to spare.

Here was a sum that then appeared far greater than it seems to be after the passage of more than a century. Excessive speculation in western land, together with the Jackson Administration's action in distributing the national surplus among the states, and the passage of the so-called "Specie Circular" which called for the payment of only gold and silver in public land sales, had suddenly drained large quantities of specie from the commercial and industrial East to the small and only partially developed communities of the West, and throughout the United States money was hard to come by.

Never before had the Hartford Fire Insurance Company occupied so important a position in the field of which it was a part, or felt so confident of the future. Nervousness, however, was apparent among the nation's more observant businessmen. Business failures were increasing in number, and as 1837 opened they increased still more. Two New York banks failed. On May 9th, $650,000 in coin was withdrawn from the remaining banks of the city and in the days that followed, specie payments were suspended entirely.

The depression of 1837 had begun.

CHAPTER 7

DEPRESSION, RECOVERY,

AND GROWTH

THE ECONOMIC depression of 1837 was by far the most serious the nation had experienced up to that time. Between 1836 and 1840, commercial failures totaled almost 35,000, and the losses directly connected with them approached half a billion dollars. Other losses resulting from the widespread depreciation in values reached an even greater total.

About nine factories in every ten throughout New England closed at one time or another. In Philadelphia, when conditions were at their worst, fully half of all the clerks and salesmen were out of work, and similar conditions prevailed in other cities throughout the country. Banks failed. Bank officials defaulted. Counterfeiting was so rampant that at one time more than a thousand different counterfeit bank notes are said to have been in circulation.

As the depression deepened, conditions grew so bad, and so many people were roaming the country in their unsuccessful search for work, that such public and private charities as existed were taxed far beyond their capacity. Poorhouses were filled to overflowing and, during the unusually severe winter of 1838, deaths by freezing and starvation were not infrequently reported in various parts of the country. It was not until 1841 that the lowest point in the depression was reached but then, as seems to be typical of such periods in America, confidence began to return and the nation, quickly making up its losses, rapidly attained new heights of prosperity that exceeded any it had ever known before.

The Hartford Fire Insurance Company, conscious though it was of the nation's economic difficulties throughout this period, was not seriously affected by them. Such businesses as were owned and operated by the company's directors and other stockholders were troubled by the depression as most other businesses were, but the great increase in the Hartford's premium income that had followed the New York fire had placed the Company in a very fortunate economic position. By comparison with the difficulties that confronted other businesses, those the Hartford faced were few. The days of limited income for the Company were over, and it was never again to return to the modest position it had occupied before.

The great increase in the Hartford's premium income had come about, in the first place, because of the promptness and efficiency that had been displayed in the payment of every claim that had resulted from the New York fire. Many fire insurance companies had failed as a result of that disaster, and even some that remained in business had been able to do so only because claims had been discounted or met by issuing notes or stock certificates. The Hartford, however, had not only established a reputation for economic soundness and financial probity, but in the period immediately following the fire capitalized on this reputation through the establishment of new agencies in many areas that the Company had not theretofore entered. In 1836 alone, agents were appointed in eleven new states* and in eastern Canada as well. In fact, more states were added in this one year to the number being served than have ever been added in any other year before or since. It is true that a few policies had already been sold in some of these states, but prior to this time no regular agents had been appointed in any of them.

Though there had been so rapid an increase in the company's business, the New York fire had clearly demonstrated that the rates that had been charged had been consistently too low. Because of this, new rates were established, and though these met with some opposition, as increased rates so often do, businessmen generally were beginning to learn the value of insurance and were even coming to understand that the financial soundness of the insurance companies was directly related to the adequacy of the rates they charged. Furthermore, increased rates made possible the payment of more adequate commissions to agents, and this, in turn, resulted in more agencies and in better ones.

* Maine, New Hampshire, Rhode Island, New Jersey, Maryland, Virginia, North Carolina, Ohio, Indiana, Illinois, and Michigan.

The fire had greatly dramatized the value of insurance and, because so many insurance companies had failed and disappeared, more business came almost automatically to each of those that remained. New companies were founded but most of these were mutual companies; and though the theory on which they were based—a theory of community of interest—made it possible for them to defend the comparatively low rates they charged, they were naturally unable to foresee the economic difficulties that were to result from the depression of 1837, and comparatively few of them survived.

Meanwhile, many policyholders whose insurance had proved valueless because of the failure of the companies that had issued the policies, began to demand legislation that would protect the holders of such policies in the future. It was not only in New York that this attitude developed. There, of course, many a policy that had been purchased in good faith had failed to provide the protection that had been promised. But other policyholders also learned that, though their property was still intact, the insurance they carried was worthless because of the failure of the companies with which they had dealt.

Those who found themselves in this position were so numerous that demands not unnaturally arose in many states for legislation that would compel the insurance companies to provide more adequately for the protection of their clients. Many ideas were discussed and many suggestions were offered, but Massachusetts was the first state to adopt a constructive statute in this field. In 1837 a law was adopted in the Bay State calling on each fire insurance company doing business there to establish a fund that would make certain that the insurance contracts into which it entered would be fulfilled. Here, and as a direct result of this new statute, an important step was taken in the creation of stronger insurance companies, for under this statute the various companies that were affected began the establishment of what have come to be known as their "unearned premium funds."

This development, important though it was to each individual policyholder, was just as important to the insurance companies themselves. Much had to be learned before the insurance companies of America could attain their present high standards, and more than a little legislation, both good and bad, was still to be recorded in the statute books of our various states. But the New York fire, terribly destructive though it had been, can nevertheless be credited, in a way, with having been constructive also, for there can be no doubt that it directly resulted in some of the earliest moves toward sound state supervision of the business of fire insurance in America.

Prior to 1837 there had been few fire insurance laws of any consequence. Now, however, legislators began to recognize the importance and the increasing dimensions of the business, and more particularly they began to view it as a field for legislation. Many early laws that were adopted were unsound, it is true. Even before the Massachusetts legislature adopted its statute requiring insurance companies to establish unearned premium funds, for example, the New York State Assembly was considering the imposition of a special tax on insurance companies. The suggestion that had been made showed little understanding of the business of insurance, and President Terry and the Directors of the Hartford no sooner had word of it than they decided to oppose it. With that in mind, they sent Secretary Bolles to Albany where he was so successful that the Hartford's Directors formally adopted a resolution on his return, commending him for his success and granting him $300 as an expression of their appreciation.

Meanwhile, developments of an entirely different nature were troubling the nation. Mexico, though independent of Spain since 1821, had for years been almost constantly racked by civil war. Rival generals, the church, the army, and the nation's privileged classes were continuously in opposition. Furthermore, to the north and east of the Rio Grande the enormous and lightly populated region known as Texas was attracting increasing numbers of settlers from the United States. By 1835 some 20,000 Americans had settled there, intending, for the most part, to become loyal citizens of Mexico. In that year, however, Antonio López de Santa Anna seized power in Mexico and, having proclaimed a new constitution, did away with certain rights that were especially prized by the new settlers in Texas. A revolt followed. Texas declared its independence of Mexico and, in the Battle of San Jacinto, not only defeated but also actually captured Santa Anna.

Although Texan independence was promptly recognized by Great Britain, France, Belgium, and the United States, Mexico refused to relinquish its claims to the region and for the next ten years border troubles were more or less continuous. Even after Texas gave up its independence in favor of American statehood, difficulties with Mexico continued, leading ultimately to the Mexican War of 1847. It was not until that unfortunate struggle was concluded and California, as well as New Mexico and Texas, had become a part of the United States, that the Mexican claims to Texas were finally given up.

Meanwhile, the depression that had begun in 1837 had run its course. It had continued unabated for four discouraging years, but by 1841 the worst was over and conditions began to improve. The Hartford Fire Insurance Company had naturally been affected by the difficult conditions that had prevailed for so long but had not been seriously hurt by them. By November 1841, in fact, the Directors found the Company's affairs so much improved that they declared the first dividend to be paid to the stockholders since November 1829.

It is not to be doubted that throughout these twelve long years the stockholders of the Hartford Fire Insurance Company—or some of them, at least—were inclined to be critical of the way the Company's affairs were being handled. In 1838 a committee was actually appointed for the purpose of suggesting improvements in the Company's methods of administration. The three Directors who made up this committee were Samuel H. Huntington, Job Allyn, and Junius S. Morgan, but no record remains of its report. It is possible that no report was ever made, but it seems more probable that the members of the committee contented themselves with verbal recommendations which never found their place in the record.

Throughout these difficult years frequent changes were made in the Board of Directors. Harvey Seymour and Henry Waterman replaced Edwin D. Morgan and Samuel Williams in 1837, and were themselves succeeded by Ezra White, Jr., and John D. Russ the following year. John Russ, in turn, was succeeded by James Goodwin, Jr., in 1840, and John P. Brace replaced Junius Morgan in 1841. These changes, however, do not seem to have been made because of any dissatisfaction with those who were replaced. Difficulties that the depression had brought to the businesses in which the retiring Directors were individually engaged could easily have provided justifiable reasons for the changes.

It would appear that by 1841 those who were responsible for the welfare of the Hartford were reasonably well satisfied with the Company's progress. Though no dividends had been paid for so long, the Company's growth had continued. In fact, its business had increased remarkably even during the depression. In the first ten years of its existence the Company's total income from premiums had amounted to only $46,-

586.45. Its second decade, however, saw the total premium income rise to $194,710.84. But during its third decade—a period that included the disastrous New York fire as well as most of the discouraging depression years—premiums that were collected reached the somewhat striking figure of $939,824.41. Furthermore, the Company's growth was only now getting well under way.

By 1845, the Company's *annual* premium had increased to more than $177,000. Unfortunately, however, a series of costly disasters began in that year, too. On July 19, 1845, an extensive fire in New York City cost the Hartford $69,691.30. Eleven months later—on June 9, 1846—St. John's, Newfoundland, was the scene of an even greater fire which caused Secretary Bolles to hurry to the stricken city where he authorized the payment of $84,014.75. Having reached Boston on his way back to Hartford, the Secretary learned that Nantucket had just been the scene of an extensive fire. Leaving at once for the offshore island, he authorized the payment of additional claims that totaled $54,521.65, before making his way back to Hartford. In other words, the Company, in addition to the usual run of lesser losses elsewhere, had been called upon during the year just passed to pay $208,227.70 in three great fires alone.

Once more the Company was forced to suspend the payment of dividends, and again its credit was being strained to the utmost. Notes were given by many of the stockholders to cover payments still due on blocks of the Company's stock, but these were not enough to fill the breach. Once again bankruptcy was just around the corner but, as had been done on several previous occasions, various Directors endorsed the Company's notes, pledging their personal fortunes with the full understanding that the Company's obligations, behind which they had agreed to stand, might fall upon them personally.

The situation was already critical but, as ill luck would have it, more disasters were still to come. On August 17, 1848, an extensive fire in Albany, New York, necessitated the payment of $57,673, while other scattered claims raised the Company's losses for that year to the staggering total of $210,391. Furthermore, only eight months later—on May 18, 1849—the first really disastrous fire ever to strike the rapidly growing city of St. Louis compelled the Hartford to pay additional claims amounting to $58,676.83.

It can be seen from this that between July 19, 1845, and May 18, 1849, five great fires had alone cost the Hartford $324,577, and with such other losses as the Company suffered during these four years, its total losses far exceeded half a million dollars. From April 1846 to April 1853 no dividends were authorized. What is more remarkable is that the Company, whose capital was still only $150,000, had been able to pay losses that totaled, in four disastrous years, more than three times its capitalization.

Though the Hartford Fire Insurance Company had been in existence for only thirty-nine years at the time of the 1849 fire in St. Louis, its reputation for financial soundness and integrity had come to be so firmly established that no question arose as to its ability or willingness to pay. Already it was being widely and almost affectionately referred to as "the old Hartford" and, in contrast to the situation that had arisen in New York fourteen years before, no one seems even to have thought of questioning the Company's reliability. Seriously impaired though its finances were during these difficult years, its reputation suffered no impairment whatever.

The long depression that ended in 1841 had fortunately been followed by a period of burgeoning national prosperity. The war with Mexico had been of short duration and, as a result, the territory of the United States now extended from the Atlantic to the Pacific. The lightly populated West had grown gigantically in area, and as endless streams of confident settlers continued to move into this great land of promise, the Hartford's business grew. In the decade of the 1840's the Company's premium income reached a total of $2,172,902.16, showing an increase of 131 per cent over the preceding ten years. And even greater increases lay ahead. Both the country and the Company, despite the striking gains that had been made, had not yet reached their stride.

In June 1849, when the annual meeting of the Hartford's stockholders was held, a letter from Eliphalet Terry was read. In it, because of his "imperfect health," he asked not to be considered for re-election either as President or as Director. He was 73 at the time and for thirty years, during fourteen of which he had been President, he had served continuously as a Director of the Hartford. Furthermore, for an even longer time, he and his brother, Roderick, had been active in the operation of the wholesale grocery house of E. & R. Terry, which was also the leading Hartford firm in the West India trade. Now, however, he was seriously ill—he was to die, in fact, the following month—and the stockholders, after having adopted a resolution expressing their warm appreciation of his ability and his faithful dedication to the Company's interests and assuring him that he would "carry with him in his retirement the affectionate remembrances of his former associates," chose a new Board of Directors* who, at their first meeting, chose Hezekiah Huntington, Jr., who had been Vice-President for thirteen years, to succeed Mr. Terry as President.

Remarkable though the Company's development had been during the fourteen years of President Terry's administration, the stockholders had benefited very little. Though the Company's premium income had increased remarkably, its losses had grown as well. For several years, in fact, they had been almost unbearable. Viewed in the light of the present day, losses such as the Hartford had suffered appear no more than moderate. As the Company then existed, however, it was almost ruined by them. Having accumulated little or no surplus, it had been compelled to borrow heavily. Every claim was paid promptly but this was due, for the most part, to the willingness of the Company's officers and Directors to shoulder personally the Company's heavy financial burden while also remaining firm in their determination to broaden its field of operations and to increase its business.

As we look back now after the passage of more than a century, it is easy to see that the Hartford Fire Insurance Company, as well as the nation generally, was about to enter a period that was filled to overflowing not only with opportunities but also with difficulties. Despite recurrent periods of economic depression, the United States had grown surprisingly. In 1810, when the Hartford Fire Insurance Company had first opened its doors for business, the population of the country had only slightly exceeded seven million. By 1850 it exceeded twenty-three million, and in the next ten years more people were added to the total than had lived in the entire United States forty years before. Nor was that all. Manufacturing and almost every other national activity had grown enormously. As Dr. Horace Bushnell, the nationally known pastor of the North Congregational Church of Hartford, pointed out in 1851, "the transition from mother- and daughter-power to water-power and steam-power" was "greater by far than many have yet begun to conceive."

Two generations earlier hardly a home had existed without its spin-

---

* The nine directors elected or re-elected at this meeting were Hezekiah Huntington, Jr., Albert Day, Junius S. Morgan, James Goodwin, Jr., Charles Boswell, Henry Keney, Calvin Day, David F. Robinson, and Job Allyn.

ning wheel and loom. Now textile manufacturing had increased enormously and, centered in New England, was rapidly doing away with textiles woven on handlooms in the country's homes. And in other fields as well factories were taking over tasks that had formerly been performed at home. Where tacks and nails, hinges, locks, and chains had formerly been made, for the most part, at little forges set up in home workshops or even beside fireplaces in the kitchens, now such work was more and more being done in factories, and New England, again, was the principal producer. Boots and shoes, as well, were largely factory-made by now, with Massachusetts leading in their production.

Transportation had progressed. Though the first railroad in the United States—a 12-mile section of the Baltimore & Ohio—was opened for operation only in 1830, by 1834 the line extended from Baltimore some ninety miles to Harper's Ferry. Within another six years, 2,799 miles of railway line had been built in various parts of the country, and ten times as many miles were added in the following two decades. By 1850, 2,500 miles of railway lines were in operation in New England alone, while 3,100 miles had been constructed in the Middle Atlantic States, and 2,000 miles in the South. By the time the Civil War broke out in 1861, more than 30,000 miles of line had been constructed, almost 2,000 miles of which lay west of the Mississippi. The first telegraph line, which extended for forty miles from Washington to Baltimore, had been completed only in 1844, but by 1851 fifty telegraph companies were in operation in the United States. Steamboats, too, had rapidly come into use on almost all of the country's great rivers, and factories, which had originally appeared for the most part in New England, were now appearing in ever-increasing numbers in western Pennsylvania and Ohio where, even as early as the 1830's, Pittsburgh and Cincinnati had begun to supply much of the South and the Southwest with manufactured goods.

Throughout the entire country reduced costs due to factory production and to the lowered cost of transportation were widening markets and bringing about a rapid increase in sales and output. A generation earlier, farmers and plantation owners had found it necessary not only to plant, cultivate, and harvest their crops by the slow methods of that day, but had also been compelled to act as veritable jacks-of-all-trades, busying themselves in such "spare" time as they could find, at workbench, kiln, and forge. Forced by the economic conditions of that day to live for months at a time without money, or almost without it, they were compelled, in large part, to be their own "manufacturers." Laboring at many tasks when time permitted, and working, literally, by hand, they created most of what they needed. They felled trees, split their own rails and shingles, and adzed such beams as they required. They molded and fired their own bricks. Their wives and daughters were forever busy at their spinning wheels and looms or, if not that, were just as busy making soap and candles. Working at their small, hand-operated forges, farmers—and even townsmen—made not only such tacks and nails as they needed, but made much more, even including many of their tools. Many of them made their own furniture, cobbled their own shoes, made yokes for their oxen and harness for their horses.

But that had been before the industrial revolution had begun to make a new America—before steam-power and water-power began to be so widely harnessed for the uses of mankind. When that time came, farmers and plantation owners found it possible to devote more of their time to agriculture, thus increasing the production of their acres, and everywhere—in rural areas and in towns and cities as well—the age of specialization began.

Both directly and indirectly, these developments had their effects on the business of insurance. Though the rural population was still growing, the nation's towns were growing much more rapidly, and the cities were growing most rapidly of all. Philadelphia grew by more than 200,000 in a single decade, and New York grew even more. Chicago, which was no more than a very small village in 1830, became a town in 1833 and a city in 1837. Even that early, those who knew this new community were confident of the greatness of its future. In 1852, when it was first reached by a railroad from the East, it entered an era of astonishing expansion, and throughout the nation other towns and cities were similarly growing.

The Hartford's prospects had been none too promising when Hezekiah Huntington, Jr., was elected President in 1849, and throughout 1850 the Directors continued to be disturbed. On October 1st of that year, for example, they reached what they must have felt to be a most discouraging conclusion when they decided "that the stock of this Company should be returned to the Comptroller this year as of no market value." And yet, all losses continued to be paid. Though the funds in the treasury were very low, and further borrowings were necessary, the Company's Directors and even the stockholders refused to admit defeat.

They not only continued to keep the Company alive, but also continued to broaden its activities and to increase the business it was doing.

Conscious, as they were, of the difficulties that confronted them, the Directors were firm in their determination to improve the Company's condition. Beginning in 1850, they regularly held meetings twice a week, and on occasion additional meetings were held as well. They usually met in the evening, though that was not invariable, and from such records as were kept it is apparent that these meetings were anything but superficial. New risks were discussed in great detail, and those that were even a little more than usually hazardous were accepted or rejected by action of the Board which sometimes issued most detailed instructions. At a meeting on March 25, 1851, for example, the Directors discussed an application that had been made by John Myer & Son of Washington, North Carolina, a small Beaufort County port on the Pamlico River some forty miles inland from Pamlico Sound. The policy for which John Myer & Son had applied was for $4,000 "on naval stores and other produce in a shed and on a wharf," and though the records provide no information as to what the "other produce" was, the Directors fully understood that "naval stores" include tar, pitch, turpentine, and other resinous products, all of which are notably inflammable.

No detailed record was kept of the discussion that took place, but the risk was accepted at a "rate fixed at three per cent provided no steamer comes nigh enough to the wharf to endanger the property—but if that is the case, then four per cent."

The Board had long since learned that prudence and caution are essential if the business of fire insurance is to be conducted successfully. On this account the Company had come to require signed and very detailed applications when risks such as those on tanneries, sugar refineries, woolen mills, cotton mills, flour mills and the like were involved. These applications, in fact, were so detailed as actually to be surveys, and the information they contained dealt not only with the construction and arrangements of the structures under consideration, but also with the financial condition of the applicants, and, very particularly, with the location, type of construction and condition of any boilers and smokestacks that had been or were to be installed.

Applications were considered on the basis of this information and, if accepted, the rates were determined on the same basis. In many cases, however, special hazards were declined or the actual writing of the poli-

HEZEKIAH HUNTINGTON, JR.
President, 1849-1864

cies was postponed until additional information could be obtained. And, while the number of the Company's agencies was growing constantly, more and more care was being taken in establishing them. Often, in fact, the Home Office refused to approve the establishment of agencies in communities that had not been adequately studied.

Though the Company often seems to have acted very conservatively, it not infrequently did the opposite. Mills of various kinds—saw mills, cotton mills, and others—were often insured up to the Company's maximum of $10,000. This was the case whether water- or steam-power was involved. At one time the Board considered a resolution that would have reduced the maximum policy to $5,000, but the idea was rejected and a little later in the 1850's the following action was taken:

> *Voted:* To authorize an increase of our present line of
> $10,000 upon a single risk to an amount not exceeding
> $20,000 in such places and upon such classes of hazards as
> the executive officers in their judgment may deem expedient.

Conservatism has long been accepted as a characteristic of New Englanders, and this was well illustrated during these very years by those who were responsible for the insurance protection of Yale College. In 1824 Timothy Dwight, the son of Timothy Dwight the Elder who had been President of the College from 1795 to 1817, was appointed an agent of the Hartford and in 1825 he wrote what seems to have been the first fire insurance policy the college ever had. This policy was for $20,000 and for sixteen years it remained unchanged. In 1841, however, it was reduced to $10,000 and this was continued until 1852, the insurance for these two periods being divided as follows:

Building	1825–1841	1841–1852
South College	$2,500	$1,250
Atheneum	....	750
South Middle College	2,000	1,000
Lyceum	2,500	1,250
North Middle College	2,000	1,000
Old Chapel	1,500	....
North Chapel	3,500	1,750
North College	3,250	1,625
President's House	1,250	625
Dining Hall or Cabinet	1,500	750

Colleges were no doubt troubled in those days, as they are now, by their too-limited means, and this may well explain why the insurance was so sharply reduced. During these very years, however, New England's factories were increasing both in number and in value, and most of them now carried insurance as a matter of course, with rates more or less standardized. Cotton mills, for example, were normally insured at rates that varied from two to two and a half per cent. Saw mills utilizing water-power usually paid two per cent though six per cent or even more was commonly paid by those that were powered by steam. The rate for steam-powered planing mills was eight per cent or even more.

Dwelling houses, on the other hand, were often insured for rates as low as thirty cents per hundred dollars per year, and stocks of merchandise commonly were rated at fifty cents while hotels, if built of brick, at seventy-five cents.

Though the Hartford's problems had been more than usually serious as the decade of the 1850's began, the nation as a whole was entering upon a period of exceptional prosperity and development. Gold had been discovered in California in 1848 and the gold rush that began in 1849 enormously increased the number of settlers that were hurrying into the West. By wagon train across the continent, under sail around Cape Horn, and by ship to Panama where, after crossing the jungle-covered isthmus, the impatient travelers again took ship for California, one of the great migrations of modern times was under way. Thousands of other migrants, too, were hurrying into the West from Europe and even from Asia. No one knows what the population of California was when John Sutter first discovered gold in 1848, but by 1850 it was 92,597, ten years later it was 380,000, and California was not the only portion of the West that was growing. By 1850 the population of the United States west of the Mississippi—a region that had contained few people beside its native Indians when the Hartford Fire Insurance Company was founded—had passed the four-and-a-half-million mark and constant streams of others continued to pour in.

New territories were being settled at such a rate as no one would have believed possible a generation earlier. Settlements were growing into busy towns almost overnight, and well-placed towns were developing into cities almost as rapidly. Furthermore, from almost every corner of these newly settled regions applications for insurance on individual risks, as well as applications for agencies, were pouring into the Company's Home Office with almost every mail. There are records of applications even from "the Sandwich Islands," as Hawaii was then known, and many were arriving from California, from Texas, from Oregon, and elsewhere.

But it was not only from beyond the Mississippi that increasing demands were being made on the Company. The population of Ohio, for example, went beyond the two-million mark in 1851, having more than doubled in twenty years. In the same year Indiana's population passed a million, having tripled in two decades, and Illinois, with a population of 850,000 in 1850, had five times as many people as had lived in the state twenty years before. The populations of New York and Pennsylvania had each increased by a million in the same period, and that of the nation, which now stood at 23,191,876, had almost doubled in those same two decades.

It is small wonder that the Home Office of the Hartford was finding it increasingly difficult to administer all the detailed affairs of the Company. Its various transactions were vastly more numerous than ever before, and their number was constantly growing. And, to complicate matters, so many of these were originating in communities remote from Hartford—communities with which it was impossible to maintain really close relations because of the slowness and uncertainty of the mails—that the officers of the Company found themselves more and more confronted by the necessity of relying on the Company's agents and even of appointing "general agents" who, subject only to general directions from Hartford, could promptly and effectively attend to whatever Company business arose in the "departments" under their control.

By 1852 it had come to be quite obvious that the Company's business in Ohio, Indiana, Illinois, and other states nearby required more adequate supervision than was possible from Hartford. Neither the mails nor any other means of communication had ever been entirely adequate, and now that the Company's business in this region had so greatly increased, administrative difficulties had mounted. Consequently, at a meeting held in May, the Directors established what they decided to call "The Western Department." This was to serve a region comprising Ohio, Indiana, Illinois, Wisconsin, Iowa, Missouri, and Kentucky, and Mr. Demas Adams was appointed General Agent. Authorized to establish the Department's headquarters in Columbus, Ohio, he succeeded from the first in improving the Company's relations with its clientele in this area, and he also laid the foundation for an even more adequate agency system in the newly organized department.

For a little more than two years, Demas Adams supervised this territory. In August 1854, however, he found it necessary to resign. Seriously ill, he had only one more month to live, and it was not until after his death in September that President Huntington, while on an inspection trip to Columbus, appointed David Alexander as the Hartford Fire Insurance Company's second Western General Agent.

Though Demas Adams was able to serve the Company for so short a time in his newly created position, he contributed importantly to the development not only of the Western Department but also to that of the Company. Under his direction, the Company's business in the Western Department increased, and he also played a constructive part in opposing the cut rates that some of the Hartford's competitors were offering. For example, in a letter written to President Huntington in September 1853, he referred to certain companies which, while doing business in Cincinnati, were making plans "to insure at fifteen to twenty-five cents less than the rates of the Board of Underwriters."

Adams described these companies in mid-nineteenth-century Cincinnati in terms that will perhaps be amusing to its present-day citizens. "They are doing great mischief," he pointed out. "They seem to suppose that the same rates that will pay in New England with its staid and permanent population will do in Cincinnati where incendiaries, rowdies, and thieves pour in from the rivers and where dishonest people find a home in the stir and bustle of a rapidly growing city after having been driven away from some point where dishonesty could not thrive. No one has made any money at insurance in Cincinnati, and after getting prices to a point that promised to pay, these silly people come in to try their hand at a game that must lose in the end—or all experience leads to a false conclusion."

Though rate-cutting was the problem that was uppermost in his mind when he wrote this letter, he failed to stop it and it continued in one form or another for years. He was just as intent, however, on urging the Hartford to increase its capital so that the Company might stand on a footing more nearly equal to that of its stronger competitors.

"I would be glad," he wrote in March 1853, "to have our capital put up to the limit of the charter—$250,000—not so much because it makes the Company safer (for the security is in the management of the business) as because of the *apparent* security it would afford. The Aetna, Protection and others with which mainly we have to contend, advertise capitals of $300,000 and upwards. An Increase, I think, would have a favorable influence."

He reverted to this subject often, and his arguments carried weight in Hartford. He was not alone, however, in favoring the increase he proposed. President Huntington was just as dissatisfied with the Company's financial position and with its limited capital. In fact, he was dissatisfied with his salary, as well. Twice he submitted his resignation, though on both occasions he was persuaded to remain. After he withdrew his first resignation his salary was increased to $3,000 a year, and after the second was withdrawn the Company's capital was increased to $300,000. Both moves seem to have pleased him, and the second especially delighted Demas Adams who, it has been suggested, might well have succeeded to the presidency had President Huntington insisted on resigning.

Unfortunately, Demas Adams' resignation and death came very shortly after the Company's capital was increased, and he never learned of the favorable effects that followed. The new stock—par value $50— was subscribed for promptly, and those who purchased it were required to pay $30 for each share within the first twelve months after it was issued, the balance being covered by notes that were callable at the pleasure of the Board.

Within the first two or three years of President Huntington's administration the Company's condition improved steadily. In 1854 the payment of dividends was resumed and, with business increasing with every passing year, the Company's capital was increased again in 1857, this time to $500,000. Throughout the first forty years of its existence the Company had frequently been confronted by the possibility of bankruptcy. On several occasions, in fact, it had been saved from disaster only by the determination of its officers, its Directors, and its stockholders. But now, in the decade of the 1850's, its premium income reached a total of $4,546,534.87 which was more than twice what it had been in the previous decade. Furthermore, by 1859 the Company's assets reached $1,000,000 and its surplus, as such matters were figured in that day, somewhat surpassed $300,000.

So far as the Company's finances were concerned, the worst was over.

After fifty years the Hartford Fire Insurance Company found itself on a firm foundation, and those who were responsible for its welfare knew that under their direction it had come to be a financial institution of important consequence. As the decade of the 1850's ended, however, the Hartford's Directors began to understand, as other thoughtful people of that day also did, that a problem of surpassing importance, and a danger of immeasurable extent, might well confront the nation in the days immediately ahead.

CHAPTER 8

THE COMING

OF THE

CIVIL WAR

For a generation prior to 1860 the people of the United States had been confronted by a problem of ever-increasing magnitude. In both Europe and America a growing interest in humanitarianism was laying the groundwork for many reforms that were to gain acceptance in the years ahead, but of them all, opposition to slavery was growing most rapidly. The idea was anything but new. For a century or more it had been evident on both sides of the Atlantic. Denmark, in 1792, had become the first European nation to abolish the slave trade, and opposition to this dreadful commerce in human beings had thereafter become general. In 1814 the Congress of Vienna had agreed that it should be abolished "as soon as possible." In 1838 Great Britain actually put an end to slavery in her possessions, and in the years that followed other European and Latin-American nations had taken similar action.

Though slavery still existed throughout the American South, opposition to it had been evident in America for a century and a half. Following Great Britain's action, however, antislavery activities in the United States grew immensely and they increased even more after the publication of Harriet Beecher Stowe's *Uncle Tom's Cabin* in 1852.

At the time of the American Revolution and during the nation's early years of independence, many leaders—Washington, Adams, and Jefferson among them—had been opposed to slavery. Washington's will provided for the emancipation of his own slaves. John Adams had urged "the total extirpation of slavery from the United States." Jefferson, in referring to slavery, had said "I tremble for my country when I reflect that God is just," and while a member of the first Continental Congress he had unsuccessfully proposed "that after the year 1800 there shall be neither slavery nor involuntary servitude . . . otherwise than in punishment for crime." None of these attitudes were governmental, of course, but under the terms of the Treaty of Ghent, signed in December 1814, Great Britain and the United States officially agreed to do all in their power to bring the slave trade to an end.

Opposition to the slave trade was one matter, however, and opposition to slavery throughout the South was another. Strangely enough, an invention of a New Englander—the cotton gin—had greatly increased the importance of slave labor upon which the production of cotton so largely depended, and, in doing so, served to rivet slavery more firmly than ever before on the cotton-growing South. Thus at the very time the Abolitionist movement was growing more extreme and more vociferous in the northern states, the prosperity of the South was coming to be more and more dependent on cotton and on the slaves who produced it. Under these circumstances, the arguments of the Abolitionists were more effective in bringing about a determined defense of slavery throughout the South than in weakening that institution. Many Southerners had formerly been inclined to criticize slavery, but as the economy of the South came to depend more and more on the production of cotton, the subject of slavery passed the point at which it could be discussed objectively. By the 1850's, in fact, it began to be apparent to the thoughtful that no settlement of the question was possible except, perhaps, by way of war.

While opposition to slavery was increasing, the people of the United States, without quite realizing it, were entering a new economic era. Though the nation was still predominantly agricultural, the urban population was growing rapidly. Methods of transportation and communication were improving, and the population, shifting from farm to city and from east to west, was ever more influenced by new ideas that were being spread abroad by increasing numbers of daily papers. Many of these, unfortunately, were given to distorting the news, and most seem to have been willing to deal in personal abuse and political vilification. During the 1840's and 1850's some improvement in newspaper ethics began to be evident but the better part of another generation was to pass before newspaper partisanship began to give way before real editorial independence, and before slanted reports of public affairs came to be replaced by objective and unbiased news accounts.

The two or three decades that just preceded the 1860's formed an era that offered the people remarkably little in the way of relaxation, and it is possible that this may explain why many mass activities of that day were marked by so much emotionalism. It was the day of the "camp meeting" and the religious "revival." Even political activities were inclined to be emotional. As James Truslow Adams points out,* "The great mass of our people in all sections were interested neither in things of the mind nor in healthy sports. There were few diversions either for those crowded into cities or living on lonely farms or clearings. The village was unutterably dull. We were emotionally starved, and in many sections the camp meeting revival . . . alone offered that release from a life of inhibitions which the normal human being craves. We have to take into consideration this starved life and the ease with which any issue appealing to the emotions would spread like fire, to understand the decades leading to the [Civil] war."

Increasing in area as no nation had ever increased before, the astonishing good fortune that attended our people led them on and on into vast new regions that had never before been organized. From the earliest days of colonialism in North America the settled areas had always been bounded on the west by frontier regions that awaited settlement, and this continued for a century even after independence had been gained. Most people, looking to the West, saw what they took to be an almost limitless land. They knew that difficulties lay there—Indians, mountains, deserts, and unknown dangers of many different kinds—but opportunities lay there too, though by 1849 the gold of California blinded many to even greater treasures that lay both there and elsewhere.

From the time California had first become known to the people of Mexico and Spain there had been talk of gold in the region. Little was found, however, until 1841 when deposits were reported not far from Los Angeles. Still, these proved to be inconsequential, and they attracted little attention. It was not until January 24, 1848, that the famous discovery of gold was made at Sutter's mill on the American River.

It was this discovery that brought about the California gold rush—

* *The March of Democracy—A History of the United States.* Vol. II, p. 216.

an astonishing migration that resulted in changes so far-reaching that within twenty months a determined convention of newcomers to California framed a constitution and applied for the admission of this remote but rapidly growing region into the Union as a state—an application that was favorably acted upon by Congress on September 9, 1850.

Dramatic though the growth and development of California proved to be, other portions of the nation were progressing almost as rapidly. Michigan had become a state in 1837 and Florida in 1845. Iowa and Wisconsin followed in 1846 and 1848, Minnesota in 1858, Oregon in 1859, and Kansas in 1861. The census of 1860 showed a national population gain of 8,250,000 over what it had been ten years earlier—a gain in a single decade that was greater by more than a million than the total population of the nation when the Hartford Fire Insurance Company was founded. Even in Connecticut, where the population had grown so slowly for half a century prior to 1840, the 1860 census showed an increase of more than fifty per cent over what it had been two decades earlier.

Despite the increasing difficulties that served to widen the political gap between the people of the North and the South, economic conditions remained good throughout the early 1850's. Many businesses were thriving, and the Hartford Fire Insurance Company, increasing its business as so many other companies were doing, steadily continued to broaden its representation in the South and West. Business was growing in Canada as well. It is true that the Directors considered withdrawing from "the Canadas" when a new law was passed requiring the deposit of $50,000 there, but they fortunately decided, instead, to comply. Furthermore, a general agent was appointed and was given authority not only to supervise the Hartford's business north of the border but also to select new agents and to adjust the Company's losses there without referring them to Hartford.

Though the Hartford's total premium income for the decade of the 1850's passed the $4,500,000 mark, more than doubling what it had been during the previous ten years, new economic difficulties were in the offing. The national economy had expanded enormously since the nation had recovered from the depression of 1837 and, as Americans seem prone to do, the people had largely forgotten such lessons as that unfortunate period had taught. Consequently, as conditions improved once more business began to expand, though the expansion was based, to a very large degree, on credit.

Since 1849, California had been producing large quantities of gold, the total having risen to $55,000,000 in a single year, and this played a part in the unhealthy expansion of credit. Throughout the early 1850's widespread economic optimism had made possible this credit-financed expansion. In the ten years following the discovery of gold, for example, more than twenty thousand miles of new railroads were built, though much of the construction was unsubstantial, and many of the lines had been planned with little thought for the traffic they would attract. It has been said that the cost of new railroads during this period alone totaled almost three quarters of a billion dollars, a gigantic sum for the day and one far greater than the national economy could afford.

As a result of such overoptimistic developments, the nation was confronted, in August 1857, by the unexpected failure of the Ohio Life Insurance and Trust Company. Widely thought to be entirely sound, this company had loaned large amounts on the new railroad lines, and its failure marked the beginning of an economic crash that forced almost every bank in the country to suspend specie payments.

In the weeks that followed, values fell enormously. Business declined and unemployment rose. In New York City where thousands were unemployed, a military guard was placed about the Federal Subtreasury as penniless mobs now and again roamed through the streets. Property values declined. Construction work of almost every kind was suspended. Railroad building came to an abrupt halt in many parts of the country. Bankruptcies were common and in the West, where almost every activity had been based on unquestioning belief in the nation's future, even towns and counties found themselves beyond their economic depth.

In New England the output of almost every factory declined. Shipping was tied up in every port. Where credit had been much too readily advanced a little while before, now it could be obtained only with the greatest difficulty. It was only in the South that economic conditions continued to be reasonably good. The 1856 cotton crop had been profitably sold, the price of slaves continued reasonably high, and months were to pass before the 1857 cotton crop would reach the market.

For the better part of three years the depression continued. It was not until 1860 that optimism fully returned, and for a time the nation's economic problems actually succeeded in displacing slavery as the leading topic of the day. Even before the depression reached its end, however, discussions of business conditions gave way once more to the perennial argument over slavery.

Despite the depression the country's more extreme abolitionists had continued their activities, and one of them—John Brown, born in Torrington, Connecticut—was called vividly to the attention of the public when, having gone to Kansas, he took part in the so-called "Pottawatomie Massacre" in the spring of 1856. In this affair, men under his orders cold-bloodedly killed five proslavery settlers in retaliation for the recent and nearby murder of five "free-state" settlers.

In the three years that followed, John Brown traveled back and forth between Kansas and the East, taking part in another raid or two and preparing a plan for the establishment of a stronghold for fugitive slaves in the mountains of Virginia. He even visited Canada where, with a small group of white and Negro sympathizers, he planned an attack on the Federal arsenal at Harper's Ferry, Virginia, which, with 18 men, he succeeded in capturing on the night of October 16, 1859.

Meanwhile, Lieutenant-Colonel Robert E. Lee, U.S. Army, was at "Arlington," his handsome, heavy-columned mansion in Fairfax County, Virginia, across the Potomac from the city of Washington. He had returned only a few days earlier from New York and, because he was preparing to rejoin his regiment and expected to be away for an extended period of time, he had asked Andrew Jamieson, the agent for the Hartford Fire Insurance Company in nearby Alexandria, to prepare an application for a fire insurance policy on "Arlington"—an application which is still in the Company's possession. Made out in detail, and in the agent's handwriting, this document bears the date of October 17, 1859, and it carries the very simply written signature of R. E. Lee.

There is no record that tells exactly the hour at which this application was signed, but Douglas Southall Freeman,* points out that Colonel Lee "was busy . . . on the morning of October 17, 1859, when Lieutenant 'Jeb' Stuart arrived with a sealed note from Colonel Drinkard, chief clerk of the War Department. The message was a brief order for Lee to report to the Secretary of War immediately."

No explanation for the order was included, but it necessitated instant action and without taking time even to change into a uniform, Colonel

* Douglas Southall Freeman, *R. E. Lee—A Biography,* Vol. 1, p. 384.

Lee called for a horse, and, accompanied by Lieutenant Stuart, set off for Washington.

It was not until three days later that he returned to Arlington. In the meantime, having been placed in command of a small force made up of marines and militia that had been sent by rail to Harper's Ferry, he joined them there and, early the following morning, he ordered an attack in which John Brown and his little band of supporters were captured hardly more than thirty hours after these fanatic Abolitionists had captured the Federal arsenal in the town at the northern end of the Shenandoah Valley.

The insurance policy for which Colonel Lee applied on the morning he was so unexpectedly ordered to Harper's Ferry was probably written in the days that followed. It was not until December that he was ordered to join his regiment, and even then his departure was delayed by an investigation of the Harper's Ferry incident. Though he had orders to go to San Antonio where he was to take command of the Department of Texas, it was not until February 6, 1860, that he finally left. Utterly unaware of the gigantic events that awaited him in the years ahead, he could not have guessed how small a portion of that troubled future he would be permitted to spend in the shelter of the home he had just insured.

Throughout the 1850's the Hartford Fire Insurance Company had continued to expand, but other companies had been expanding, too, and not infrequently the Hartford agents called for help in meeting their more active competitors. In 1859, for example, the Hartford's agent in Toledo, Ohio, asked the Company for a loan that would make it possible for him "to defray for a time extra office and other expenses necessary to counteract the efforts now being made by . . . other companies to obtain business by increased compensation to their agents and liberal expenditures otherwise." In enlarging on his problem the agent asked that the loan be made "at a nominal interest of from five to seven per cent and payable in one and two years."

How commonly loans of this nature were made is not apparent, but in this case the Directors authorized a loan of $1,000 at six per cent, "the security to be made satisfactory to the executive officers."

Moreover, during this decade the Company's agents continued to grow in numbers. The South had long since been reasonably well covered, and now the West was demanding more attention. For example, at a meeting of the Company's Directors on August 25, 1857, an "Application of Edmund McLean for an agency of this Company at San Francisco, California, was discussed and postponed for further consideration," but five weeks later "The Application of Edmund McLean, postponed August 25th, was taken up and after discussion it was Voted, To establish an agency at San Francisco, California, and to appoint Mr. McLean, the applicant, the Agent at that point."

By the time this appointment was made California had been a state for seven years, but it was still very remote from the Company's headquarters in Hartford. It took sixty days or more for a letter to reach Hartford from San Francisco, and the payment of losses was a slow procedure. On April 18, 1858, however, a letter from Agent McLean reached Hartford, proposing that he and a certain John Fowler, Esq., be granted "a joint commission . . . as Agents for this Company and asking for additional powers for the adjustment and payment of losses."

The Directors agreed, and for a time McLean and Fowler, who established their office at the northeast corner of Clay and Battery Streets, not only represented the Hartford and several other insurance companies in San Francisco, but also appointed sub-agents in other California towns. For a time, they were unusually successful, too. Property owners in San Francisco and other California communities, most of which were very inadequately provided with fire-fighting equipment, were eager to obtain policies, and premiums often came in unsolicited. But the office of McLean and Fowler was to learn that there was more to the business of insurance than the mere acceptance of premiums. A series of bad fires developed and there were heavy losses in various parts of the state. Fires were so widespread, in fact, that some small companies failed, and some of the larger ones, having paid their losses, withdrew from California. The Hartford, however, was less easily discouraged. When The Pony Express and the transcontinental telegraph were inaugurated in 1860 and 1861, they greatly improved communications between the East and the West, and California was developing rapidly. In 1863, however, new difficulties took Secretary Timothy C. Allyn to San Francisco; and while he was there he chose a new agency—Bigelow Brothers—to replace McLean and Fowler. Even now, however, Edmund McLean and the firm he established are widely credited with having acquainted the Pacific Coast with the importance of insurance.

Meanwhile, the difficulties under which the nation was laboring continued to increase. Congress, having remained in session throughout the winter of 1859–60, was filled with tension. Many members of the Senate and the House actually went armed as they attended to their duties, and it has been said that armed supporters of both the proslavery and antislavery groups in Congress commonly occupied places in the galleries.

Bitter though these animosities had come to be, the Hartford Fire Insurance Company continued to increase its business throughout the South. Even in Charleston, South Carolina, where Southern loyalties were especially strong, the Company's popularity was undiminished. Some twenty years earlier—in 1838—a disastrous fire in Charleston had destroyed a large section of the city, leaving thousands of people homeless. The only insurance companies doing business in South Carolina at the time were local ones, all others being debarred by law, and these local companies, faced with losses so extensive, found it impossible to meet them. The result was that every company failed and, for a time, no single fire insurance company was in operation in the entire state.

As luck would have it, however, H. P. Gleason, who had formerly been a resident of Hartford, had moved to Charleston some time before the fire, and had opened a china, glassware, and crockery store at the corner of King and Wentworth Streets. He understood the importance of fire insurance and had arranged with the Home Office of the Hartford for a $10,000 policy on the stock that lined the shelves of his Charleston store.

His place of business, like many others all about, was destroyed in the fire and his stock was ruined. Unlike the other sufferers, however, his claim was promptly met—in full—and the South Carolina legislature, suddenly conscious of the unsoundness of the law it had passed, removed the restriction that had kept all but local companies from operating in the state, and the Hartford was the very first to take advantage of the change. The Charleston firm of Hayden, Gregg & Company—who were jewelers, incidentally—became the Hartford's first agents in South Carolina, and in their hands the Hartford's business prospered up to the very outbreak of the Civil War.

Though 1860 was a year of increasing political tension, the record that was kept of the meetings of the Hartford's Directors tells little of their political point of view. By late summer bitter antagonisms were apparent in every one of the nation's thirty-three states, but the Hartford's Directors, meeting regularly as they had for years, seem to have devoted their meetings entirely to Company affairs. Not even between the lines is it possible to detect any sign of their political point of view. At a meeting held in August, for example, the minutes explain only that "The subject of state agencies laid over from the last meeting was taken up and a plan for the organization of the system and specifying the principal duties of state agents was submitted and fully explained by the President, and the plan as submitted was approved and adopted by the Board." And at a later meeting the Directors decided that it was "not deemed expedient to establish an agency at Denver City, K. T.,* at present," though no reason was given.

There were four candidates for President in the election of 1860—Lincoln, Douglas, Breckinridge, and Bell—and of the 4,692,069 votes that were cast, Lincoln received only 1,866,452. In the electoral college, however, he stood far in the lead. Long before the vote was cast it was clear that Lincoln's election would be followed by secession. Many Southern leaders had openly declared that that would be the case, though in the North, and particularly among Republicans, such threats and warnings were thought to have comparatively little support among the people below the Mason and Dixon Line. Had it not been for this belief, it is not unlikely that Lincoln's vote would have been measurably smaller than it was. But even among those who had foreseen this outcome many were startled by the rapidity with which the secession movement developed.

The election was held on November 6, 1860, and four days later South Carolina issued a call for a convention to consider the situation that had arisen. The members of the convention, who were chosen in a special election held on December 6th, met first in Columbia. But because of an outbreak of smallpox there they transferred their meeting to Charleston. Meeting again on December 17th, they spent three days in fiery discussion, finally repealing the Act of 1788 which had ratified the Federal Constitution, and declaring "that the union now subsisting between

* This was before Colorado had been organized as a territory and "Denver City" was consequently still in Kansas Territory.

South Carolina and other States, under the name of 'The United States of America' is hereby dissolved."

As yet, opinion in the South was far from unanimous. Dissatisfaction was general, and secession was being widely proposed but—in Virginia, for example, and elsewhere as well—no actual move in that direction had been taken. Throughout the South, in fact, important leaders—Jefferson Davis and Alexander H. Stephens among them—were advising caution. Robert E. Lee, writing to his son from Texas on November 24th, was deeply troubled. "My little personal troubles," he admitted, "sink into insignificance when I contemplate the condition of the country, and I feel as if I could easily lay down my life for its safety." And some ten days later, still uncertain as to what might happen, he wrote again: "If the Union is dissolved, which God in his mercy forbid, I shall return to you."

Opinion in the North had not truly taken form as yet. Horace Greeley's New York *Tribune,* commenting on secession before the South Carolina convention had met, insisted that "The right to secede may be a revolutionary right, but it exists, nevertheless." And on the very day the South Carolina delegates met in Charleston, Greeley went further. "If the Declaration of Independence justified the secession of three millions of Colonists in 1776, *we do not see why it should not* JUSTIFY the secession of five millions of Southerners in 1861."

Nor was the *Tribune* alone in holding this opinion, though ideas changed as events began to force the people of both the North and the South to take their stand in favor of the Union or of the still unorganized Confederacy.

What secession might ultimately mean to the Hartford Fire Insurance Company was not immediately apparent. As individuals, the Company's Directors no doubt had opinions of their own, but collectively no opinion became evident for a time. It is not unlikely that even those who were strongest in their opposition to secession were uncertain as to what action the Company should take. It was entirely possible, as the Hartford's experience in Canada had shown, that the Company's business in South Carolina, for example, might be carried on as successfully after the state had seceded as before. Even those most heartily opposed to the idea of secession might well have argued that right and wrong, so far as that question was concerned, need not necessarily affect the Company's business one way or the other in such states as chose to secede. For a time, however, the Directors took no action whatever. So far as the record shows it was not until a meeting was called at 11 A.M. on January 12, 1861, that any discussion of this new problem occurred.

Though the Secretary's minutes refer to this meeting of the Board as a "special" one, no reason is given for its having been called. The hour that was set was in itself unusual, for meetings were usually held in the evening or late in the afternoon. It would appear, however, that the Directors had no thought that anything of outstanding importance was to be discussed for, in addition to President Huntington and Secretary Allyn, only five were present.

Having approved the minutes of the previous meeting, the meeting was told that no insurance had been "made since last meeting," and were asked to approve the appointment of six new agents in six different Pennsylvania cities.

Those who were present at this meeting were apparently well-informed about the progress of secession. They knew that South Carolina had seceded some three weeks before. They also knew that Mississippi, acting on January 9th, had followed South Carolina's example, though it is possible that word of Florida's secession on January 10th and Alabama's on the 11th had not yet reached Hartford. But even without these two latest reports enough was known to make it clear that a situation of grave significance had arisen.

It would appear that the secession of South Carolina had failed to arouse the Hartford's Directors to any action. Surprised by the suddenness of that move, perhaps, and uncertain as to what should be done to protect the Company's interests, no action whatever had been taken. When word of Mississippi's secession reached Hartford, however, it seems to have shocked the Directors into action. In all probability, the arrival of this news was what brought about the special meeting on the morning of January 12th. Once the meeting had been called to order, however, other matters were considered first.

Among those present it would appear that Director Calvin Day was most deeply troubled by the news from the South. "The subject of a discontinuance of business in the seceding Southern States," the Secretary's minutes read, "was laid before the Board, and a motion made by C. Day, Esq., That the Agencies of the Company in the State of Mississippi be withdrawn, and all outstanding policies cancelled by return of unearned premium, was referred, after lengthy discussion, to the next meeting of the Board."

Apparently because it was felt to be a part of this same problem, the meeting then

> *Voted:* To appoint the President and C. Boswell, Esq.,
> a Committee to confer with the officers of the Aetna Ins.
> Company in relation to Southern business, and report at
> the next meeting of the Board."

It was only three days later—on January 15th—that the next meeting was held. According to Secretary Allyn's minutes, "The Committee consisting of the President and C. Boswell, Esqs. appointed at the last meeting to confer with the 'Aetna' Company relative to any action taken by them in reference to Southern business, made a verbal report. That no action had been taken by said Company farther than to recommend additional care and caution to their several Agents in the taking of new and continuance of old risks.

"On motion of C. Day Esq. referred from last meeting, it was then

> *Voted:* That the Agencies of the Company in the State
> of Mississippi be withdrawn, and all outstanding Policies
> be cancelled by return of unearned premium."

Though the minutes of the Directors' meetings are often lacking in detail, they are strangely so during this very difficult period. By the time the Directors voted "That the Agencies of the Company in the State of Mississippi be withdrawn," four separate Southern states had seceded from the Union,* and by May 21st seven others had followed their example. So far as the minutes of the Directors' meetings show, however, action was taken to withdraw the Company's agents only from the State of Mississippi.

On April 14, 1861, the war actually began and the Hartford, even without further action on the part of its Directors, was effectively cut off from its agents in the South. What influence this would have on the Company no one could say. How the Southern agents would react no one knew. Before long, however, it began to be apparent that many of them felt that *de facto,* at least, and probably *de jure,* as well, they were agents of the Company no longer.

---

* South Carolina, December 20, 1860; Mississippi, January 9, 1861; Florida, January 10, 1861; and Alabama, January 11, 1861.

CHAPTER 9

A DIVIDED NATION

ABRAHAM LINCOLN, elected President of the United States early in November 1860, was not inaugurated until March 4, 1861. Having been at home in Springfield at the time of his election, he remained there except for a brief trip to Chicago. The room in the old state capitol that he had used during his campaign still served him as an office, though he received many important visitors at home. He had bought his house—a simple, two-storied structure and the only one he ever owned—in 1844, two years after his marriage, and following the election he and his family remained in it until February 11th when they left for Washington. It was during this period of waiting that he found a tenant for the house —Lucian A. Tilton, then President of the Great Western Railroad. He also sold some of its furnishings and, as the day for his departure approached, he asked James L. Hill, the local agent of the Hartford Fire Insurance Company, to inspect the property and to write a fire insurance policy on it. Hill attended to the matter promptly and, on February 8th, personally delivered the policy to the President-elect—a policy for $3,200 which called for the payment of a premium of $24.00 and an added fee of $2.00 to cover the expense of making the survey and issuing the policy.

The policy that was issued is now a treasured possession of the Hartford Fire Insurance Company, for, at the request of Jim Hill who originally made it out, Robert Todd Lincoln, several years after his father's death, presented it to the firm of Hill & Flower who, by then, had succeeded James L. Hill & Company as the Hartford's agents in Springfield, and they, in turn, later gave it to the Company.

In this connection it should be added that this famous document is not the only "Lincoln policy" that the Hartford Fire Insurance Company has issued. The original policy was renewed each year until 1867, but was then apparently replaced by a new one. Later, too, Robert Todd Lincoln, who maintained his summer home in Manchester, Vermont, insured it with the Hartford, as his great granddaughter, who inherited it, still does. Interestingly enough, when in 1950 the work of restoration began on Abraham Lincoln's Springfield home in order that the house and its attendant structures might be returned to their original condition, "the most valuable lead" the architects and other experts were given was the original fire insurance policy that was issued just three days before the President-elect left for Washington.

Though the minutes of the meetings that were held by the Hartford's Directors during the tragic 1860's are less detailed than might have been expected, other evidence now and again explains their point of view. Whatever opinions the various Directors may have had insofar as the secession was concerned, they seem to have been unanimous in believing that the Company's responsibilities remained unchanged so long as any policies they had written remained in force. By early January 1861, they were clearly conscious of the difficulties that were likely to arise as a result of secession, and with these in mind, Secretary Timothy Allyn wrote a letter to one of the Company's more important Southern agents— Dewitt F. Willcox, who had represented the Hartford in Columbus, Georgia, since 1852 (and whose descendants still do to this day).

"The probabilities of a peaceful solution of our national difficulties," this letter read in part, "are now so far distant that it seems proper for us to adopt some measure to protect ourselves against heavy losses arising from the derangement of business affairs, or that will probably arise. We do not know how you southern insurance men look at this matter, but it is very evident to us that the hazards are very much increased. *Personally*, we are very friendly to the South, but we must not allow our feelings to interfere with our judgment in a business point of view. We therefore recommend additional caution & watchfulness on the part of our Agents. Let the distant risks & doubtful ones run off at expiration. Leave wide margins at owner's risk & look over the risks now on the books with a view to cutting off all that are at all doubtful or you may have any fears of."

It is obvious from this that despite the January vote of the Directors to withdraw from the State of Mississippi, the Company was determined to do its best to carry on elsewhere. During the next three months, however, conditions changed. The seven states that had so far seceded sent delegates to Montgomery, Alabama, where they organized the Confederate States of America. A provisional government was established and Jefferson Davis was inaugurated as President on February 18th.

It was not until March 4th, two weeks after Davis had assumed the Presidency of the newly organized Confederacy, that Abraham Lincoln was inaugurated in Washington. Then, for more than a month, each side tried to force the other to make some move that would constitute a *casus belli*, and, on April 12th, fearing that Fort Sumter, the one remaining fort in Charleston harbor, was to be supplied by Union forces, the Confederates began a bombardment which led to the fort's surrender two days later.

Here, President Lincoln felt, was the actual military move that would justify him in making a military move of his own, and the next day, with the people of the North suddenly unified behind him, he called for 75,000 militia for three months' service.

The Directors of the Hartford, conscious now that the Company could no longer hope to operate in the Southern states as it had before, ordered a circular prepared for distribution to the Company's agents throughout the new Confederacy. The circular directed them "upon receipt of these instructions to decline all new applications for Insurance in this Company, and not to renew any outstanding policies, but drop them as they expire, until otherwise advised . . . . If ever the time should come when peace and harmony shall prevail, we can then resume our business, if all things concur to make it expedient.

"You are therefore requested and instructed to make a package, under seal, of all the Books and Papers belonging to this Company in your possession, and deposit them in a safe place, subject to the orders of the Company."

A few additional instructions were added, and the circular, bearing the date of April 23rd, was mailed, though how many agents actually received it has never been determined. Mails—or some of them—were still going through, however, as a letter written by President Huntington shows. Bearing the date of May 2nd, it was addressed to Agent Willcox of Columbus, Georgia.

"We are in receipt of your favour of the 23," it read, "and in answer to that part of it, in relation to the validity of our contracts under the present condition of our country, I answer that we fully & unreservedly confirm your reply to policy holders of this Co. The old Hartford holds each policy issued legally, as a contract, which we are legally, equitably, & in honour bound to fulfill, under any circumstances, and any just claim under such policy will be promptly & honourably paid. Since you wrote yours, I presume you have received the circular from this office of same date. That circular disposes of all future business. We thought this step prudent, under the present aspect of political affairs. In regards to a formal declaration of war, I have no idea that any such declaration will be made by the Government of the United States, if it is not done by the Confederate States. I cannot conceive that it can make any difference —we are in an actual state of civil war now, and any public declaration of such fact on the part of the Confederate States cannot change matters for the worse. The law of nations does, I suppose, suspend all liabilities from either side to the other during a state of war, but the law does not, I think, apply in this case. The separate and independent Government of the Confederate States is not acknowledged by any Government, therefore the law of nations does not apply. If however it did, I do not think it would make any difference in our contract, or our disposition to pay all honest claims. In answer to your question—if either Government should by proclamation forbid liquidation of claims due citizens of the other, I say that no such proclamation will ever be issued by the United States or any of the States in the North composing it. If they did, I think it would be a better cause of rebellion in the North than you have in the South. Such a measure might embarrass our settlement but could not release us from the moral obligation to pay.

"Very truly yours

"H. Huntington, Prest."

President Huntington's letter clearly shows how seriously the Company accepted its responsibilities. Though this letter was written at a time when feelings were running high and animosities, both in the North and the South, were growing in intensity, the Company's unquestioning willingness to abide by the terms of its policies goes far toward explaining not only the reputation "the old Hartford" had long since gained, but also the reputation it retained so widely in the South through four long and terrible years of civil war.

On April 17th Virginia's move to secede was ratified by popular vote and early in May both Arkansas and Tennessee also joined the Confederacy. North Carolina, as yet, had not reached a decision but with this one exception, the lines had formed and communications between the North and South, long since slowed to a trickle, had finally ended completely.

Late in 1860 a fire in Albany, Georgia, had damaged a hotel owned and operated by James L. Byington. Fortunately, Mr. Byington had long since arranged with Captain John A. Davis, the Hartford Fire Insurance Company's agent in Albany, for a fire insurance policy on his property and, in due course, the necessary proof of loss was prepared.

With the whole South troubled by the occurrences of that eventful winter, the papers that were ultimately sent to Hartford were slow in leaving. Still, they reached the Company's office in Hartford at last where, following the office's usual routine, the check to cover the loss—a check for $800, payable in gold—was made out, signed by the proper officers of the Company, and sent on its way to Georgia. As luck would have it, however, it reached its destination by the very last mail to get through before communications between the North and South were broken, and Mr. Byington, with a perfectly good check in his hands, was unable to cash it because no one could safely send it back to the North for clearance.

Under the circumstances, the hotel proprietor may very well have wondered just how good the check was to him after all. It presently occurred to him, however, that even though the check could not be cashed, its essential worth was questioned by no one, and, offered as collateral security, it should provide an excellent basis for a loan.

The local bank agreed and made the loan. Then, when it was repaid, the check was used as collateral for another. In fact, it was hypothecated so often during the four war years that followed, that it came to be recognized by the bankers and businessmen of the community almost as a legal tender though, being payable in gold, its value actually increased as the fortunes of war turned more and more against the Confederacy.

Unable to cash the check so long as the war continued, the hotel-keeper nevertheless saw it develop into an asset on which he actually succeeded in basing a postwar competency. In the meantime, a long slip of paper containing its many endorsements was added and, according to Captain Davis who represented the Hartford in Albany for almost fifty years, this long list of endorsements was still attached when, at the conclusion of the war, the check, having been sent North, was accepted for clearance and promptly paid.

As the first year of the war approached its end the struggle had assumed proportions far greater than anyone had foreseen when the Confederacy had originally been formed. Lincoln's call for 75,000 volunteers to serve three months had been followed a few weeks later by a call for 40,000 who were to serve three years or "for the duration." Then, late in June, after the half-trained Union army under General McDowell was defeated at the first Battle of Bull Run, and was driven from the field in a rout by a Confederate army under General Beauregard, Congress, shocked into action, authorized the enlistment of half a million.

Meanwhile, hoping for recognition by Great Britain and other foreign powers, the Confederate Government ordered John Slidell of Louisiana and James M. Mason of Virginia to join a Confederate Commission that was already in England. Hurrying to Havana, Mason and Slidell took passage on the British mail steamer *Trent*. Learning of their departure, Captain Wilkes, of the U.S.S. *Jacinto*, intercepted the *Trent* and removed both of the Confederate commissioners. The American public was delighted and Congress publicly thanked Captain Wilkes, but the action was illegal, nevertheless. The British Government, naturally angered, ordered 8,000 troops to Canada. A peremptory demand for an apology was also written by Lord Russell, the Foreign Secretary (though before it was sent it was fortunately modified by the Prince Consort).

Being demonstrably in the wrong, the American authorities ultimately released the two Southerners, sending them on their way again aboard another British ship, but while the matter was pending a special meeting of the Hartford's Board of Directors was called. Dated "Thursday, Dec. 26, 1861," the Secretary's minutes read as follows:

> At a special meeting of the Board duly notified and held this day at 4 o'clock P.M. there were present the President and Messrs. A. Day, Goodwin & Roberts.
>
> A communication was submitted to the Board from A. Ballock, Agent at St. John, N.B. under date of the 16th inst. deriving information in relation to the course that would be processed by the Company toward its policyholders in the Provinces, in case of hostilities between Great Britain & the United States, and it was
>
> *Voted:* That in the event of a declaration of war between Great Britain and the United States this Company will cancel all outstanding policies of Insurance in the British Provinces returning to the assessed the unearned premium, in accordance with office rules.

Fortunately, the authorities in Washington released both Mason and Slidell only a few days after this meeting of the Board was held, and the danger that had arisen faded away. While the problem was at its height, however, a lesser event laid the foundation for another Company problem that was not finally settled until the war had been concluded.

On December 13, 1861, the city of Charleston, South Carolina, was badly damaged by fire. Many structures on Meeting Street, along with others on Hayne and King Streets, were destroyed or badly damaged, and despite the fact that war had long since cut all normal communications between South Carolina and the North, three of these buildings were still covered by fire insurance policies issued long before by the Hartford Fire Insurance Company and still in effect.

Because it was impossible to communicate with Hartford at the time, A. H. Hayden, the Company's agent in Charleston, was compelled to act as no agent had ever been forced to act before. Consulted by anxious policyholders who had paid their premiums in good faith but who were now unable to make any claim on the Hartford, he was asked what they should do.

Troubled, no doubt, by the problem that had arisen, and far from certain that the only idea that occurred to him was the best one under the circumstances, he did his best to conceal his doubts.

"Make out your proofs of loss," he said in effect, "and give them to me. Obviously we can't send them to Hartford now, but I'll take care of them. The war will end sometime, and when it does, the necessary papers will be sent to Hartford, and you will get your money."

Just how convincing this sounded to those who heard it no one can say, but having no other recourse, the three claimants prepared the papers for which he had asked and turned them over. Agent Hayden, however, was entirely conscious that these very important papers were susceptible to damage or destruction, especially in time of war. As a citizen of Charleston he had seen the sturdy ramparts of Fort Sumter battered into rubble less than a year before. He was conscious, also, of the presence of the blockading fleet of Union warships that maintained their ceaseless watch just outside the harbor entrance, and knew that the island of Port Royal, at the head of Port Royal Sound only fifty miles or so from Charleston, had already been captured by the Union Navy. Charleston was defended, he knew, but Union ships were almost constantly visible from the harbor, and it was impossible that the city would never be attacked. And if attack were to come, even the safest vault in town might fail to protect the papers that had been entrusted to his care.

It was impossible for him to solve his problem instantly, but ultimately an idea occurred to him. Without explaining what he was about, he obtained a sturdy wooden keg and, gathering together certain private papers of his own, he added the various papers his policyholders had given him and made a package of them. Wrapping this package carefully so as to protect it as best he could against moisture, insects, and harm in other forms, he put it in the keg, fastened the head as firmly as he could, and, with the keg covered from view in the back of his buggy, he harnessed his horse and drove out Meeting Street and on into the country.

So far, he had taken no one into his confidence, but now he needed help. It was with that in mind that he made his way to a plantation that he knew, the owner of which was a thoroughly trustworthy gentleman of his acquaintance. Having reached the place he explained his need, and asked what might be done to hide the keg against any possibility of discovery; and together the two worked out the final steps in the plan that was adopted.

Waiting until after dark, Agent Hayden and his planter friend located a spot in an open field far removed from any landmarks, and there they dug a hole and buried the keg, covering it carefully and determining its exact location in relation to certain trees at the edge of the field. Though the hole they had dug had carefully been filled, they hid the spot more thoroughly by having the field plowed the next day, and there the documents remained until the war ended in 1865. It was only then that the keg was recovered and, once the papers were removed, the various proofs of loss that had been prepared late in 1861 were sent to Hartford.

General Lee had surrendered at Appomattox on April 9th. President Lincoln had been assassinated five days later. Before the end of May the last remaining Confederate forces gave up the hopeless struggle, and on Monday, June 12th, 1865, a special meeting of the Hartford Board of Directors was held at "3½ o'clock P.M."

What word the Company had received from its former agents in the South does not appear. Certainly no word had arrived as yet from Charleston, and perhaps none had actually arrived from any Southerner. Nevertheless, after discussing other matters, "The subject of resuming business at the South was also discussed and it was thought best to be in no haste to occupy the ground, and to postpone the transaction of any but a very limited business until the state of the country and matters generally were more settled and better established."

It was not until August that any mention of the long-buried Charleston papers appear in the minutes of any of the Directors' meetings, but then the following action was taken:

Tuesday, August 15th, 1865

At a special meeting of the Board held at their office this day at 11 o'clock A.M. There were present the President and Messrs. Albert Day, James Goodwin, Harry Keney, Calvin Day, Job Allyn and C. C. Lyman.

The minutes of the last meeting were read and approved.

The President presented for consideration of the Board the Proofs and claims for loss under Policies 823, 1999 & 2050 of the Charleston S. Company, which occurred in Dec. 1861: after some consideration

Voted: on motion of Mr. Albert Day, that decision upon the claims be postponed for further consideration and till more definite information can be obtained as to the loyalty of the parties.

On motion of Mr. Albert Day,

Voted: that the President be authorized to reappoint Mr. Hayden our former agent at Charleston, with instructions to do a very limited business.

It was not until December 12th that the Charleston claims came up for discussion again, but, according to the minutes, "the subject was postponed until the next meeting," which was held on Tuesday, December 19th. Even then, however, final action was not taken, as the following extract from the minutes shows:

The subject of the Charleston losses, postponed from the last meeting, was brought forward and again discussed, and on motion by Mr. Albert Day, it was

Voted: That the answer be given the claimants that the Company acknowledges no legal claim under the Policies, but that after South Carolina assumes her constitutional obligations and her civil government is re-established, the claims may be considered under principles of equity.

No reference in the minutes of the Directors' meetings tells exactly when the Charleston claims were finally settled, though several resolutions refer to the reappointment of A. H. Hayden as the Company's agent in Charleston. Even as late as September 16, 1867, "the following resolution was adopted. Resolved, that Mr. A. H. Hayden is our duly authorized Agent for the City of Charleston, S.C. and its vicinity, his appointment dating March 1st, 1866." And on Oct. 2nd, 1867, a "Power of Attorney was voted, to our Agent at Charleston, Mr. A. H. Hayden, to acknowledge service of legal process, for the Company in said State."

But long before this Power of Attorney was voted, the three claims that had arisen from the fire that had taken place in December 1861 had been paid. The bitter days of Reconstruction created even greater animosities than those that had resulted from the war, but the Hartford Fire Insurance Company, despite its Yankee origin, soon re-established its business in the South where it had succeeded in maintaining the reputation it had long since earned.

Though the Company stood firmly behind every Hartford policy that remained in effect in any part of the South when the war began, its premium income from the eleven states that made up the Confederacy was instantly cut off. Even had they been willing to do so, it was quite impossible, while the war was being fought, for Southern policyholders or agents to communicate with the Company's home office. No remittances of any kind could be made in either direction and, under war conditions, it would have been impossible for the Company even to establish rates. Necessarily, therefore, the Company's income from the eleven Confederate states ended the moment communications between the North and South were broken and, as policy after policy expired, the Company's responsibilities in the South grew smaller until none remained.

While there is little in the record to tell us how the Company's Directors felt about this very great loss of business, there is no question that they were conscious of it. But, fortunately for the Company, the rapidly expanding West, which continued to grow even during the four terrible years of the Civil War, made it possible for the Company to gain far more new business there than it had lost in the South. Furthermore, the war years were remarkably exempt from destructive fires and the Company's losses were consequently moderate. Thus, with its business increasing rapidly in the West—as well as in New England and elsewhere in the East where wartime industries were expanding so greatly—and with its losses moderating, too, the Company found itself more prosperous as the war came to an end than it had ever been before.

The Western Department, which had been established in 1852 with headquarters in Columbus, Ohio, had been under the direction of David Alexander from 1854 to early in 1863, when he resigned. In the meantime, George F. Bissell, a local agent in Dubuque, Iowa, had been appointed "traveling supervisor" and had established his headquarters in Chicago. Well known by the officials of the Company as a man of exceptional force and ability, and as an unusually capable underwriter, George Bissell was appointed to succeed David Alexander as General Agent in charge of the Western Department, and the Department's headquarters were transferred from Columbus to Chicago.

By 1864 Hezekiah Huntington had been President of the Hartford for fifteen years. Under his direction the Company had made enormous progress, and despite the war years, he had seen its business increase to a point far beyond his prewar expectations. Now, however, with his sixty-ninth birthday not far off and with his health not what it had been, he resigned, being succeeded by Timothy C. Allyn who had served as Secretary since 1858, and whose father had been one of the founders of the Company and one of the original Directors.

Though 1864 had been one of the most tragically eventful years of the Civil War, the records of the Hartford Fire Insurance Company for that period are more than usually lacking in color. At a meeting that had been held in February the Directors discussed the purchase of a tract of land in Chicago and the possible erection on it of a building for the use of the Western Department. At a meeting in March, General Agent Bissell, of the Western Department, was authorized to purchase a lot "with building thereon, on La Salle Street at $15,500." Later, too, the Secretary was sent to Chicago in order to arrange for the construction of the new building which was completed and occupied before the end of the year.

In the meantime General Grant and General Lee, fighting the bloody battles that led from the Wilderness to Petersburg, were daily bringing the war closer to its conclusion, and General Sherman, having finally captured Atlanta, began his march to the sea. As 1864 reached its conclusion the outcome of the war was plain, and late the following spring the end came when General Lee asked for a meeting with General Grant at Appomattox.

No sooner had the war reached its long-delayed ending than the

Hartford began to appoint new agents in the South or, as often happened, to reappoint old ones. The very first Southern agency to be reopened was in June 1865, and thereafter new agents and reappointed ones rapidly took their places throughout the South.

In 1853 the Company had been authorized to increase its capital to $300,000 and to change the par value of its shares from $50 to $100. In 1857 the Company's capitalization had been increased to $500,000 and in June 1864 the Directors had taken advantage of an authorization the stockholders had previously granted to double the capital stock—a move that was accomplished by means of a stock dividend of $500,000. Thus, as 1864 ended, the Hartford's capitalization was $1,000,000, and as a result of wartime profits and wartime inflation, the Company's surplus was $200,799.76.

The Company entered the year of 1865 in sound condition but was soon confronted with major losses. On September 16, 1865, a fire in Augusta, Maine, called for the payment of $57,000 in claims. In 1866 a fire in Portland, Maine, necessitated the payment of $151,000, and Vicksburg, Mississippi, doing its best to rebuild itself after the destructive years of the war, suffered from a fire that cost the Hartford $55,000.

Had this been all, no great difficulty would have faced the Company, but, as always happens after a war has ended, a period of deflation developed and the Company's surplus, which had been more than $200,000 only a little while before, completely disappeared.

For two years, fire insurance companies everywhere found conditions difficult. In a report prepared in the spring of 1867 the Superintendent of the New York Fire Insurance Department made it clear that he was still concerned.

"With low or diminishing net premiums," he wrote, "the moral hazards have been woefully increased, and the sad results are now historic in years 1865 and 1866—two consecutive years of excessive and unprecedented loss."

And yet, so far as the Hartford was concerned, better days lay ahead. By the end of 1868 the Company's surplus once more stood at a little more than $200,000; and by the last day of December one year later that figure had more than doubled.

CHAPTER 10

COMPETITION, LEGISLATION,

AND A

SUPREME COURT DECISION

IN THE years immediately following the Civil War the fire insurance companies became more and more concerned about the laws under which they were compelled to operate. Federal laws played no part in this problem for insurance legislation had been left in the hands of the states. In the years to come, this legislation was to reach such a high degree of intelligence and unanimity that insurance companies became stanch defenders of state control. But, at this time, the states were anything but consistent in outlook. This had resulted not only in laws that were conflicting but also in many that were burdensome, oppressive, and unsound. Here and there legislation was so ill-considered as actually to be harmful to the best interests of the people and the companies alike.

Problems such as these were universally apparent to insurance executives. By the time the War had ended and the nation found it possible to turn its attention to peacetime development again, they widely understood the need for some association through which the many individual companies could act in promoting the best interests of all.

It was with this in mind that a group of insurance executives, in October 1865, succeeded in calling a convention made up of representatives of all interested companies. Primarily concerned with "unfriendly legislation in several of the States toward the insurance companies of other States, which . . . has caused the gravest apprehensions," the convention apparently felt that its most important act was the adoption of a resolution which urged "that Congress at its next session be memorialized to consider and enact such laws as shall essentially nationalize the busi-

TIMOTHY C. ALLYN
President, 1864-1867

ness of insurance in all the States of this Union." In addition, however—and more importantly, as developments were later to prove—a second meeting, held on June 18, 1866, succeeded in organizing the National Board of Fire Underwriters.

It was the hope of many insurance executives of that day that Congress could be persuaded to enact "one general law for the government of insurance companies throughout the Union." But Congress, despite the best efforts of the companies, showed little interest in entering this field of legislation—so little, in fact, that ultimately the more determined advocates of Federal legislation decided to try to force the adoption of Federal legislation by questioning the constitutionality of State regulation in the courts.

In 1866 the legislature of the State of Virginia enacted a law which required every nonresident insurance company wishing to do business in that state to obtain a license before transacting any business there, and to deposit certain prescribed sums in the state as security. The law also required each agent of such a company to procure a license.

Determined to test the constitutionality of this law, Colonel Samuel B. Paul, an attorney of Petersburg, Virginia, who was also the local agent for the New York Underwriters Agency, applied for licenses and, as he was directed to do by Alexander Stoddart, who headed the Agency, agreed to comply with all the provisions of the law except that which called for the deposit of security.

When licenses were refused him, Colonel Paul nevertheless continued to transact fire insurance business in Virginia and, as he had expected, was indicted, convicted, and fined. By writ of error, the case, now known as Paul vs. Virginia, went to the Supreme Court of Appeals of the State, where the decision of the lower court was affirmed. But again the case was appealed.

It was under the 25th section of the Judiciary Act that Paul vs. Virginia finally reached the United States Supreme Court, and, on behalf of the Colonel and the insurance companies he represented, the argument advanced was (1) that the business of insurance was commerce, (2) that insurance written by nonresident insurance companies on risks in Virginia was commerce among the several states, and (3) that the Virginia statute amounted to regulation of commerce among the several states which was invalid because power to regulate such commerce was placed in Congress by the Constitution. Therefore, it was argued, the Virginia statute was unconstitutional.

The unanimous opinion of the Court was delivered by Justice Stephen J. Field. Holding that the fallacy in the contention of the plaintiff lay in the nature of the transaction involved, the opinion continued as follows:

> Issuing a policy of insurance is not a transaction of commerce. The policies are simple contracts of indemnity against loss by fire, entered into between the corporations and the assured, for a consideration paid by the latter. These contracts are not articles of commerce in any proper meaning of the word. They are not subjects of trade and barter offered in the market as something having an existence and value independent of the parties to them. They are not commodities to be shipped or forwarded from one State to another, and then put up for sale. They are like other personal contracts between parties which are completed by their signature and the transfer of the consideration. Such contracts are not inter-state transactions, though the parties may be domiciled in different States. The policies do not take effect—are not executed contracts—until delivered by the agent in Virginia. They are, then, local transactions, and are governed by local law. They do not constitute a part of the commerce between the States any more than a contract for the purchase and sale of goods in Virginia by a citizen of New York whilst in Virginia would constitute a portion of such commerce.

Insurance companies generally had hoped that Colonel Paul's contentions would be upheld. It was their belief that Federal regulation would be greatly more desirable than the often differing and sometimes contradictory regulation of the separate states. The Supreme Court decision was so clear, however, that their one-time hopes were cast aside, and state regulation, despite the problems that accompanied it, was everywhere accepted as unchangeable—was accepted, that is, for three quarters of a century. And even then, as events were to prove, the change that came was only temporary.

Timothy Allyn, having succeeded Hezekiah Huntington as President of the Hartford in 1864, resigned in 1867 in order to move to New York City and to form a partnership with Ezra White who had long been the Company's agent there.

In the fifty-seven years the Company had now been active, each new President who had been elected had had deep roots in Hartford. Even yet that was true of all the members of the Board. At the time President Allyn resigned, only one of the eight remaining Directors had served in that capacity for less than twenty years, while two had served for twenty-five, two for twenty-seven, and one for thirty-two.

The members of the Board, in other words, were not notable for their youth, and none seems to have felt that the new president should be chosen from among themselves. Even elsewhere in Hartford no one seemed sufficiently well fitted for the position and, wondering where a really competent person might be found, the Directors decided to consult George F. Bissell, the Company's Western General Agent.

It was George L. Chase, the Assistant General Agent of the Western Department, whom Mr. Bissell recommended. Thirty-nine at the time, he had been born in Millbury, Massachusetts, where, having graduated from Millbury Academy at the age of nineteen, he had become the local agent for an insurance company. A year later he had been appointed traveling agent for the People's Insurance Company of Worcester, Massachusetts, and, after four years in that position, had been offered an appointment as assistant superintendent of the Central Ohio Railway—an unusually responsible position for a man so young.

After a year in this position he became general superintendent of the railroad, and for eight years he continued in railroad work. Then, having been offered the western agency of the New England Fire and Marine Insurance Company of Hartford, he returned to his original occupation, transferring to the Western Department of the Hartford Fire Insurance Company in 1863 when that office, under General Agent Bissell, was moved from Columbus to Chicago.

Called to Hartford as a result of General Agent Bissell's recommendation, George Chase met the Company's Directors for the first time. He gained their unanimous approval, and on June 6, 1867, was elected to the presidency—a position he was destined to hold for forty-one eventful years.

Though 1865 and 1866 had been years "of excessive and unprecedented loss" according to the Superintendent of the New York Fire Insurance Department, the Hartford's Directors do not seem to have been discouraged. The Company's business was still expanding and almost a year before the new President had been chosen it had become clear that the Company badly needed a new and more commodious office. Housed, as it was, in a four-story building on Main Street, to which it had moved in 1859, the Company occupied only three first-floor rooms. The office staff was small, consisting of only half a dozen people in 1866 and not more than eight two years later, but more employees were needed and before they could be added, more space was required to accommodate them. It was because of this that the Directors, at a special meeting on August 29, 1866,

> *Voted,* That the President and Messrs. Goodwin &
> C. Day be a committee with power to select and purchase
> a lot for a new office for this Co. and to procure plans
> for said building.

Two years earlier, because of the growth of business in the Western Department following its transfer to Chicago, a lot had been purchased at 49 La Salle Street and a three-story building had been erected there. Oddly enough, the Company, despite what it knew about the destructiveness of fire, seems never, prior to this time, to have given any serious consideration to the need for a "fire-proof" vault for the protection of its securities and records. No such vault existed or had ever existed in the home office in Hartford, and plans for the new building in Chicago seem to have been well under way before it was suggested that a vault be included there. And even when the Directors approved the idea, they failed to authorize a *"fire-proof"* vault, telling the Western Agent, instead, to arrange for a contract for "a steam-heating plant and a burglar-proof vault, with proper doors and locks." As luck would have it, however—and as events were to prove before many years had passed—when the building at 49 La Salle Street was completed late in 1864, the big three-story vault that it contained was just as resistant to fire as it was to burglars.

In Hartford, the proposed new building had not yet been planned when George Chase arrived from Chicago and was elected President. Though a year had passed since a committee had been authorized to purchase a lot and "procure plans for said building" nothing had been done. But President Chase was nothing if not vigorous and, determined to have a Hartford agency "at every settlement in the United States and Canada where income bid fair to exceed outgo,"* he seems to have been equally determined to prepare the home office for the expansion he foresaw. But even he seems to have been willing to make haste slowly. It was not until he had been President for two years that a large lot was purchased at the corner of Pearl and Trumbull Streets in Hartford, and an architect was selected to design the new home office that was to be.

* P. Henry Woodward, *op. cit.,* p. 18.

In the meantime, the Company's position had shown remarkable improvement. Where, six months after George Chase had been elected President, the Company's surplus amounted to only $26,744.69, two years later, at the close of 1869, the Company's statement showed a surplus of $412,422.22 with full premium reserve based on modern standards.

By 1870, anyone familiar with the position the Hartford occupied among the fire insurance companies of America must have realized that it was an enviable one. But fire insurance generally was still confronted by many difficulties, and some years were to pass before the worst of these were mastered. For example, according to an old "loss register" that was in use by the Company during the 1860's, a good many fires were listed as having been due to "external exposure." Others were listed as of unknown origin, but the cause of fire most frequently given was "incendiary." In fact, fires of incendiary origin and others caused by "external exposure" came to be so frequent in San Francisco in the early 1860's that a Company representative made the long journey to the West Coast city late in 1862 in order to investigate. New agents were appointed and stricter regulations were adopted but little improvement resulted, and in 1864 the Company withdrew from California and did not renew its agencies there until President Chase visited San Francisco in 1869 and reached the conclusion that the Company would be warranted in re-entering that field.

Always theretofore, the great distance that separated California from the East had made it difficult for the home office to maintain close contact with agents on the West Coast, but the opening of the transcontinental railroad in 1869 simplified that problem. Porter P. Heywood was appointed as the San Francisco General Agent in November 1869, and in 1870, when the Pacific Department was organized, he and Augustus P. Flint, having organized the firm of Flint & Heywood, became General Agents for the Company in charge of the new Department which included not only the State of California, but also Oregon, Washington, Idaho, Montana, Utah, Nevada, Arizona, and even British Columbia, Alaska, and the Hawaiian Islands.

With the organization of the Pacific Department, the Company and its General Agents were confronted by an enormous task. The appointment and control of agents in so vast an area when communications still left so much to be desired was an almost superhuman task. The West was developing rapidly, however, and though much time was still to pass before agents could be found for the more remote and lightly settled regions, the Company soon had an agency system in this new territory that has continued to expand down to the present day.

By the time the Pacific Department was organized, the Western Department, with its headquarters now long established in Chicago, had come to be immensely productive. It is true that the business of fire insurance was without any widely accepted controls. Sometimes, in fact, the industry seemed to be almost in a state of anarchy. Policies were anything but standard. Forms and questionnaires differed widely. The rules and regulations of the various companies not only differed but were also constantly undergoing minor modifications and even basic changes. No formal or widely accepted method of establishing rates had yet been evolved. Ostensibly based on experience and sound judgment, they were often influenced—or even determined—by competition. Added to this, no sound basis for the establishment of commissions had yet been evolved and commission wars were perennial. Solutions ultimately began to be found for these intolerable practices, but for more than a decade after the Civil War such progress as was made in this connection was usually traceable to the stronger and wiser fire insurance executives of the day.

Competing companies now and again permitted, or even urged, their agents to cut established rates, and exaggerated campaigns of rate-cutting now and again developed. There were even instances in which prospective purchasers of policies, haggling with one agent after another, or going over an agent's head to some unwise home office, succeeded in greatly reducing—almost in actually setting—the rates they were willing to pay.

Usually the most extreme rate wars took place in reasonably narrow areas in which short-sighted agents, looking for quick profits, were urged on by the companies they represented, but campaigns of this nature were always opposed by thoughtful agents as well as by the more understanding executives and the sounder, stronger companies. But in the absence of any agency powerful enough to bring rate-cutting to an end, the problem usually lay largely in the hands of the wiser insurance men in the affected areas.

Perhaps the most outstanding insurance executive in the Middle West in the greatly booming period following the Civil War was George F. Bissell, General Agent for the Hartford in charge of the Company's Western Department. The record clearly shows that he was a man of unusual ability, and as one of Chicago's leading citizens he was active in many civic and charitable enterprises. He was one of the founders and was later president of the Union League Club. He was an active member of the Presbyterian Church. He served for ten years as treasurer of the Old People's Home, and, for a time, was president of the Illinois Society of the Sons of the Revolution. In fact, he was active in so many societies and organizations that one can only wonder where he found the time for them, in view of the great responsibilities that rested on him as General Agent of the Western Department of the Hartford Fire Insurance Company.

As a fire insurance executive, he had the responsibility of keeping himself informed as to conditions throughout the whole of the Western Department, an enormous and rapidly developing region of half a million square miles or so. And his task, which would have been difficult and complicated even under the best of conditions, was now and again exceedingly trying because the business of fire insurance was then so little subject to control.

In the matter of rate-cutting it is probable that the states that made up the Western Department differed little from some of the others. George Bissell, however, was an especially sturdy opponent of the practice, and such instances as came to his attention always sent him into action.

For example, there is a story that has to do with an especially exaggerated rate war. It has been told and retold for at least three generations, but always by word of mouth and never, it would appear, as a part of the written record.

Even if the story is hearsay, it rings true and is worth recording as a picture of those somewhat distant days even though no one can tell it now without including much that is apocryphal. It is certain, however, that the story fits the character of George F. Bissell and, when it is told, he is always the principal character.

Mr. Bissell, on one occasion—according to this story—was told of a rate-cutting campaign that had broken out in Iowa where it was centered in and about Dubuque. Always interested in problems of this nature, he was especially interested in this instance for Dubuque, in addition to being in the Western Department, was also the town in which he had lived when, as a young man, he had been a local Hartford agent. And, in addition, this particular rate war was rapidly progressing from bad to worse.

Well informed about the situation from reports that had come from a Hartford agent in Dubuque, he decided to do something about it. He refused to permit any of the Company's agents to meet cut-rate competition by cutting their own rates, if the Hartford's rates were justifiable, as he was convinced they were, it was because they had been established at a level below which the sound operation of the Company would be impossible. On the other hand, the Company's business in Dubuque was falling off and its agent there badly needed help. On that account Mr. Bissell left for Iowa with the firm intention of bringing the rate war to an end, but at as little cost to the Company as possible.

Arriving in Dubuque he lost no time in discussing the matter with the agent from whom his reports had come, and he made a list of ten or a dozen of the more important policies that had been lost to the Hartford's rate-cutting competitor. Then, armed with the information he had obtained, he asked the agent to accompany him while he called on the former holders of the policies he had listed, all of whom had now taken out new policies at cut rates.

Dubuque, though the oldest town in Iowa, was a small, informal place at the time, and Mr. Bissell, tall, slender, refined, and aristocratic in appearance, would have been received readily enough even had he made his calls unannounced and alone. Accompanied as he was, however, by the Hartford's well-known local agent, and introduced as the General Agent of the Western Department of the Hartford Fire Insurance Company, he had little need to explain why he was there.

"I understand," Mr. Bissell began when he had been introduced to the first businessman on whom he and the agent called, "that you have recently taken out a fire insurance policy on this property of yours at a premium somewhat lower than our agent would have had to charge."

The one-time Hartford client nodded.

"The matter has been reported to me," Mr. Bissell continued, "and I would like to tell you what the Hartford is now prepared to do if you will cancel the policy you have purchased."

"Cancel it?" was the reply. "Why should I do that?"

"I'll explain," Mr. Bissell nodded. "If you cancel your present policy, our agent here will write a Hartford policy identical in every way with the Hartford policy you formerly held. But the premium on the policy we now offer will be less —a good deal less—even than the premium you have paid on your present cut-rate policy. Are you interested?"

"But I've got a policy," the one-time Hartford client objected.

"I know," Mr. Bissell agreed, "but you can cancel that, and when you do, you will recover all but a small percentage of the premium you have paid."

"But your premium. You haven't told me what that would be."

"That's true," Mr. Bissell nodded, "but I'll tell you now.

"If you agree to cancel your present policy and replace it with the one I now offer, we will not charge our usual premium which, when you insured with us before, was $125. We will not even charge you $100 which your present cut-rate policy cost. Instead, the premium for the Hartford policy I now suggest, will be—*one* dollar.

"By canceling your present policy you will have most of the $100 you have paid returned to you. And for one dollar you will have a new policy to replace it—a Hartford policy, the value of which you already know."

According to the story, Mr. Bissell made only a few such calls in Dubuque. Not unnaturally, the men to whom he talked were easy to convince. But it must be obvious that Mr. Bissell had no intention of carrying his own campaign too far. In a town as small and intimate as Dubuque, word of what the Chicago insurance man was doing must have run ahead of him—"by moccasin telegraph," as the saying then was.

Just how many dollar policies he sold is not a matter of record, but very few probably served his purpose. When the competitors who had started the rate war began to be asked to cancel policies they had so recently sold, and to return the major portion of each premium, they quickly saw that they were utterly unable to compete on this new basis. It is not surprising that they promptly agreed to reinstate the rates that had formerly been in effect—rates to which even Mr. Bissell was entirely happy to return. Indeed, Mr. Bissell's action was not rate-cutting as such. No one dreamed that any such dollar rate had been established permanently.

Apocryphal or not, this story could have happened in those days. Forceful individualism of this kind was characteristic of the leaders of that generation. Men were everywhere expected to solve their own problems and the outstanding leaders were those who did so most successfully.

Unfortunately, however, the important problem of rate-cutting was not susceptible to permanent solution even by the most forceful individual insurance executives of the period. Victories were sometimes won, and, human nature being what it is, rate-cutting was far less frequent wherever opposition to the practice was strong. But years were to pass before it was eliminated, and even when it was, the victory was due far less to individual than to collective effort. And in the meantime, George Bissell and other insurance executives were confronted by other problems among which some of the most important were soon to result from one of the greatest peacetime tragedies of the century.

CHAPTER 11

THE

GREAT CHICAGO FIRE

Had anyone thought to suggest it, President Chase and the Directors of the Hartford Fire Insurance Company might have decided, in the spring of 1870, to celebrate the sixtieth anniversary of the Company's founding. It appears, however, that nothing was done about it, perhaps because tentative plans were already being considered for another event that was to take place later in the year.

Half a century earlier, genial suppers had often been arranged in celebration of events less notable than Company anniversaries, but by 1870 the Company and its Directors were less inclined to give much time to gatherings of this nature. And now, as the summer of 1870 approached, everyone connected with the Company must have been keenly alive to the progress that was being made in the construction, at the corner of Pearl and Trumbull Streets in Hartford, of the new office building the Company was to occupy before the year was out—"a palatial" four-story structure built of stone and said, at the time, to be "one of the largest and most beautiful buildings in the city of Hartford."

Until the new building could be completed, the Company's office would remain where it had been since 1859—in the three rather poorly lighted rooms that occupied about half of the ground floor of an unimpressive four-story structure on Main Street. These rooms, which ran through the building from front to back, were notably unpretentious, and though, at first glance, it appeared that the Hartford and the bank next door had equally divided the ground floor of the building between them, it was out of the Hartford's "half" that the space had been taken for the hall and the stairway that led very steeply up to the second-, third-, and fourth-floor offices of several attorneys and a dentist, to certain "Photographic Rooms," and to William Draper's tailor shop which occupied a room on the second floor immediately above the entrance to the Hartford office.

By 1870 the Hartford Fire Insurance Company had come to be a business establishment of consequence. Nationally known, and with increasing numbers of agencies in almost every state, as well as in many areas of Canada, it was as well and favorably known as any of its competitors, and far better known than most. The Company was strong financially as it awaited the completion of the new office building that was under construction. Even after dividend payments of twenty per cent that year, there remained "an excess of income of about $112,000," and as the year ended, the Company's surplus was comfortably over $500,000.

President Chase and the Directors seem to have been more than usually well satisfied as the new office building approached completion. Every plan that they had made was moving smoothly to fruition. Business was steadily increasing. Agencies were not only growing in number but were also growing in productivity, and the Home Office, which had been operated by only six employees when President Chase had first arrived from Chicago, was shortly to move into the "palatial" new quarters where plans already made would necessitate, for the first time in the Company's history, a great increase in the number of employees.

It was in November 1870 that the Company's new building was finally ready for occupancy, and an entertainment of consequence was planned. Every insurance executive in the city was invited to be present at the opening, and even by 1870 insurance companies had established themselves in Hartford in numbers disproportionate to the city's size. But others were invited, too, and the Hartford's Directors, more than usually pleased with themselves and their accomplishments, called a meeting that was timed to adjourn at just the moment their responsibilities as hosts would call upon them to receive their guests.

No business was to be transacted at this Directors' Meeting—no business, that is, except the important business of congratulating themselves. And that, in essence, is what they did, as the following extract from the minutes shows:

"The President congratulated the gentlemen present on
the completion and occupancy of their new and beautiful
office, so strikingly in contrast with former accommodations,
and so eminently fit and proper as indicative of the standing and stability of the Company.

"The old time records were examined and discussed and
many interesting reminiscences in the history of the Company revived by the gentlemen of the Board, one of whom*
had been in the direction of its affairs for thirty-five years
and others† for a quarter of a century. General satisfaction
with the convenient arrangement and substantial and elegant finish and furnishing of the rooms was expressed, and
the final deserved and assured success of the Company
and its permanent establishment in a commodious, substantial, and elegant building of its own, after sixty years
of business with varying and uncertain fortunes as well as
habitations, was considered an occasion for mutual con-
gratulation.

"The officers of the fire and life insurance companies of
the city having been invited to an entertainment to be
given by the officers and directors of this Company on the
occasion of the opening of the new building—at nine o'clock
P.M.—and the hour being arrived, the Board adjourned."

Except for the opening of the Company's new office building, the
most important development in 1870, so far as the Hartford was concerned, resulted from President Chase's vigorous campaign to increase
the number of the Company's agencies. Subject only to the perennial
problem of finding good men, he not only steadily increased the number
of representatives but also labored ceaselessly to increase their efficiency.
The work done in this field was largely undramatic, but in the long run
it is likely that President Chase's success in enlarging and improving the
agency system contributed more to the Company's growth than anything
else this unusually able and successful executive accomplished in his
forty-one-year career as President of the Hartford.

The five years that preceded the opening of the Hartford's new home
office had witnessed a period of national prosperity quite unparalleled

* Albert Day.
† Actually James Goodwin, Jr., had been a director for thirty years, while both Charles
Boswell and William T. Lee had served for twenty-eight.

in the earlier history of the country. Actually the nation had entered a new era in its development. Industrialization had made remarkable progress throughout the North even during the War, when easy money and wartime demands had called for ever-increasing quantities of military supplies. But the War had no sooner ended than expansion began in almost every field. The West was being settled and developed at a remarkably rapid rate. Where, formerly, the nation's wealth had never given the impression of being especially great, now gold and silver had called the excited attention of the world to California and the Mountain States. Coal had been found in almost unbelievable quantities in Pennsylvania and elsewhere, and, with rail and canal transportation rapidly reaching into almost every settled area in the country, the production of coal was increasing as never before. Vast deposits of iron ore had been found in Michigan and much greater ones were soon to be discovered in Wisconsin and Minnesota. Important copper and lead deposits had been located. Though the first oil well in the United States had been drilled only in 1859, the Standard Oil Company, with a capital of $1,-000,000, was incorporated in 1870.

Manufacturing plants of every description were increasing both in number and in output. In a single decade their number had grown from about 120,000 to more than 250,000, and the manufacture of steel was increasing as never before.

Cattle were being raised in larger and larger numbers in the vast open range country that extended north from Texas to where the newly built Union Pacific Railroad crossed Kansas and Nebraska. Meat-packing plants in Chicago, aided by the invention of the refrigerator car, were already supplying New York, Boston, and other cities of the East with "fresh" meat.

The former Confederate states, struggling to recover from the dreadful destruction of war, were heavily handicapped by the problems of "Reconstruction," but elsewhere in the country a furious outburst of energy led to astonishing developments in almost every field—developments which, in many spectacular instances, were directed or controlled by men who were strikingly bold and energetic, and who were unscrupulous and grasping as well.

Except for the South, almost every corner of the country was expanding at a prodigious rate. But Chicago more adequately typified the tumultuous energy and excessive confidence of the day than any other city of the nation. By 1870 its population had reached 306,605, having more than doubled in the preceding ten years. Hurriedly and, for the most part, cheaply built, hardly a third of the city's 60,000 structures were built of masonry, and even among these, many were roofed with wooden shingles. Even on State Street, where land values were highest, structures of seeming elegance were often no more than hurriedly built firetraps with ostentatious fronts. Fire laws, such as they were, were more honored in the breach than in the observance, and though fire-fighting equipment had improved, volunteer fire companies had yet to be displaced by professional fire departments. Only in Cincinnati, New York, and one or two other forward-looking communities had this important step been taken.

It goes almost without saying that fire insurance in Chicago was growing at much the same rate everything else was, and locally organized fire insurance companies, most of which had little in the way of surplus or reserve, and few of whose officials were sufficiently experienced, were busy selling policies and declaring dividends while shrugging off, or even failing to notice, the critical comments of better-trained and more conservative insurance men.

Little rain had fallen in Chicago during the late summer and early autumn of 1871, and the sun, shining day after day in a cloudless sky, had drawn every drop of moisture from the city's shingled roofs. Such lawns as existed had been scorched and brown since August, and the weeds stood tall and dry in vacant lots and in the ditches beside the railroad tracks.

Fires had been frequent in the city throughout this period of drought, but the volunteer fire companies had kept them under control. The great fire bell on which alarms were given had seldom pounded out the general alarm which was sounded only when some fire seemed likely to get out of hand.

As evening came on Sunday, October 8, 1871, a strong wind was blowing across Chicago. The waves of Lake Michigan, noticeably higher than usual, broke into foam beside the railroad track that paralleled the lake front, but the weather was otherwise mild. As darkness fell, even the wind, as it eddied through the largely deserted streets, did little to enliven the normal Sunday evening quiet.

Rapid though Chicago's growth had been, and large though the city seemed by comparison with any other community in the rapidly expanding West, it was less than a tenth as large as it later came to be. The business section lay almost entirely between the Chicago River and Lake Michigan, and though the city's growth had already pushed its limits beyond the river to the west and north, it soon gave way to the prairie in both directions save here and there where early suburbs already revealed their scant beginnings.

What was then known as "the west side,"—a somewhat indefinite area west of the river—was an unkempt district filled with lumber yards and cluttered accumulations of builders' supplies. Occasional rows of gaunt frame houses lined certain West Side streets. Barns, sheds, and outhouses, often unpainted and untidy, were scattered here and there; and separate from, yet vaguely a part of, this same region was an even less attractive district given over largely to the city's outcasts.

It is probable that the wind, as it swept across Chicago on that October Sunday evening in 1871, seemed stronger among the houses, barns, and lumber yards of the West Side than among the many blocks of larger structures that filled the city's business section. It shifted its direction and, changing in intensity, sometimes blew in sudden gusts that made the lighter structures quiver. Now and again a loosened shingle blew from some steep roof, or a board, caught by the wind, went clattering through the darkness of some lumber yard.

At 49 La Salle Street the offices of the Western Department of the Hartford Fire Insurance Company stood dark and deserted like all its neighbors. A few blocks away, beside the fire alarm bell in the tower of the City Hall, a guard on fire watch, sheltering himself as best he could from the wind, casually glanced from time to time across the dark expanse of city roofs. Clustered together near the mouth of the Chicago River, several schooners and a barge or two, straining now and again against the hawsers that held them, rolled a little as the waves swept by. And far off on the West Side, Mrs. Jeremiah O'Leary, whose house was at 137 De Koven Street, had no inkling of the fact that she was about to become a character in the history—and even in the mythology—of Chicago.

The fact is that no one knows just how the Great Chicago Fire began. It would appear from much convincing evidence that it actually started in Mrs. O'Leary's barn, but the oft-repeated story that her cow caused it by kicking over a lamp while being milked is certainly open to question. For one thing, Mrs. O'Leary had five cows, not merely one, and the

considerable chore of milking them was always attended to by daylight—
or so she later said. Furthermore, it was not Mrs. O'Leary who first reported her barn on fire. It was a neighbor who did so, and by then the
flames had spread so far that nothing could be done to save either the
barn or the five cows and a horse it contained.

Oddly enough, the O'Leary house remained unharmed, but, fanned
by the strong and gusty wind, the flames, in one great uncontrollable
leap, attacked a nearby row of tinder-dry wooden tenements. All in a
moment they were furiously ablaze. Their flaming wooden shingles, torn
free by the wind, sailed upward in the heat to scatter and fall on other
dried-out roofs, there to be fanned into new fires by the increasing wind.

Fourteen weeks of drought in a city mostly built of wood had created
conditions that were ideal for such a holocaust as followed. But there
were other reasons. The fire had first been seen about 9:25 on that windy
evening, and a shouted alarm had been given. Even the fire watch in
the City Hall tower had pounded out his more far-reaching alarm on
the great fire bell. But, unable to decide as to the location of the distant
blaze, he had pounded out a signal that misdirected the first fire companies by a mile or more at a time when any delay at all added immensely to the fury of the spreading and gale-driven flames.

Out of hand almost from the moment it began, the fire spread furiously across the structures and the lumber yards of the West Side. Here
and there a shingled roof, bursting suddenly into flame, provided flaming
embers enough to start additional fires in an adjoining block or two.
Torn loose by the wind, burning shingles were scattered over everything
nearby. Within a quarter of an hour, any number of these and larger
firebrands, vividly aflame and uncontrollable, had crossed the Chicago
River. Fires broke out on Wells Street—on La Salle Street—on Adams.
Wind-driven streamers of fire leaped from roof to roof, and the flames,
growing more and more furious as the burning area enlarged, created
heat so terrible that observers scores of miles away actually felt it on
their upturned faces as they watched the red light in the sky.

Well started before ten o'clock in the evening, the fire had crossed
the river and advanced more than two miles by four in the morning.
From the very first the fire companies had been all but helpless, and as
the flaming tragedy grew greater thousands of people, driven from
homes, hotels, and rooming houses, fled toward the lake ahead of the

ever-spreading flames. Taking refuge beside the water, many of them were actually forced by the advancing fire into the lake itself.

Bravery and even heroism were common throughout the city as the fire advanced. Generous helpfulness was often apparent even amid the most unpromising surroundings. But the opposite was evident, too. Now and then some frightened person, caught in the press of traffic on some narrow Chicago River bridge, perhaps, slipped and fell and was trampled under foot. Elsewhere the night was marked by robbery and pillage, and extortion was the answer sometimes given to those who asked for help.

As the sun rose on the morning of October 9th, the fire, which had long since reached the lake front with a northwest wind behind it, was making its destructive way toward the city's south side. But here it was met by troops ordered into action by General Philip Sheridan. Hurrying his men toward the city from the reserve headquarters of the army's Western Department, he ordered them to blast a firebreak across the path of the advancing flames. Though halted there, the fire encountered no such opposition on the city's other side. The water works had already been destroyed, and when the flames once more leaped the Chicago River and began to make their way toward the north, nothing could be done to halt them. It was not until twenty-seven hours of destruction had passed, and the fire had made its way almost to the open prairie near what is now known as Lincoln Park, that the wind dropped and a heavy fall of rain providentially brought the conflagration to an end.

The very heart of the city—an area five square miles in extent—had been destroyed. More than a hundred thousand people were homeless. Not less than 250 were dead. Every important public building had been burned. Newspaper offices, hotels, and railroad stations—all were smoking ruins. Churches, stores, and business houses had given way to ashes. In all, 17,450 buildings and property valued at $196,000,000 had been consumed.

The first word of the Chicago fire reached Hartford on the morning of Monday, October 9th. Throughout that week the Directors of the Hartford Fire Insurance Company met frequently. From time to time additional information about the extent of the fire arrived, but because the headquarters building of the Western Department had been destroyed, it was impossible for George Bissell or his assistants to turn to their records in order to learn just what losses the Company had suffered.

Instead, the Home Office, having first obtained a list of all the streets in the burned district, had to check the monthly reports of the Western Department against them. In this way, even before any detailed information arrived from Chicago, President Chase and the Directors had learned that the Company's losses in the fire might reach $2,240,000—a truly staggering figure in view of the fact that the Company's assets were less than $1,700,000 at the time.

It was not until this estimate had been made that the Directors had anything upon which they could depend in determining what the Company's policy was to be. But with this before them, they reached their decision in a single meeting.

"On motion of Mr. Lyman," the minutes of the Directors' meeting of October 10, 1871, reads, "it was voted to advise the agents of the Company immediately to continue business at advanced rates as from present information and after a careful survey of the field such seems to be the only proper and expedient course to pursue."

It was as a result of this motion that President Chase, while the ruins of Chicago were still smoking and the Western Department's great three-story vault was still too hot to open, wrote out a message that was sent by telegraph to every Hartford agent. It read as follows:

HARTFORD, CONN.

OCT. 10

THE OLD HARTFORD WILL PROMPTLY MEET ITS OBLIGATIONS IN CHICAGO & ELSEWHERE AS USUAL. CONTINUE BUSINESS AND ADVANCE RATES FIFTY TO ONE HUNDRED PER CENT.

GEO. L. CHASE

PRES'T

In Chicago, meanwhile, General Agent Bissell had been laboring under exceptional difficulties. With his La Salle Street office destroyed, and with the Company's vaults too hot to approach, he had no records to which to turn in order to determine the Hartford's losses. At 128 La Salle Street, however, the important insurance agency of Moore, Case, Lyman, & Hubbard, which had represented the Hartford in Chicago since 1864, had had its office. It, too, had been destroyed, but its vault appeared to be intact and, because it was smaller than the Western Department's great three-story vault, as well as because it had apparently been subjected to less heat, it was not unlikely that it could safely be opened long before the great overheated mass of the Western Department's vault had cooled down enough to touch. And here, as well as in the Western Department's vault, were books—if they were still intact— that would provide the information the Hartford Fire Insurance Company and the four other companies the agency represented, so urgently needed.

"The vault in our office was intact," James H. Moore, the senior partner in the agency wrote many years later,[*] "but we did not open it until Thursday afternoon. Meantime we had dispatched messengers to locate the street numbers of buildings destroyed around the entire burned district on our street books and ascertain the liability of each company [we represented] . . .

"George F. Bissell . . . met me at our vault Thursday afternoon. Upon opening the door we found everything inside uninjured, though the books were so hot we had to wear gloves to handle them. We carted them over to my house on West Monroe Street, and with the aid of a half dozen clerks, made a schedule of the different policies involved. . . . We completed the work before midnight and sent a man to the nearest telegraph office available—Joliet, Ill.[†]—to advise the Home Offices of the amount of their total liability. Afterward these messages proved to be the first ones sent from any agency that gave a definite estimate of the companies' losses, and these original estimates were nearly correct."

Incidentally, because of the disruption of telegraph service in Chicago, it was not until the next morning—Friday, October 13th—that the message President Chase had telegraphed to all Hartford agents, reached Moore, Case, Lyman & Hubbard at a little temporary office they had opened on Canal Street.

"It was, so far as I know," wrote Mr. Moore in the same account from which the above quotation was taken, "the first intimation received [in Chicago] from any company as to their condition and willingness to pay. . . . This message from the Hartford did much to give men courage . . . and it was the beginning of the new enterprise that rebuilt Chicago."

Because of the excessive demands on Chicago's badly damaged telegraph facilities, General Agent Bissell's first report to the home office of the Hartford did not arrive until a week after the fire was over. But even before receiving the information he had been able to send, arrange-

---

[*] *The Hartford Agent,* Vol. XIII, No. 4, p. 117.
[†] Joliet is about thirty miles from Chicago.

ments had been made for the Company to meet its losses, and the moment these had been completed President Chase left for Chicago to work with General Agent Bissell in seeing to the adjustment of claims and in guarding the Company's interests.

Even before the fire had ended, Chicago was beginning to ask what the fire insurance companies would do. Though no one except the better-informed insurance men had any clear idea of the number of insurance companies that were involved, and some time was still to pass before any accurate estimate of the total property loss could be compiled, it was clear from the first that failure was inevitable for many insurance companies.

Ultimately it was learned that property valued at $196,000,000 had been destroyed, little more than half of which had been insured. But the tragedy was greater because of another fact. Of the 202 insurance companies involved, 68 failed immediately, and 83 more settled their claims only in part. Following this great tragedy only 51 insurance companies paid their losses in full. Of a hundred million dollars in insurance claims, only half was ever paid, the unpaid balance of $50,119,977 falling on unfortunate property owners in Chicago who had to bear additional losses of some $96,000,000 on property not covered by insurance of any kind.

Though President Chase and the Directors of the Hartford had instantly decided that the Company would fully "meet its obligations in Chicago & elsewhere," plans had to be made to do so. The Hartford National Bank, to which the Hartford Fire Insurance Company had so often turned, immediately agreed to lend to the limit of its resources. The Connecticut Mutual Life Insurance Company granted a loan of $500,000, and another loan was arranged at the office of the Connecticut Trust and Safe Deposit Company.

It was fortunately unnecessary for the Hartford to sell any of its securities, but all of them had to be used as collateral. Though seriously concerned because of the extent of the catastrophe, the Directors never for a moment lost confidence. At the very meeting at which General Agent Bissell's first estimate of the Company's Chicago losses was read, they adopted a resolution to keep the Company's capital at $1,000,000, and agreed to maintain "a reinsurance fund sufficient to meet the requirements of the several states; and should any deficiency appear in the re-insurance reserve after settlement of Chicago losses, the same shall be made good."

In all, about $700,000 was borrowed, and, under the direction of President Chase and General Agent Bissell, every loss was settled in full. Unfortunately, however, only about $1,000,000 was left in the treasury, a sum too small to meet the requirements of the reinsurance fund.

Confronted with this problem, the Directors promptly voted to reduce the Company's capital to $500,000, and then immediately increased it to $1,000,000 again by issuing $500,000 in new stock at $100 par. And, in demonstration of the fact that no one had lost confidence, the demand for this new stock was so great that rights to subscribe commanded a premium of $85 a share.

General Agent Bissell of the Hartford's Western Department, instantly conscious of the problems confronting the Company, was the first fire insurance manager in Chicago to open an office after the fire. Even before President Chase arrived from Hartford, the entire staff of the Hartford's Western Department was working day and night under his direction. Nor were the tasks that they assumed related only to the adjustment of claims resulting from the fire. These claims were given priority, it is true, but the Company's vault had not yet cooled when George Bissell took President Chase to inspect the ruins of the former office. Having temporarily installed his clerks and assistants in an inadequate little office he had fortunately been able to rent, the Chicago General Agent had already obtained an estimate on the cost of rebuilding the ruined structure that had housed the offices of the Western Department. President Chase, seeing the need the moment he arrived, and quick to agree with the General Agent's idea, sent the following telegram to the Company's Directors only nine days after the fire had ended:

VAULTS COMPARATIVELY UNINJURED. CONSIDERABLE OLD MATERIAL AVAILABLE. CAN REBUILD THREE STORIES HIGH, NINETY DAYS FOR TEN THOUSAND DOLLARS. CAN RENT FOUR ROOMS NEW BUILDING FOUR THOUSAND DOLLARS. NOW PAYING FIFTEEN HUNDRED RENT NO VAULTS. I RECOMMEND REBUILDING IMMEDIATELY. PLEASE ACT PROMPTLY AND ADVISE BY TELEGRAPH.

A reply by wire gave immediate approval and the new building, when it was completed, bore the following words high up on its plain brick side:

HARTFORD BUILDING
ERECTED
A.D.   1864
DESTROYED OCT. 9TH, 1871
REBUILT DEC. 1871

Much has been written of what the insurance companies did and failed to do in the difficult days that followed the Chicago fire. The weaknesses that brought about so many failures have especially been a subject for discussion, but the Hartford Fire Insurance Company even yet likes to recall that it was one of the fifty-one companies that paid every claim it owed. In all, the Hartford adjusted Chicago claims that totaled $1,968,225, and in proof of the Company's fairness and consideration, all of these were paid without a single case of litigation.

The Hartford losses, said an insurance publication of the day, "were adjusted correctly and promptly and paid within the regular time limit— the best piece of insurance adjustment and payment ever executed in this country."

It is a record of which any company might be proud.

CHAPTER 12

A CO-OPERATIVE

BEGINNING

THOUGH the Chicago fire had been so enormously destructive, it was directly responsible for much that was good. The generosity of the people of the United States and Europe made possible the creation of a system of relief that remained in effective operation for five years, and the energy that has always marked Chicago went a long way toward rebuilding the destroyed business district within a year. Taking the lesson of the fire to heart, wooden construction was very largely barred and when, two or three years later, the last of the fire scars had disappeared, the "new" Chicago—a city of brick and stone—was not only larger and finer than ever before, but was actually wealthier as well.

Even the insurance companies had undergone a somewhat similar experience. The weaker ones, as had been the case with the wooden structures of the city's business section, had disappeared, but those that remained—and especially those like the Hartford that had promptly and unhesitatingly paid every dollar of loss—instantly entered upon a new era of expanding business. Immediately inheriting the business that had formerly gone to the companies that had failed, they also gained new business as a result of the unanswerable argument the fire had advanced. Just as Chicago continued to advance in business and in population despite the fire, so the sound insurance companies, despite their heavy losses—even, in a way, because of them—were able to increase their business on a greater scale than ever before.

Frederick Samson, later Secretary of the Hartford Fire Insurance

Company, was a clerk in the Home Office at the time of the fire and in an account of what he saw take place,[*] he referred to the telegrams sent to the Company's agents by President Chase in order to assure them that "the old Hartford will promptly meet its obligations in Chicago & elsewhere."

"The telegrams had their proper effect," he wrote. "It seemed as if we could see the money coming in the front door by the basketful. We certainly could see business roll in so fast that it was hard to take care of it. It was like handling a year's business in a month."

Referring to the $700,000 that was borrowed, and to the half-million-dollar assessment, he added, "Money on new business did the rest . . . and we could say 'All's well that ends well.' "

How well it ended is proved by the fact that when Boston suffered an $80,000,000 fire in November the following year, "the old Hartford" promptly paid losses amounting to $485,000. Furthermore, this disaster was no more than mentioned in the minutes of a meeting of the Board of Directors—a meeting during which "the President made a verbal report relative to the disastrous conflagrations in Boston yesterday."

During 1871 and 1872, the Hartford Fire Insurance Company had received $4,090,222 in premiums, a sum more than six hundred thousand dollars greater than the Company's total premium income for the first forty years of its existence. In those same two years, however, it had been called upon to pay losses that totaled $4,451,612—almost nine per cent more than it had received in premiums—and, in addition, had had to meet all of its costs of operation. Because of this, the Company's books, when the New Year of 1873 began, showed that its capital was impaired by about $147,000.

Even under the best of conditions this would have been a problem of some consequence, but for many reasons economic conditions in the country were irregular and not invariably good. The South, as yet, had made comparatively little headway in rebuilding its economic structure. Many Southern states were still being plundered by "carpet-baggers" and "scalawags." On the other hand, an expansive era of railroad building was actively under way in the West. The vast herds of buffalo were being decimated and with every passing year the Indians were steadily losing out in their efforts to maintain their former way of life.

[*] "In the Old Times," by Fred'k Samson. *The Hartford Agent,* June 1917, p. 446.

GEORGE L. CHASE
President, 1867-1908

The West that has since become a land of legend had suddenly evolved. Cattle were being driven north from Texas by tens of thousands to the cattle towns and railroads of Kansas and Nebraska. The cowboy, unknown to the world a generation earlier, had appeared and taken his place in a picturesque economy that could not have existed without him—an economy that began to be replaced as soon as it appeared, and that covered, from first to last, a span of little more than two or three decades.

In the East, meanwhile, many business opportunities awaited bold, unscrupulous men. Some of the more prominent men who now appeared in the fields of commerce and finance were as thoughtless of the rights of others as any robber baron of the Middle Ages. Though among them there were a few who succeeded in founding some of the greatest fortunes America has produced, their inclinations were often purely predatory. Nevertheless, so great were the opportunities of the day, some of their activities resulted in gigantic enterprises—railroads, oil, steel, and others—that later played important parts in the creation of the America that was to be. Monopolists, speculators, and men of doubtful economic morals though many of them were, some among them nevertheless laid strong foundations upon which worthy structures were later to be built.

In politics, meanwhile, corruption often seemed to be the order of the day. In New York City, conservative estimates place the amount directly stolen by the "Tweed Ring" in 1869, 1870, and 1871 at $45,000,-000, while indirect losses to the city were probably four times as great. Nor was New York alone. Pennsylvania, in the dishonest grip of Simon Cameron, the former Secretary of War, was in no sense better; and notorious financiers of the day, conscious that President Ulysses S. Grant was easy to hoodwink, went so far as to give their bribes in the very shadow of the White House. Not infrequently, men in public life—including representatives and senators—accepted bribes. Often enough, franchises and even legislative acts were paid for. Congress itself, on the day before President Grant was to be inaugurated for his second term, not only increased Congressional salaries fifty per cent, but also made the act retroactive so as to give each member of Congress an additional $5,000 in back pay.

Under conditions such as these, it is entirely understandable that the national economy was being weakened. Though President Grant and his supporters gladly claimed credit for the prosperity that had continued throughout his first term, there had been signs for a year or more that trouble was on the way. Four savings banks in New York had failed during 1872. In the spring of 1873 European financiers, obviously troubled by a stock exchange panic in Vienna, checked the flow of credit to America. On September 18th the greatest banking house in the United States—the firm of Jay Cooke & Co., which had invested too heavily in the half-built Northern Pacific Railway—was forced to close its doors. Immediately thereafter, nineteen Stock Exchange firms collapsed. The Union Trust Company failed, and other companies followed.

A new panic had come—a panic that was to prove longer and more destructive of values than any other the country had yet experienced.

Fortunately, a vitally important step had been taken some seven years earlier by the more responsible fire insurance companies of the United States. Following the Civil War, fire losses had increased so tremendously that the fire insurance companies of the nation, with a total capitalization of only about $65,000,000, were actually in danger, unless incendiarism could be controlled and fire-fighting methods immensely improved, of being driven out of business. Greatly troubled by this prospect, they were troubled also by rate-cutting and other harmful methods of competition. And, as if that were not enough, small, inadequately financed companies that were incapable of meeting their responsibilities when losses proved more than very moderate, were constantly being organized. It was because of difficulties such as these, and there were many more, that representatives of a large number of the nation's soundest companies finally succeeded in organizing The National Board of Fire Underwriters of the United States.

Efforts had been made before to create some such association of companies in the hope of eliminating their more troublesome problems, but nothing had been permanently accomplished. Even now that the National Board had been formed, the difficulties that had brought it into existence were not soon to be eliminated. Years were to pass before the purposes for which it was organized were ultimately to be attained. The first step had been taken, however, and though the new association came close to outright failure more than once in its first half-dozen years of existence, good fortune, seconded by wise and determined leadership, enabled it not only to remain in existence but also to contribute greatly to the future of fire insurance in America.

The new organization, which was formed at a meeting of seventy-five companies in New York on July 18, 1866, itemized its purposes as follows:

1. To establish and maintain, as far as practicable, a system of uniform rates of premium.

2. To establish and maintain a uniform rate of compensation to agents and brokers.

3. To repress incendiarism and arson by combining in suitable measures for the apprehension, conviction, and punishment of criminals engaged in this nefarious business.

4. To devise and give effect to measures for the protection of our common interests and the promotion of our general prosperity.

In the years that followed, these simply stated purposes were subjected to many alterations and improvements, but the conditions that existed in the field of fire insurance were so chaotic that, even with the best intentions, the companies that were represented in this new association were unable to find any quick and easy way to successful collaboration.

Fortunately, the officers chosen to head the board were men of vision and ability. James M. McLean, President of the Citizens' Insurance Company of New York, was elected President. Timothy C. Allyn, President of the Hartford Fire Insurance Company at the time, became Vice-President. Frank W. Ballard, Secretary of the New York Board of Fire Underwriters, was elected Secretary of the new Board, and J. S. Parish, President of the Atlantic Fire and Marine Insurance Company of Providence, was elected Treasurer.

Though "underwriting" was a term that had long been in use by insurance men both in Great Britain and America, its origin, and even its meaning, were little understood by others. The term seems to have originated late in the seventeenth century when Lloyd's Coffee House, in London, gradually became the center for the marine insurance activities of that day. Merchants and shipowners, congregating there, ultimately began to list the values of their various cargoes on a blackboard provided by the coffee house, and such businessmen as cared to guarantee the owners of these cargoes—for a fee, of course—against "the perils of the sea," wrote their names under the particular cargo lists they were willing to accept as "risks." First used in reference to this practice, the term "underwriters" ultimately came into use throughout the whole field of insurance where it remained as an accepted term even after the black-board at Lloyd's Coffee House gave way to a better system of records.

The first annual meeting of the new National Board, which was held in February 1867, only seven months after its organization, gave evidence of some progress. Where representatives of only seventy-five companies had attended the original meeting, ninety-nine companies and thirty-two local boards were represented at the second. The importance the new board had already attained was apparent from the fact that those who attended the meeting were, for the most part, the presidents of the companies and boards they represented.

Such growth as took place in the next several years was remarkably uneven. Hundreds of local boards were organized, and much progress was made in the adoption of uniform rates. Various standards and classifications were set. A report warned against the danger that attended the increasing use of kerosene, and another report on "gas-machines," inadequate though it appears today, was nevertheless an early step in the Board's progress toward the establishment of the invaluable Underwriters' Laboratories of a later day.

The new National Board, hoping to see Federal legislation replace state laws in the regulation and control of insurance, was even represented by counsel in the famous case of Paul vs. Virginia. For the most part, however, the subjects that most interested the organization were those having to do with the standardization of premiums and commissions.

For a time it seemed that the National Board was making excellent progress. By 1869 a Rating Bureau had been organized, tariffs had been written for almost two thousand separate communities, and the entire country had been divided into six departments, each with a committee, an office, and such paid representatives as were necessary. The National Board's Policy Form was widely accepted and, under the terms of the famous "Chicago Compact," thirty-seven companies agreed to remove any local agent who was guilty, for a second time, of failing to abide by the rates established by the National Board.

Under these newly adopted rules and regulations conditions definitely improved, and, at least among those who were more than usually given to optimism, a bright new day seemed about to dawn. By 1870, however, doubts began to materialize. Many local boards were seen to be weak and ineffective. Demands for cheaper insurance were made by many local agents, and some of the companies, weakening in their support of the National Board, permitted their rates to be cut.

"If this . . . goes much further," said E. W. Crowell, Chairman of the National Board's Executive Committee, "it is only a question of time . . . [before] the matter of rates will be a thing of the past."

As a matter of fact, this unfortunate development made such headway that the Executive Committee, meeting on February 24, 1870, authorized the various local boards to "modify, suspend, or declare advisory any or all rates fixed by them."

The excellent beginning, in other words, turned into failure within a period of four years, and the 1870's began with the National Board in a condition not far removed from suspended animation—a condition from which it was ultimately rescued by the unparalleled catastrophe of the Chicago fire.

It was clear, even before the smoke of the Chicago disaster had drifted away, that cheap insurance was usually not worth its cost. Weak companies had gone to the wall by scores, and even the strongest firms were strained. It was evident, too, that some of the companies that succeeded in paying their losses were in a position to do so only, or very largely, because, for a time, they had been controlled by the rules and regulations laid down by the National Board.

With these facts so apparent, the National Board of Fire Underwriters was given a new lease on life. The local boards came to life again as well, and rate-cutting, ruinous as it was now known to be, disappeared completely—disappeared, that is, for a time. Sharp though the lesson had been, some began to forget it before many months had passed.

Despite the high mortality among the weaker companies that resulted from the Chicago fire, inadequately financed companies now began to be organized by scores in order to profit from the increased demand for insurance that followed the Chicago fire. Supervision and control again fell on evil days and when, only thirteen months after the Chicago fire, Boston suffered from its great fire, thirty more fire insurance companies went bankrupt, their total assets amounting to only about half their total losses.

Now fire insurance executives again bethought themselves of the sound principles the National Board had endeavored to enforce. Once more conscious of the danger that was certain to arise from inadequate rates, they agreed on a general increase—an increase of 30 per cent in towns of less than 50,000 population, and of 50 per cent in all the larger cities.

For the time being, at least, they were once more in agreement.

For a time after the Chicago and Boston fires, it appeared that much constructive thought was being given to the subject of fire prevention. In Chicago, for example, brick and stone came into much more general use. Except in New York, however, few laws had been adopted with the idea of providing for the erection of "fire-proof" or fire-resistant buildings. Even in New York, where certain desirable regulations had been adopted, they accomplished very little because of the lack of any adequate method of enforcement. Furthermore, architecture was in the midst of a notably stagnant period, and the structures of the day, covered as they often were with unsubstantial and often tawdry ornaments, were rarely designed with any thought of fire resistance.

Thoughtful fire insurance executives now and again made it clear that they understood the need for legislation that would aid in the prevention or control of fires, but few communities did anything about it. Even in Chicago, where everyone still recalled the tragedy of the great fire, few regulations were adopted with the idea of compelling the construction of truly fire-resistant structures. And those that were designed with that end in view were none too well enforced. A member of the National Board, troubled by this fact, called attention to "four or five new, large buildings, just finished in Chicago, having the worst mansard roofs ever erected. It is scarcely possible that worse could be built. . . . I think some action should be taken, for we are not unlikely to have another fire there shortly."

As buildings grew taller, elevators came more and more into use, and the open shafts in which they operated were wonderfully effective in spreading flames up through any number of floors.

Obvious though these weaknesses were, the legislation that was needed was slow in coming—so slow, in fact, that the National Board, conscious not only of this need but also of the shocking inadequacy of the firemen and fire-fighting equipment of that day, sent a telegram, late in July 1874, to its local board in Chicago.

"We demand," this message read, "the immediate establishment of a special fire-patrol of at least a hundred men, by the city. No committee will come, but National Board companies will forward their demands to be complied with within a fixed time, or companies will retire."

Chicago, that is to say, had best see to it that the National Board's demands were met or the city would awaken some morning to find all its fire insurance policies canceled.

The local Chicago board passed the demands on to the mayor, and when he agreed to ask the city council for appropriate action, the National Board sent six demands, threatening to bring the Chicago business of its fire insurance companies to an end if they were not complied with.

The demands were as follows:

1. The establishment of permanent fire limits.

2. The enactment of a stringent building law, and provisions for its enforcement.

3. The complete reorganization of the Fire Department, the eradication of political influence, the establishment of discipline, and the improvement of equipment.

4. An increase in water facilities.

5. The establishment of a Fire Marshal's Bureau.

6. The passage of a law for the gradual removal of special hazards.

Confident that these demands would be met, the National Board was astonished when nothing of the kind happened. The next step, however, had already been decided on, and on September 23, 1874, the Executive Committee of the National Board officially called on all the companies represented by the Board to suspend business in Chicago and withdraw from the city on October 1st.

The mayor and the city council still failed to act, but the Chicago Citizens Association, more impressed than the politicians were by the Board's threat, brought all their influence to bear. It was plain to the National Board that this Association would ultimately force the city government to adopt the Board's suggestions, but the fire insurance companies that were associated with the Board, and even some that were not, nevertheless withdrew from the city when October 1st arrived.

This proved to be the final argument. The city administration, confronted not only by the action of the insurance companies but also by the highly aroused Citizens Association, promptly capitulated. Before the end of November so much had been accomplished that the National Board recommended to its member companies that they reopen their Chicago offices.

Successful though the National Board had been in its contest with Chicago, it did not thus succeed in solving all its problems. For a time the Chicago victory made it easy for the Board to hold its member companies in line, and other communities, unwilling to see the Board treat them as it had treated Chicago, themselves took steps to improve their fire departments, their water systems, and their building restriction laws. Here again, however, the millenium was slow in coming, and the Board, using its new-found power, increased insurance rates in certain cities that had failed to initiate the improvements the Board considered necessary. Rochester, New York, for example, had an inadequate water system and, late in 1872, when the city administration failed to take steps to improve it, the National Board increased fire insurance rates in the city by 20 per cent. This brought action, and when a new water works system that supplied a large part of the city ultimately went into operation, the National Board instructed its local board in Rochester "to abate the 20 per cent advance, of December, '72, on all risks covered by the new water works of the city—and no other—to take effect from the date at which the water works were accepted by the city authorities."

As will be noted in the pages that follow, the National Board ultimately concluded that its rating and policing activities were doomed to failure and that these could be better supervised by other bodies. During the succeeding years and up to this day the Board continued active and now is widely recognized as a public-spirited organization through which its member companies continue to provide service in the fields of fire protection standards, arson investigation, actuarial work and accounting, legislation, public relations, and kindred fields.

CHAPTER 13

ECONOMIC STRENGTH

AND

ECONOMIC WEAKNESS

Tʜᴏᴜɢʜ fire-fighting equipment of a sort had been in use for generations, it was notably ineffective until the steam fire engine first
appeared shortly before the Civil War. Even this important instrument
was of little or no use if water in considerable quantities was not widely
available. Water works capable of supplying whole cities were late in
coming. At the close of the Civil War steam fire engines were in use in
only fifteen cities in the United States. Within the next ten years, however, fire-fighting equipment was greatly improved and by 1876—largely,
perhaps, because of the National Board's increasing influence—about
280 communities had invested in fire engines, and professional, full-time
fire departments were rapidly increasing in numbers.

During these years the National Board of Fire Underwriters had had
a hand in many improvements and more than a few experiments. Here
and there—as in Chicago—it had greatly benefited the public. In other
fields, too, as in the establishment of its Bureau of Statistics, it proved
to be forward-looking and constructive. But, in a way, the success it had
attained had come somewhat too easily. In particular, its power to establish and maintain rates had been unwisely used. Determined, as it was,
to oppose rate-cutting, the harmful effects of which had long been evident, the Board seems to have overlooked the fact that the establishment of excessive rates could not fail, in the long run, to be just as
harmful.

At first, the opposition of the new companies unassociated with the National Board had little effect. As such companies grew in number, however, this influence increased. Competing actively for business, and conscious, as many of their potential clients also were, that the rates established by the National Board were unjustifiably high, they set their own rates lower.

The result was what might have been expected. Already troubled by the business depression which grew steadily worse from 1873 to 1878, the insurance companies that continued to support the National Board also found themselves losing more and more business to their rate-cutting competitors. During these five depression years more than 50,000 business firms went bankrupt. Factories closed. Wages fell. Unemployment increased.

Under such circumstances more and more fire insurance companies either withdrew from the National Board or, casually continuing their membership, nevertheless began to meet the cut rates of their competitors with cut rates of their own.

A National Board committee, of which President Chase of the Hartford was a member, made a report of the situation in April 1876. Referring to the fact that the committee had "acted upon over four thousand applications for revisions in rates and new ratings," the report added the following very long sentence:

"The withdrawal of companies from our organization with the argument that they shall stay in the board when it suits them, and go out when and where they please, observing National Board rules and principles where it is for their interest; in other words taking advantage of board experience and labor without lending it any sympathy or support, pecuniarily or otherwise, and who believe in the board simply because it ties other companies up to rates, and allows them to shade them just enough to steal the business, is, at best, a narrow, selfish, and extremely unwise policy."

Justifiable though this statement was, it did little good. Even before it was written, the National Board had been greatly harmed, and when in April 1876 President Chase of the Hartford succeeded Henry A. Oakley as President of the National Board, one of its first duties was to accept the resignation of a score of companies and to drop that many more for having failed to live up to the Board's requirements.

For the next two years a discouraging rear-guard action was fought by the defenders of the greatly weakened Board. President Chase was succeeded by Alfred B. Baker of the Franklin Insurance Company of Philadelphia. It was during his administration that the National Board's attempt to control rates was permanently abandoned, and for ten discouraging years the Board's fortunes continued to decline.

From the time the National Board of Fire Underwriters was formed, the Hartford Fire Insurance Company had been one of its most consistent supporters. Having learned long before how perilous cut-rate competition could be, the Company did its utmost to maintain the rates established by the National Board. Perhaps it was because of this—in part, at least—that the economic depression that steadily grew worse from 1873 to 1878 seems to have affected the Company only moderately. In 1876, for example, the stockholders were granted a stock dividend of 25 per cent, thus increasing the Company's capital stock to $1,250,000, and losses of almost a million dollars due to fires in 1877 seem to have been paid with no great difficulty.

Because the attempts of the National Board to establish and maintain rates had failed, competition not unnaturally reverted to the methods that had formerly existed. Rate wars—openly acknowledged or furtively indulged in—came to be commonplace once more, though here and there strong local boards or determined agents and executives successfully opposed them. In general, however, the business of fire insurance was adversely affected, and the Hartford felt the effects along with the rest.

Though the Company's premium income for the decade of the 1870's was $18,253,000, an increase of more than $7,000,000 over that of the preceding ten years, the income for 1879 was actually less than it had been in 1870. On the whole, however, the record was a good one. Despite losses of almost two million dollars in Chicago, of almost half a million in Boston, and of more than nine million in other, lesser fires, and despite the difficulties that the collapse of rate controls had caused, the Company showed an underwriting profit for the decade of $630,000 and was able to pay dividends in every one of those ten years with the single exception of 1872.

In the whole of the Company's existence no other decade appears to have been so filled with difficulties. And yet, as the New Year of 1880 dawned, the Company, in addition to its capital of $1,250,000, could point to a net surplus of $935,399.12—a sum almost two and a half times as great as it had been ten years before.

Though the Hartford had made so remarkable a recovery, internal difficulties of which the public knew little or nothing had gradually assumed serious proportions. While he continued as a director for six more years, "differences with the management" had caused C. C. Lyman to resign in 1878 after forty-three years as Assistant Secretary, and in 1880 John D. Browne, who had been Secretary for ten years, came "to the point of terminating the official relations which, in past years, I had hoped might be life-long."

It is apparent that both these resignations were influenced by "differences" that had arisen in connection with the policy and management of the Company, but there is little doubt that the strong personalities of Secretary Browne and President Chase made it difficult for them to collaborate smoothly. It was because of this, apparently, that Secretary Browne accepted the Presidency of the Connecticut Fire Insurance Company when that position was offered him in October 1880, and it is interesting to note that in this new capacity his self-confidence and firmly held opinions, serving him in good stead, made his administration notably successful.

The Hartford, in turn, chose C. B. Whiting as its new Secretary. Philander C. Royce, Secretary of the Girard Fire Insurance Company of Philadelphia and formerly a special agent and adjuster in the Hartford's Western Department, later accepted an invitation to return to the Hartford as Assistant Secretary. Five years later, Secretary Whiting resigned and accepted the Presidency of the Orient Insurance Company. Assistant Secretary Royce succeeded him as Secretary and continued in that position for twenty years.

As a result of these changes, and of modifications in policy that naturally followed, the business of the Company was prosecuted with renewed vigor. This, as events were later to prove, was fortunate for, as the historian, David S. Muzzey, later pointed out, the United States of America had reached "dead center," and for a time the nation's progress was definitely retarded.

Half a generation had passed since the close of the Civil War, and the deep enmities it had brought into being had somewhat lessened. At the same time, however, both political and economic ethics had sharply deteriorated. Political morality, in fact, had degenerated almost unbelievably during the early postwar years, and despite some improvement that had come during the administration of Rutherford B. Hayes, conditions still left much to be desired. Furthermore, the business depression, starting in 1873 and reaching its belated end six years later, had transmitted to the nation a troublesome legacy of unsound economic thinking and discreditable business practices that was to bedevil the country for another score of years.

Widespread opposition to the Resumption Act of 1875 had failed to overthrow that piece of legislation. Despite the best efforts of the Greenback Party, the "Free-Silverites," and others, specie payments which had been halted for years had been resumed on January 1, 1879, and the country was once more back on the gold standard. Thus an important step had been taken in preparation for the period of expansion that was ultimately to come. But that lay far in the future. The national economy still lacked the necessary dynamism. The country's more powerful monopolists all too often failed to recognize the fact that great economic power properly entails at least a modicum of social responsibility. Railroads, with little thought for the national good, not infrequently indulged in bribery, gave lower rates and even rebates to favored shippers, and, on occasion, paid for such votes as were necessary to the election of some willing but inglorious politician even to the august Senate of the United States. Fortunately, however, even when such practices were most widespread, other and better things gave some promise for the nation's future.

Despite the rapid growth of manufacturing and the increase in the population of the nation's cities, the rural population of the country still accounted for almost two thirds of the total. In fact, from 1840 to 1880, the actual numerical increase in rural areas had been greater than in urban ones, and farmers, who had been enormously hard hit by the depression, felt—and with some justification—that they were consistently imposed upon by railroads, monopolists, tariff-protected manufacturers, and bankers who widely held mortgages on farms. In earlier days farmers had only occasionally banded together for political action, but now various agrarian movements attracted them in large numbers; and their opposition to railroads, monopolies, and tariffs, as well as their support of all kinds of inflationary legislation, began to play an important part in American politics.

As early as 1871 the farmers of Illinois, having gained control of the state legislature, obtained the passage of an act that somewhat restricted excessive freight rates and partially controlled certain discriminatory railroad practices. The people of other states were not slow to follow this example, and though the railroads objected, similar controls were widely adopted, especially after the Supreme Court held, in 1876, that "When . . . one devotes his property to a use in which the public has an interest, he . . . must submit to be controlled by the public for the common good."

James A. Garfield's election to the Presidency in 1880 and his assassination the following year introduced a decade of political change. Bad crops throughout the Middle West in 1881, coupled with widespread dissatisfaction with boss rule and the spoils system, greatly strengthened the Democratic Party in the Congressional election of 1882. Two years later, for the first time in twenty-eight years, a Democrat—Grover Cleveland of New York—was elected President.

Throughout this period the population of the country continued to increase, but nowhere was the growth so rapid as in the Middle West. In thirty years the people of Illinois had more than tripled in number, and other states in the territory assigned to the Hartford Fire Insurance Company's Western Department had grown at an even greater rate.

Even during the depression years of the 1870's this growth continued, and, largely because of it, the business of the Western Department increased so greatly that the rebuilt building at 49 La Salle Street was outgrown by 1881 and larger quarters were taken in what was said to be the first fire-resistant building ever erected in Chicago—the Montauk Block at 115 Monroe Street.

Following the fire of 1871, Chicago had not only been rebuilt with surprising rapidity but had also continued to grow. In 1870 its population was 306,000, but by 1880, despite the fire and six years of depression, the city had half a million people; and ten years later, with a population of a million, it took its place as the second largest city in the country.

Economically, too, it had made great strides. Because of its fortunate location it had come to be the railroad center of the nation. This, in turn, resulted in the rapid growth of its manufactures and its wholesale trade. As agricultural production increased throughout the Middle West, Chicago's grain elevators and meat-packing plants also increased spectacularly.

With business expansion going forward on so great a scale, the city naturally became an insurance center of importance. On that account, the reduction in scope of the National Board of Fire Underwriters in 1878 led some of the more forward-looking insurance men of the city to consider the possibility of forming an association of their own.

Warned by the difficulties that had brought about the decline of the National Board, the Chicago group was careful in drafting the original statement of its aims. Meeting on July 12, 1879, to form a new association to be called "The Union," and to draw up a compact upon which they could agree, the thirty-eight representatives of fire insurance companies and agencies that assembled were careful not to be too specific in stating the purposes they had in mind.

"We the undersigned," they wrote, "whose signatures are hereto appended, agree to form an Association for the purpose of promoting reforms in Underwriting, to be known as The Union."

Six simple paragraphs then outlined the method of organization and the rules that were to be followed, and finally, near the bottom of the large single sheet of paper on which this statement was engrossed, the names of the thirty-eight companies and agencies that were represented—one of which was the "Hartford of Hartford"—were listed.

It was on September 22, 1879, that "The Union," which has been known since 1929 as the Western Underwriters Association, actually came into existence, for it was on that date that its basic document was ratified. In the years that followed, the new organization played a most constructive part in bringing order to the highly disordered field of fire insurance in the Middle West. It led in the establishment of the Underwriters' Laboratories, the Western Factory Insurance Association, and the Underwriters Salvage Company. The active part it played in legislative matters greatly influenced the related activities of the National Board of Fire Underwriters, and even the ultimate re-establishment of the influence of the National Board was due, in part, to the constructive activities of The Union.

The success of The Union in the Middle West naturally attracted the attention of insurance men elsewhere, and because conditions in the East were as troubled and chaotic as they had been in the Middle West, the "Eastern Union," later renamed the Eastern Underwriters Association, was soon founded. This organization and the related body in the Middle West proved to be stabilizing influences from the first, and they may properly be credited with having played a leading part in correcting the chaotic conditions that threatened, at one time, to bring disaster to the whole field of insurance. The South Eastern Underwriters Association and the Board of Underwriters of the Pacific performed similar services in their geographic areas. The directions and trends of the business, however, have wiped out the geographical differences. As a result, these regional organizations which served the industry so well have now had their functions transferred to two national organizations, Interregional Insurance Conference and Insurance Information Institute.

By the time these organizations had been founded, a number of the nation's stronger insurance companies had come to be national institutions known to almost everyone. They were widely represented, with their agents active almost everywhere, and among their trademarks some had attained almost universal acceptance.

In all probability the Hartford Fire Insurance Company's trademark—an engraved adaptation of the famous Landseer painting of the "Monarch of the Glen"—is the most widely known symbol in the fire insurance field. It is an odd fact, however, that no one seems to know exactly how or when this engraving came to occupy the position it now so clearly holds.

The Hartford Fire Insurance Company has not infrequently been asked what possible connection a deer has with fire insurance, and it must be admitted that the connection does not become apparent even when it is pointed out that the deer in question is an adult male—a stag—of the red deer family, which is a European species smaller than, but closely related to, the American elk.

In medieval times, as well as later, such a stag, which was also known in England as a hart, was one of the very greatest prizes of the chase. These animals were often used as "supporters" in the complicated symbolism of heraldry as the lion and the unicorn are used even yet in the royal coat-of-arms of Great Britain.

Because of this use of the stag—or, more properly in this connection, the hart—it was entirely natural for the English town of Hertford, which got its name in Anglo-Saxon times and to this day is called "här-ferd" or "härt-ferd," to have adopted a coat-of-arms showing a *hart* crossing a *ford*. And Hartford, Connecticut, named, as it apparently was, after the English town of Hertford, used the same idea when the city's official seal was designed.

So far as it is now possible to determine, the Hartford Fire Insurance Company, sometime in the 1850's, began to use a reproduction of the seal of the city of Hartford as a part of its letterhead. In the years that followed, variations of this design were used on various policies and certificates, and even on calendars and blotters.

It would appear that the hart of the city seal somehow succeeded in establishing a kind of place for itself in connection with the Hartford Fire Insurance Company. On the other hand, the frequent variations in the design suggest that some time elapsed before a drawing was found that was entirely satisfactory. And even in this connection, oddly enough, England had a hand in the matter.

In 1850 Great Britain completed the erection of her handsome new Houses of Parliament, and Sir Edwin H. Landseer, a very successful artist of the day who later modeled the four lions that guard the base of the Nelson monument in Trafalgar Square, was commissioned to paint for the Houses of Parliament three subjects connected with the chase. One of these—the famous painting known as "Monarch of the Glen"—was completed in 1851, but by then the commission had come to nothing because the House of Commons refused to appropriate more than £1,500 for the paintings, and the "Monarch" found a private purchaser. Landseer's paintings were very popular at the time and engraved reproductions of many of them, including one "Monarch of the Glen" done for John A. Lowell & Co. of Boston by E. G. Farmer in 1890, sold widely both in Great Britain and America.

Here, at last, was the symbol the Hartford Fire Insurance Company had been hoping to find, and so the majestic stag has come to represent the Hartford visually for more than half a century.

Throughout the 1880's the Company's business grew. On the whole, however, its percentage of increase was little more than enough to match the growing population of the country.

The fact is that though the age of steam and machinery had begun to change the lives of the people, the changes, as yet, were comparatively slight. Factory production had increased the growth of cities. Labor-saving machinery, though still but little developed, had reduced the more wearing tasks both in factories and on the farm. Travel was more rapid and more comfortable and, in the cities, leisure as well as productivity had increased.

Life had grown a little easier even on the farms. Scythes had given way almost completely to mowing machines and binders, and windmills, all across the Middle West, pumped the water. In other ways too life was more convenient. The railroads had made travel much easier and had reduced the cost of freight. The telegraph and cable, together with improved printing presses, had increased the number and improved the quality of the country's newspapers.

At home, however, few changes had been made as yet. Home life in 1890 differed little from what it had been just prior to the Civil War. Except in the cities and larger towns pavements were almost unknown. Country roads, with only the rarest of exceptions, were utterly unpaved—unbelievably muddy at times, and at other times badly rutted, deep in dust, or difficult to traverse because of snow and ice. Farms, and even some of the smaller and more remote villages, were sometimes very nearly isolated. So despite the growth of factories and the prosperity that attended them, rural areas, for the most part, found life anything but easy.

The depression years of the 1870's had been felt throughout every portion of the country but the improved conditions of the 1880's were far less general. The South, greatly delayed in rebuilding its shattered economy, was improving only slowly, and the rapidly growing Middle West, which was still predominantly agricultural, was hurt as much by droughts, grasshoppers, and the high cost of what it had to buy as it was aided by its great production when its crops were good.

The unsettled politics of the period had defeated President Cleveland in 1888 but in 1892 he was elected again. In the meantime, however, the price of farm products had been falling. Industrial conditions had deteriorated, too, and at Homestead, on the Monongahela River near Pittsburgh, a strike of steel workers not only killed seven men and wounded a score or more, but also led the anarchist, Alexander Berkman, to attack and seriously wound H. C. Frick, a powerful financier and steel manufacturer. Prices on most commodities were declining and wage reductions followed.

The bankruptcy of the Philadelphia & Reading Railroad was announced just before President Cleveland's inauguration, and some two months later, with the Government's gold reserve rapidly dwindling, a widespread series of bankruptcies brought on a disastrous panic.

The depression of 1893 had come—an economic disaster far worse than any the nation had yet experienced.

CHAPTER 14

GREAT LOSSES

AND

GREAT GAINS

THOUGH the 1880's had been a period of expansion and relative prosperity throughout most of the country, it had also been a period of much social unrest. Industrial combinations, placing great power in the hands of industrial leaders and financiers, had forced labor to organize, and strikes, many of which were carried out in a spirit of bitterness new to the United States, had been numerous and prolonged. Political and economic discontent had also been widespread in the newly settled prairie states where drought and crop failures had driven many farmers from the land and left many others debt-ridden and helpless.

Because of these conditions marked economic contrasts had come to be apparent in the country. Here and there great fortunes were being accumulated, sometimes by monopolists and manipulators who gave little thought to the public welfare. On the other hand, large numbers of farmers and factory workers found themselves hard-pressed and pessimistic, with the result that socialistic—and even anarchistic—ideas were gaining acceptance among them.

Despite conditions such as these, much had been accomplished in the years that followed the depression of the 1870's. In the field of transportation enormous strides had been taken, and great advances had been made in industry. The Hartford Fire Insurance Company, however, had made less progress than its officers and stockholders might have wished.

In the 1870's, despite six years of economic depression, the Company's premium income had shown an increase of some 65 per cent over that of the previous decade, but in the 1880's the percentage of growth was somewhat less than half as great.

Judging from comments made by Company officials of that day, the last two decades of the nineteenth century formed a somewhat colorless period in the Company's history. Even during the 1890's little that was dramatic seems to have occurred.

"Between the first of January, 1890, and December 31, 1899," wrote Richard Bissell, President of the Company from 1914 to 1941, "there is nothing very spectacular to record in the history of our company."

But though that may have been true of the Company, there was little that would justify any such remark about the decade itself. Later generations, with less justification than they seem to have imagined, have long referred to this decade as "the gay 'nineties." There was little gayety, of course, during the depression of 1893. The silver-mining states were all but ruined. The farmers of the Middle West, discontented even before the panic, were frightened and embittered when they found themselves beset by the depression. Many farmers, and even townsmen, of the Middle West burned corn for which there was no market instead of coal they could not afford to buy. Thousands of commercial bankruptcies increased the number of the unemployed, and bitterness grew when fiscal manipulations made it possible for strong financial combinations to increase their power at the cost of smaller companies and individual owners who were unable to defend themselves.

The election of William McKinley to the Presidency in 1896 was followed within the next two years by the welcome return of prosperity. Farm conditions and farm production improved. Business conditions grew better and employment increased. The Spanish-American War, having broken out in April 1898, was brought to an end by the signing of an armistice four months later; and when the Treaty of Paris was signed on December 10th, both Europeans and Americans began to realize that the United States had not only added to its prestige and its territory, but had also acquired a place of greatly increased importance among the nations of the world.

Though President Bissell was later to write that the Hartford Fire Insurance Company had done "nothing very spectacular" during the nineties, any examination of the record will show that it had improved immensely on the previous decade. Furthermore, as the new century began, the Company found itself in a position to make more progress than it had ever made before.

The Hartford had worked hard to increase its premium income. It had succeeded, too, and had reason to be proud of what had been accomplished, the greatest part of the increase having come from two unusually important transactions.

In 1890 the Company's net premiums had passed the three-million-dollar mark, and each of the next three years had shown reasonably comfortable gains. In 1894, however, a much larger gain materialized despite the adverse effects accompanying the depression. This was due to two new insurance connections that the Company had made—one with the New York Underwriters Agency and the other with the Citizens Insurance Company of New York.*

In 1863, when the New York Underwriters Agency had been organized, owners of valuable property often found it difficult to protect themselves adequately against fire. This was owing to the fact that the insurance companies of that day invariably limited the size of the risks they were willing to accept. It was possible for the owner whose property warranted it to protect himself by taking out several policies in several different companies so that the total they represented would approximate the value of the property he wanted to insure, but many businessmen found this difficult, and they knew that many fire insurance companies were unreliable. On this account, an opportunity awaited any soundly financed organization that could somehow provide coverage in several strong companies at once but in a single policy.

This was one of the services that the New York Underwriters Agency was established to perform, and for thirty years it had operated successfully, building up in that time a worth-while business that was largely concentrated in the Middle West. At one time five separate fire insurance companies underwrote the Agency's policies, but in 1893 there were only two—the Hanover Fire Insurance Company and the Citizens Insurance Company of New York. Furthermore, their contracts with the Agency were due to expire on December 31, 1893. Normally, no doubt, they would have been renewed, but the Hanover Fire Insurance Company had decided to enter the territory in which the Agency was operat-

* This company should not be confused with the Citizens Insurance Company of Missouri or the Citizens Insurance Company of New Jersey.

ing and wished to terminate its arrangement with the Agency. In addition to this, the Hartford Fire Insurance Company agreed to reinsure that portion of the business of the Citizens Insurance Company of New York that had come from the New York Underwriters Agency and was still outstanding, and a contract was prepared under the terms of which the Hartford alone was to guarantee the policies thereafter written by the Agency.

It was this transaction that accounted for the Company's large increase in premiums in 1894. Without this new arrangement, premiums for that year would have totaled $4,070,901.91, but with it the total increased to $5,690,233.68.

This new arrangement, coming as it did so early in the depression, was especially fortunate. During the next four years the nation's economic recovery was slow, and the Hartford's premium income increased only at a very moderate pace. In 1898, for example, it was only $35,000 more than it had been in 1894. Late in 1898, however, the Hartford acquired the Citizens Insurance Company of Missouri and reinsured its outstanding business as of January 1, 1899. This move added about $500,000 to the Company's premium income for that year, bringing it to $6,224,178 and increasing the total for the decade to $52,864,743.48. This was a figure which, despite a depression far worse than any the country had previously seen, was 118 per cent greater than the corresponding figure ten years earlier.

This, it must be admitted, tells only a part of the story. Expenses had been met and losses had been paid, but because of the two new ventures the expense ratio had reached what was then an unprecedented 34.87 per cent, and the loss ratio for the decade was 57.02 per cent. Because of this, the Company's underwriting profit was less than one or two earlier decades had shown. Still, interest rates had been high, investments had been profitable, and the Company's total income over outgo, including dividends, surpassed four million dollars. Few other companies had done anywhere near as well, so it may be fair to say, President Bissell to the contrary notwithstanding, that during that difficult decade the Company had accomplished something spectacular after all.

The final years of the nineteenth century had witnessed a number of developments that were important in the progress of the Hartford Fire Insurance Company, and these same years also witnessed the gradual return of the National Board of Fire Underwriters to a position of influence.

In 1895 the Hartford lost an executive of unusual ability when George F. Bissell, the General Agent of the Company's Western Department, died after forty years with the Company. And his successor, Porter P. Heywood, who had been transferred to the Western Department from San Francisco twenty-three years earlier, unfortunately survived in his new position less than one full year.

In filling the position that had been held for so many years by George Bissell, and for so short a time by Porter Heywood, the Company chose two men. The first of these—John W. G. Cofran—had been transferred to Chicago from San Francisco the year before, and had been appointed Assistant General Agent of the Western Department. The second was Richard M. Bissell, son of the former Agent and Second Assistant General Agent of the Department. These two now formed the firm of Cofran & Bissell, and in that capacity they each became an Associate General Agent of the Western Department.

While these changes were being made in Chicago, comparable changes had been necessitated elsewhere. In San Francisco the firm of Belden & Cofran had managed the Hartford's Pacific Department since 1885, but when Mr. Cofran was transferred to Chicago, the firm was dissolved and the other partner, H. K. Belden, was appointed Manager, with Whitney Palache as Assistant Manager.

At the Home Office in Hartford, too, important changes had been necessitated by the greatly increased scale on which the Company was now operating. Until George L. Chase became President in 1867, the number of employees in the Home Office had always been remarkably small. Even when President Chase first took over his new position the office force consisted only of the Company's secretary, an assistant secretary, an examiner, a bookkeeper-clerk, and an office boy.

As we have seen, it was during President Chase's first years in Hartford that the Home Office really began to grow. Within three years the Directors had begun to realize that new and larger offices were needed, and in 1871 "one of the largest and most beautiful buildings in Hartford" had been erected for the Company's occupancy. But the Company's growth had continued. By 1897 this building had been outgrown and additions were made to the structure which almost doubled its size. Oddly enough, however, the Company seems to have confined itself only to the ground floor and basement. Writing in 1897, P. Henry Woodward[*] pointed out that after the change was made, the first floor was "thrown into a single room, sixty-four by seventy feet. Here the main clerical work of the company is performed under the eyes of the officers. . . . In the rear of the office, besides a large room for private consultations, is an additional fire-proof vault." And this somewhat detailed description then concludes by pointing out that "the upper floors are rented for offices and bachelor apartments."

Though mathematical minds insisted that the new year of 1900 was actually the one-hundredth year of the nineteenth century and not the first year of the twentieth, few others would have it so. To almost everyone, the stroke of midnight, 1899, had ushered in not merely a New Year but also a New Century. And the fact was—though few Americans, as yet, were ready to accept it—that a New Era in the development of our country had arrived as well.

Looking back now, after the passage of so many additional years, it is hard to realize how comparatively youthful the nation was in 1900. Unnumbered men and women who had crossed the prairies and the mountains in covered wagons were still active in the affairs of the West. Hundreds of thousands of sturdy men who had fought for one side or the other in the Civil War were to be found throughout the nation. Here and there in Massachusetts and Virginia a few elderly men and women were still to be found who, as children, had personally known John Adams or Thomas Jefferson. And in Connecticut the story of the founding of the Hartford Fire Insurance Company could still be told by men and women who had heard it at first hand from one or another of those who had played an active part in that beginning.

Despite these close connections with the past, the people of America had their minds on other matters. Surprising developments had recently broadened the horizons of the nation, and new ideas, many of which were little understood as yet, were changing the outlook of the people.

For the better part of three hundred years the frontier had greatly influenced the development of the nation, the evolution of its institutions, and the outlook of its people. But, with surprising suddenness, the frontier had disappeared, and a nation that had been little inclined to look for opportunities outside its own extensive territory had suddenly,

[*] *Insurance in Connecticut*, p. 20.

as one result of an unexpected and easily won war, been compelled to look upon itself as a world power with colonial possessions half a world away.

The national population now stood at 76,000,000, a figure surpassed in all the world only by Russia, India, and China; and almost as many Americans were urban as had made up the entire population of the nation forty years before. Nevertheless, the fortunes of the Hartford Fire Insurance Company were none too good, and the same was true for several years thereafter. But this was in no sense individual. Many other companies also found the going difficult, for fires of unusual proportions followed one another so frequently that fire insurance leaders everywhere were seriously discouraged.

The Hartford's premium income for the single year of 1900 was $6,684,747—a figure that would have been very impressive indeed at any earlier time in the Company's history. In fact, the figure for this single year approximated that for the twenty years prior to 1860. But, along with this remarkably creditable income, went losses greater than the Company had ever known before—losses that reached the record-breaking total of $4,371,522.

The largest single loss in 1900—$177,785—had resulted from a fire in the Canadian city of Ottawa, Ontario. This alone would have troubled the Company comparatively little. The difficulty arose because other lesser losses, scattered here and there all about the country, had been so numerous as to raise the total to a figure 40 per cent greater even than the Company's total losses for the entire year of the Chicago fire.

With this unfortunate beginning, the Hartford's officers and Directors must have been encouraged when the premium income for 1901 showed a marked increase. The total for the year, when at last that could be determined, was $9,653,783, a figure almost 45 per cent greater than that of the year before. By any ordinary measurement, this was excellent, but once more the Company's losses were enormous. In Jacksonville, Florida, an extensive fire necessitated the payment of $215,900, and scores of other losses increased the total to a figure 32 per cent higher even than the staggering losses of the previous year.

Time and again, as one looks into the story of fire insurance in America, it is apparent that bad years—and good ones, too—often come together. The great fires in Chicago and Boston, for example, had come in 1871 and 1872, and now two disastrous years had once more come together. But this was not the end. In 1902, when the premium income declined a trifle from the record-breaking figure of the year before, losses again surpassed five million dollars, bringing the total for these three discouraging years to more than fifteen million, a sum that later proved to be about one eighth of the Company's total losses for the first century of its existence.

Even viewed alone, this record of a single company's losses would have been impressive, but the Hartford was not the only company that was suffering. The entire industry had been somewhat similarly affected, and the National Board of Fire Underwriters, revivified and once more influential, called together a large committee of the fire insurance executives in the hope of finding an answer to what had become a vital insurance problem.

Though some opposition materialized, this committee ultimately recommended a twenty-five per cent advance in rates—an increase that sounded greater than it was. For eight years rates had been declining, and the change that was now adopted was modified in certain cases. In fact, where the improvement of risks warranted it, rates were actually reduced, and after the change had been made the average rate proved to be only about four cents on the hundred dollars higher than the rates of 1894.

In 1903—partly because of this change but perhaps more importantly because fires were fewer and no great conflagration materialized—conditions throughout the fire insurance industry improved. The Hartford's premium income showed another welcome increase, actually passing the ten-million-dollar mark, and, with losses substantially less than in any of the three preceding years, the Company's assets, as the year ended, comfortably surpassed fourteen million dollars—a gain of more than a million over the year before.

As 1904 opened, the Company's prospects seemed definitely brighter, but on February 7th a tragic fire broke out in the business section of Baltimore. Up to this time the city had retained much of its earlier appearance. Many of its busiest streets were narrow and winding. Its system of water supply was entirely inadequate and, except for one or two new skyscrapers and a few other buildings of unusual solidity, the threatened area contained nothing that was fire-proof and little that was fire-resisting.

As had been the case in Chicago thirty-three years earlier, a high wind was blowing across the city, and the flames, spreading rapidly from building to building and readily leaping the narrow streets, was almost instantly out of hand. Heat grew so intense that furious updrafts filled the air with flaming embers that fell upon great stretches of unprotected roofs. Now and again some flaming tin-roofed structure, with every floor burned through, became so vast a furnace that the heat, pushing up against the burning rafters of the roof, lifted great sections of red-hot tin into the air and sent them twisting and turning in the gale onto adjacent buildings or down into the narrow streets, there to imperil the city's exhausted firemen.

Ultimately, when fire-fighting equipment had been rushed from Washington and elsewhere, the fire was mastered and extinguished. Here and there an occasional structure had survived but, taken as a whole, the business section of the city had been destroyed. The total loss was estimated at some fifty million dollars, about thirty million of which was covered by insurance.

The Hartford's losses in Baltimore amounted to $1,213,843—a sum two thirds as great as the Company's losses in the Chicago fire of 1871, and, with that exception, the largest the Company had ever suffered up to that time in a single conflagration. But 1904 had only begun, and before it ended, fires in many parts of the country had been so numerous and disastrous that the Company's total losses had mounted to an unprecedented seven and a quarter million dollars, a sum 30 per cent greater than the Company had ever lost in a single year before. Still, when the New Year came, assets showed an increase of more than a million dollars over the previous year and the Company's surplus to policyholders of more than five and a quarter million dollars was higher, by a comfortable margin, than it had ever been before—truly a remarkable record in view of the fact that losses totaling some twenty-five million dollars had been paid in the five years just concluded.

Though the Hartford Fire Insurance Company had increased in importance from decade to decade ever since its founding, and though it had been among the leading companies of the country at least from the time of the New York fire of 1835, it was only as the twentieth century dawned that it began to assume in the minds of the people of the country the really great position it has occupied ever since. One reason for this was that the agents of the Company had increased so greatly in number that they were to be found in almost every community in the

United States and Canada. The Hartford stag had come to be one of the best known trademarks of the day.

Local insurance agents, as most people realize, are independent businessmen remunerated on a commission basis like salesmen. But unlike salesmen, they perform services that do not end when a sale is made. Licensed by the states in which they operate, and regulated by state laws as well as by the terms of their agency contracts, they serve their clients so intimately and so well—in times of tragedy and stress especially—that they are an influential part of the company whose policies they sell.

From its earliest beginnings the Hartford had understood its need for agents. Originally, it is true, any agent at a distance had had little intimate contact with the Company. He might have reported only once a month, or even only once in six months, and the Home Office had then been entirely without the statistics and the wonderfully detailed maps that now make it possible, along with the remarkable system of daily reports, to keep so close and accurate a check on all the business that is done. But as business developed in areas remote from Hartford, the need for more intimate contacts between the agents and the Company brought about the establishment, first, of the Western Department and, second, the Pacific Department.

As the twentieth century opened, both of these Departments, each of which was responsible for an enormous geographical area, had come to be highly important in the Hartford's scheme of things, and because of them the Company was well known and strongly represented not merely in Chicago and San Francisco, where the Departments had their headquarters, but actually in every community of any consequence from the Ohio River to California, Oregon, Washington, and British Columbia.

San Francisco's reputation prior to 1857 had been none too savory. From the time of the gold rush in 1849 the town had been a tough and, often, a lawless place. Gambling was not merely present. It went on almost everywhere. The cost of everything was exorbitant and, with an inefficient and indifferent city government, the city was overrun with crime. George Bancroft, in his *History of California*, makes the statement that in 1855 there were 585 deaths by violence in San Francisco alone, and that up to 1854 there had been 4,200 homicides and 1,200 suicides.

As early as 1851 crime and sudden death were almost omnipresent. To cope with the situation the Vigilance Committee was formed. Fortunately, it was effective and, after the worst of the lawless element had been hanged or driven out of town, conditions improved. The moment the Vigilance Committee suspended its activities, however, the old conditions returned and in 1856 the vigilantes had to clean the place up once more.

The fact is that by 1857 San Francisco had begun to be an orderly city and by 1869, when the Hartford returned to California after having withdrawn from the state three years before, its new agents—the firm of Flint & Heywood—were able to make excellent progress from the very first. It was because of this that Augustus P. Flint and Porter Heywood, by way of the company they had organized, were chosen to act as General Agents when the Hartford's Pacific Department was established in 1870.

It was in 1872, as has already been explained, that Porter Heywood was transferred to Chicago as Assistant General Agent of the Western Department. Augustus Flint, remaining in San Francisco, continued as General Agent of the Pacific Department until his death in 1885. It was then that Henry K. Belden joined John W. G. Cofran in forming the firm of Belden & Cofran, and these two, having become the new General Agents of the Pacific Department, were largely responsible for the great expansion of the Department that soon began. In 1895 John Cofran was transferred to the Western Department as Assistant General Agent, leaving Henry Belden as manager of the Pacific Department with Whitney Palache as his assistant. Seven years later, these two, having formed the firm of Belden & Palache, were appointed Associate General Agents. A year later, however, Mr. Belden died, and when Dixwell Hewitt joined Mr. Palache as an Associate General Agent of the Pacific Department, the firm of Belden & Palache made way for the newly organized firm of Palache & Hewitt.

Throughout this period of development and change, the business of the Pacific Department had steadily increased. Agencies had been established in Montana as early as 1870, in Nevada in 1874, in Utah in 1877, in Idaho in 1879. New Mexico had followed in 1880; Oregon and Washington in 1881; and Arizona in 1882. The population of the West had multiplied, and San Francisco had grown in half a century from a community containing the Presidio, a Spanish mission, and a nondescript huddle of hurriedly built structures, into a handsome and impressive city that was surpassed in size by only eleven others in the country. In 1906 it was a community of 343,000, and was already well on the way toward what it has since become—one of the most beautiful and distinctive cities in the world.

This was the community in which the headquarters of the Pacific Department of the Hartford Fire Insurance Company had been established in 1870, and though the Department's agencies were to be found throughout almost the whole of the Rocky Mountain and the Pacific Coast areas, San Francisco itself had always provided an especially consequential part of the Department's business. The maps that were on file in the Department's office at 313 California Street—large-scale maps that showed every portion of the city as well as every structure in it—were an important part of the Department's equipment, and on these maps, carefully penciled wherever a structure with a Hartford policy was shown as standing, was a notation giving enough information to enable anyone to tell almost at a glance not only where the structure stood, but also its type and size, its construction, and the face value of the policy that had been issued.

When the Pacific Department first established itself in the three-story building it occupied on California Street there was far more space than was needed. But the Department's business, increasing from year to year, ultimately necessitated the use of most of the structure, and in 1906 only the third floor and a small part of the second were available for tenants.

Even as late as 1903 the annual premium income of the Pacific Department was somewhat less than half a million dollars—a little less than five per cent of the Company's total for the year. But under the energetic management of Whitney Palache and Dixwell Hewitt business was growing and the Department's prospects were bright. In 1879 a unique form of fire insurance had been "invented" in California—insurance against fire for growing crops of grain. The Hartford's Pacific Department was not only writing more and more such policies but was also finding the business profitable. The increasing acreage of crops in the great valleys of California, and the large areas given over to the production of wheat in Oregon and Washington had opened a new and reasonably productive field for such fire insurance companies as were represented in the Far West. Many of these crops grew more and more inflammable as harvest time approached, and farmers, conscious of the danger, were receptive to the idea of protecting themselves by way of these new policies.

In San Francisco the Department's business, like business of many other kinds, was growing faster than the city, and the atmosphere of the whole community was permeated with confidence. The people of the city had long been conscious of the fact that the peninsula on which they lived, as well as other areas of California, was subject to earth tremors. In 1868, and again in 1898 and 1900, minor earthquakes had shaken the area, and it was widely known that the San Andreas fault—a fracture in the earth's crust which runs for several hundred miles from southeast to northwest near the coast of California—passes through a region that had long been understood to be more than usually unstable. But the idea of earthquakes troubled the people of San Francisco not at all. Even on April 17, 1906, when the late afternoon papers carried a news item about a disastrous earthquake that had badly damaged the city of Valparaiso, Chile, the average San Franciscan gave the story little attention and went to bed that evening without thinking seriously about the matter.

Oddly enough, on April 16th, the day before the Valparaiso quake, L. R. Ingham, a San Francisco police officer, had called at the California Street office of the Hartford's Pacific Department and, admitting that a premonition warned him that a terrible disaster was about to occur, asked for a $2,000 fire insurance policy on his house. Laughed at and asked why he did not take out a larger policy, he said he didn't think the Company would give him a larger one, and it is true that no one urged him to increase the amount. Still, the policy for which he had asked was made out, the modest premium was paid, and those in the Hartford office who had been momentarily amused, promptly forgot the matter—for a time.

So far as the record shows, no one else in San Francisco seems to have been bothered by any premonitory warnings. As evening fell on April 17th everything about the city appeared entirely normal. Even when early dawn arrived on the 18th no change whatever had materialized, and the clock in the tower of the Ferry Building at the foot of Market Street marked five o'clock as faithfully and unobtrusively as it had done for years. But somewhere along the length of the great San Andreas fault certain geological strains and stresses, of which no one, as yet, was conscious, were building up to a vast and uncontrollable seismic readjustment. It is possible that somewhere, deep within the earth, some preliminary warning of what was about to happen was given off, but if so it failed to impress itself on anyone in San Francisco. For the most part, the city was still asleep, but at about 5:12 A.M.—the time differed by several minutes in various parts of the affected area—the geological strains that had been building up throughout an indefinite period overcame the forces that until that moment had been successful in maintaining the *status quo*.

Even a later era that has learned a little of the almost unbelievable power of the hydrogen bomb is unable to estimate the forces that now were suddenly released all the way from San Benito County some eighty miles southeast of San Francisco to Humboldt County almost two hundred miles to the north and west. The "fault break" that had taken place was the longest ever recorded, and the earthquake shock that accompanied it was felt all the way from Los Angeles in the south to Coos Bay on the coast of Oregon, a distance of more than seven hundred miles. Even to the east the quake was felt for a distance of three hundred miles or more.

The main shock lasted no more than forty seconds, yet in that time enormous damage was done not only in communities near which the fault passed but also in others that lay miles away. San Francisco was instantly shaken into wakefulness. Immeasurable forces, suddenly released, were torturing the peninsula on the end of which the city stands. The earth heaved. Buildings swayed. Irregular fissures opened in the streets, and elsewhere the broken pavements were lifted into mounds. Masonry crashed down from cornices and walls. Here and there a structure collapsed completely and, as other shocks followed, tens of thousands of frightened and just awakened people scurried into the streets. Like a giant ants' nest abruptly broken open, the damaged city suddenly swarmed with life.

CHAPTER 15

DISASTER

IN SAN FRANCISCO

THE PENINSULA San Francisco occupies had hardly ceased its ter-
rifying trembling when fires broke out in many scattered places.
Chimneys had fallen. Stoves and furnaces had been overturned. Electric
wires were down. Gas pipes had been broken.

Making their way through rubble-strewn streets, heedless of earthquake damage they were helpless to correct, the city's firemen were
confident of their ability to control the incipient fires to which, after some
delay, they had been called. Hurrying to the nearest fire hydrants they
quickly coupled their hoses and opened the valves.

To their shocked astonishment there was no water pressure. Many
hydrants failed to flow at all and, as fire company after company reported this tragic news to their troubled chiefs, it began to be apparent
that the earthquake shock, in addition to damaging the structures of the
city, had dealt the fire department a deadly blow.

The water mains had broken.

Before dawn that morning and well before the earthquake, there
had been a three-alarm fire at the corner of Bay and Mason Streets. Most
of the firemen in the business section of the city had answered the call
and, worn out by that struggle with the flames, had just turned in when
the city was first shaken by the quake.

Startled into wakefulness, they were momentarily relieved when no
fire alarms came through. Only later did they learn that the entire fire
alarm system had broken down. Of 600 glass wet batteries on which the

system operated, 556 had been broken by the earthquake shock and, because of that, no alarm was sounded. No single fire house was alerted to the danger until frightened and breathless messengers brought word of the city's scattered fires.

Within three hours or a little more, 52 fires had started, but long before that the fire department had learned that almost no water would be available. The city's most important reservoirs were twenty miles away, and the principal conduit leading to the city, closely following the earthquake's "fault line" for six miles of that distance, had been twisted and broken in many places. There were lesser pipe lines but all of these led across filled, unstable ground and all were broken.

Here and there a few cisterns provided a little water, but they soon ran dry. Now and again the crew of a fire engine was able to pump water for a time from some sewer. Along the water front two fireboats were hard at work, and in one case, out in "the Western Addition," three fire engines, working in tandem, pumped water 3,000 feet from the Bay.

At the very outbreak of the enormous tragedy, D. J. Sullivan, the Chief of the city's fire department, had been fatally injured in a firehouse by a falling wall, but all through the disaster the department kept going. Men dropped exhausted beside their equipment. During the first twenty-four hours no one was relieved, and many fell asleep on the pavement, returning to their work when they wakened.

General Frederick Funston, who had long since won the Congressional Medal of Honor and had also captured Aguinaldo, the Philippine revolutionary leader, was in command at the Presidio. Awakened by the earthquake, he watched as smoke began to rise over the distant business section of the city.

With both telephone and telegraph wires down, he was unable to get any specific news, but the increasing columns of smoke told him that something serious had occurred, and on his own responsibility, with no word whatever from Washington—or even from San Francisco—he ordered out his men. Marching them into the burning city he established martial law.

"Survivors have often told me of Funston's dramatic entry," wrote Wallace Irwin some thirty years later after reading the proofs of Mark Sullivan's *Our Times*. "The disaster; the fires rising; a series of lighter shocks; the police inadequate in numbers; the Fire Chief dead in his own fire house; the people just standing around in groups as though paralyzed. Then, at about 8 o'clock in the morning, comes a regiment of

U.S. infantry four abreast, picking its way through the debris of Market Street—and everyone woke to life."

It was largely because of General Funston that the burning city was policed. Furthermore, it was under his direction that the soldiers, coming to the aid of the firemen, brought explosives into use, blasting broad fire guards in order to contain the furiously spreading fire.

For three disastrous days and two nights the fire continued. In that time hundreds of lives were lost. An area consisting of 497 city blocks was completely devastated. According to official records, 28,188 buildings were destroyed. In the whole of the business section no single structure remained undamaged. The Ferry Terminal had escaped serious harm, but the hands of its great clock still marked the hour at which the quake had struck, and all the way up Market Street such buildings as still stood were little more than gaunt and blackened skeletons.

The City Hall was in ruins and two policemen lay dead beneath one of its fallen walls. The burned-out tower of the Call Building still stood high above the ruins that surrounded it. In every direction almost everything was gone—east to the waters of the bay—south across the wholesale district—north and beyond to Nob Hill where the proudest mansions of the city had stood a little while before—northeast through Chinatown, and west to where General Funston's explosives and the 120-foot width of Van Ness Avenue had finally made a path the flames were unable to leap. Fragments of ruins stood. A few blocks near the water front had escaped the fire, but elsewhere only two little islands of safety still existed in more than four square miles of ruin.

Hundreds of thousands of people were homeless. Within eight days 216,000—more than half of the city's population—left the ruined city by ferry and by railroad, and thousands more were camping in Golden Gate Park, at the Presidio, and elsewhere.

Stunned by the tragedy, the people at first had seemed half paralyzed, but with remarkable rapidity they regained their confidence. Even before the fire was finally extinguished, plans were under way for the reconstruction of the city.

The Hartford office, at the time of the earthquake, had been occupied by the Pacific Department since early in the 1870's. It was on the south side of California Street, three blocks from where that thoroughfare meets Market not far from the Ferry Terminal. In the other direction, two blocks away, California Street began its steep climb up Nob Hill, the top of which supported the handsome marble mass of the

Fairmont Hotel and an impressive group of the city's greatest mansions.

Because of the early hour at which the city had been awakened by the earthquake, the business section was largely deserted. None of the offices was open as yet, and few passengers were on the cable cars that were abruptly halted when both rails and cables were twisted out of alignment.

The staff that manned the office of the Hartford's Pacific Department was small and, scattered all about in their widely separated homes, its various members were naturally confronted by different conditions. Most of them made no attempt to reach the office at all that day. Concerned for the safety of family and friends, they gave the office little thought. But Adam Gilliland, the Department's City Agent and General Adjuster, shaken awake as the whole city was, found his home at 2019 Broderick Street, and even the neighborhood in which he lived, almost entirely unhurt. Here and there a window had been broken or a picture, insecurely hung, had dropped to the floor. Off in the distance, however, columns of smoke began to climb into the sky and it was soon apparent that fires were raging in the city's business section. And fires, as Adam Gilliland intimately understood, meant work at the office. In this case, in fact, it most especially meant work for him. Though his title was "City Agent," he might better have been called the manager of the metropolitan department. His responsibilities, though not confined to the city, were largely connected with it. It had long been an important part of his work, for example, to see that Hartford policies in the city of San Francisco were kept within the "block limits" of liability that careful studies had established—limits that kept the Company from covering any area too solidly with its policies.

Several very hilly miles lay between Adam Gilliland's Broderick Street home and the California Street office of the Pacific Department not far from which those distant columns of smoke were rising. But the city's transportation system was entirely paralyzed. The California Street cable car, which passed directly in front of the Pacific Department's office, led up across Nob Hill and on to the west for another two miles or so, but its cable had stopped running and its cars, motionless from the moment of the first great temblor, stood helpless and deserted along three and a half miles of track.

No one seems to know how Adam Gilliland reached the office that morning, but he probably walked. It may be, too, that he followed California Street across Nob Hill, and if so he must have seen that the greatest columns of smoke were rising from areas south of Market Street. That meant that the Hartford office was not being threatened as yet, but when he finally reached it he saw that the fire was coming closer.

He unlocked the door and hurried in, uncertain what to do. He was the first to arrive, and, realizing how important the office records were, he did what he could to save them. He knew that the most important records were in the two big vaults. The one in the basement contained the all-important maps, while most of the other records were in the upper vault. Both were locked, of course, and had best stay locked, he thought. He had no idea what he could possibly do with such a mass of records even if he were able to get them into the street through which, by now, a growing stream of frightened people was already flowing.

Let the vaults alone, he thought. But how about the desks?

He opened drawer after drawer, and hauled their contents forth. He had no time to sort the stuff. He merely bundled it together, hauling it through the door and down the flight of ten iron steps to the narrow sidewalk.

He knew that the fire was spreading. The sky was heavy with smoke which no longer rose in separate columns. Instead, it drifted up to an enormous altitude from a burning area that extended far to the westward from near the water front.

He had no time to watch the fire. He had to protect the bundle of papers he had collected. More and more people were hurrying past—heading for the ferry apparently. He did not think to ask for help and no one offered it, but he knew that a vacant lot lay only a stone's throw away and he hurried toward it. He would dig a hole and bury the papers, whether or not the Hartford office burned, then they would be safe.

But when he reached the lot he found it difficult to dig any hole at all. He had no tools and, forced to scratch and kick the dirt away, it was only with the greatest difficulty that he was able to excavate a little pit that barely contained the papers he had brought. Still, he put the bundle in, protected it as best he could, and covered it with the dirt he had removed. It was not the best job in the world, but it would have to do, so he left it and hurried back.

The fire was closer now, and immensely greater, too. He could hear the roar of flames and the occasional rending crash of falling floors. Now and again a heavy wall came crashing down, and he began to realize that the fire, which had furiously attacked many of the city's greatest buildings on the south side of Market Street, had somehow crossed that unusually wide street and was rapidly spreading—across O'Farrell Street and Geary—across Post and Sutter.

Off in the smoke-covered distance, explosions told of the soldiers' efforts to halt the progress of the fire, but now that it had made its way across Market Street it seemed to gather speed. It swept north along both sides of Montgomery Street. It crossed Pine and reached California little more than a block from the Hartford office. Block after block burst suddenly into flames and nothing remained for Adam Gilliland to do but make his way as best he could back across the tortured city to the safety of his home on Broderick Street.

The building occupied by the Hartford was destroyed within four or five hours of the time the earthquake struck. Though the business section of the city had been little hurt by the quake itself, the broken water mains had made it impossible to fight the fire effectively, and the rapidity with which it spread was frightening.

By dusk on the third day the fire had been checked on the west at Van Ness Avenue, and on the north it had all but burned itself out not far beyond the crest of Telegraph Hill. Most of the water front was quite untouched, and the Ferry Terminal, the most important exit from the city, had been very little hurt.

The exhausted city, with unknown numbers dead and with tens of thousands of helpless people crowded together in tents and temporary shelters in parks and other open places, had very nearly reached the limit of its strength. But unexpectedly a rising wind fanned the flames into renewed activity and all night long the exhausted firemen, aided by General Funston's soldiers and by sailors from warships in the harbor, fought to save the water front. Blocks of buildings were dynamited. Fireboats fought to keep the flames from warehouses and piers. Finally, as the sun rose on the morning of the fourth day—Saturday, April 21st— the fire was under control. Great stores of grain were still burning on the water front half a mile north of the Ferry Terminal. Smoke still rose from beneath four square miles of ashes that once had been a city. But in a few more hours the fire was out.

Adam Gilliland had been forced to leave the Hartford office within an hour or so of the time he had arrived. Many years later in a modest and incomplete account he wrote for *The Hartford Agent*,[*] he explained that "the building occupied by the Hartford was destroyed about four or five hours after the fire was started." Even the papers he had buried

[*] October 1937, p. 67.

were destroyed, and days later, when an inspection of the ruins was possible, it was found that the Company's "upper vault" had gone as well, though "the basement vault was not in such a bad condition." Under the circumstances, in fact, the basement vault proved to be in remarkably good condition. When it was opened, after many days of waiting for it to cool, the Company's important San Francisco maps were found "badly scorched but not illegible."

Maps of this nature are always important, but in this case they were vital. All the other Company records had been destroyed. Nothing remained but such minor notes and memoranda as the various members of the staff may have had in their pockets when the office closed the day before the quake. The most important papers of all had been locked in "the upper vault" which had been utterly destroyed, and without the maps, on which notes of the Company's risks had been penciled, no record whatever would have remained of the Company's enormous liability.

Nothing but ruins remained where 28,188 buildings had formerly stood in the four and a half square miles east of Van Ness Avenue, and the Hartford's basement vault had no sooner been opened than the scorched but invaluable maps were hurried out to 2019 Broderick Street. Still intent on protecting them from any possibility of damage or destruction, a large packing case was lined with zinc and fitted with a cover. A hole was dug at the rear of Adam Gilliland's lot, as far away as possible from anything inflammable, and every night the maps were placed in the box and carefully covered with dirt.

Meanwhile, with no other place in which to work, the Hartford's Pacific Department established itself in Adam Gilliland's home. Shelves of unfinished lumber that had been installed in the basement were removed and transformed into an office counter. Tables served as desks and boxes as filing cabinets, and for two months the crowded home served as headquarters of the Pacific Department.

Almost entirely on the basis of those fortunately salvaged maps, the enormous task of adjusting claims went on. Some claimants, of course, were able to show the policies the Company had issued. Many others, however, had nothing on which to depend but their memory. Because of some official's wisdom, a thorough survey had been made by the Fire Patrol as soon as the fire had been extinguished, and the earthquake damage to foundations and walls was determined and recorded as accurately as possible under the circumstances. This information was given to all the fire insurance companies and, in the Hartford's temporary office, it was posted on the carefully guarded city maps. Consequently, whenever a claimant arrived, the adjuster to whom he was assigned could turn to the appropriate map, see at a glance what the earthquake damage had been, and arrive at a settlement accordingly.

While this was going on, astonishing progress was being made at clearing the wreckage and beginning the reconstruction of the city. Everywhere the work was being pressed, and about the middle of June, two months after the fire, when P. J. Hobbs, the Hartford's Chief Adjuster, arrived in San Francisco, the Pacific Department's office was transferred from Adam Gilliland's home to the fourth floor of the Merchants Exchange Building. Even here the Company's quarters were only temporary, for the interior of the building had been entirely destroyed. But by now it had been newly floored with lumber, and in the space the Hartford had been able to obtain, booths were set up for the Company's adjusters and for the lines of claimants. It was here, under the direction of Chief Adjuster Hobbs, that the greatest task of claim adjustment in the Company's history was carried to completion. Day after day claimants waited in lines. In all, 4,972 claims were presented. The adjusters, often with little to guide them but the statements of the claimants and such penciled notations as had been written on the maps, approved thousands of claims that added up to a rapidly growing total of millions of dollars.

Now and again even the invaluable maps proved useless. After all, the penciled notes that they contained had never been intended to be any actual part of the Company's authoritative records. They had been written on the maps merely as a matter of convenience. So it had sometimes happened that, in the rush of business, no such notes had been made. Thus even the maps were of little or no help on occasion, and troubled adjusters were hard put to find some basis on which they might arrive at justifiable conclusions.

One such problem arose in connection with a claim made by a large coffee company—Folger's Coffee. Like many other business structures in the city, this company's property had been completely destroyed by the fire, and its books and office records had disappeared with all the rest. As the story is usually told, the company's officers, bookkeepers, and clerks did their best to gather together such facts as they could remember.

Among these was a statement that a Hartford fire insurance policy had been taken out on some forgotten date long before—a policy for $100,000. There was no longer any record of the policy, and even those who recalled it were shy on details. They remembered the policy and the amount for which it had been written, but further than that none of them could go. The Hartford adjusters, however, were not especially troubled. Other claimants had found themselves in similar situations. But when the maps were studied in this instance no notation having to do with the Folger policy was to be found. The Folger plant was clearly represented on one of the maps, but no notation of any kind suggested that any policy whatever had ever been issued to cover it.

Here, obviously, was an impasse. No doubt existed that the Folger Company was an entirely reputable firm, and its claim was obviously being presented in all honesty. But $100,000 is a very large sum, and in the absence of any written record whatever, it was hard to see how the claim could be recognized or how any adjustment could possibly be made.

The adjusters were naturally concerned. Quite unprepared to say "No," they were equally unprepared to say "Yes"—for the moment, at least.

"Who sold that policy?" someone asked at last.

The Folger representative did not know, but offered to do what he could to find out. And finally someone in the company remembered—or thought he did.

"We think it was Mr. Gilliland," he reported.

"Adam Gilliland?" asked the adjuster. "He's our City Agent. I'll ask him to come in."

"Do you remember ever selling a policy to the Folger Company?" the adjuster asked when Mr. Gilliland arrived.

Mr. Gilliland nodded thoughtfully. "Yes," he declared. "I handled that. It was a policy for $100,000."

More followed, of course, though no record of any kind was found, and in the end—primarily on the basis of Adam Gilliland's memory—the hundred-thousand-dollar claim was paid.

The first great earthquake shock had instantly broken all telephone and telegraph contact between San Francisco and the outside world. Then, an hour or so later, a single Postal Telegraph wire opened to Chicago, and over it the first report of the catastrophe had gone. Thus the first account dealt only with the earthquake, except as scattered fires had been incidentally mentioned. And then the urgent news that was flowing through that single wire abruptly stopped and all news from San Francisco stopped as well. It was because of this that newspapers all across the country and the world were able to tell only of the earthquake. Though San

Francisco burned for three days, most of the country, lacking all information except what had been sent during that one hour, imagined that such damage as the city had suffered had been due entirely to the quake.

Days passed before much in the way of details reached Hartford from its San Francisco office. There had consequently been a long delay before any adequate idea could be formed of the extent of the fire loss. Finally, however, the truth came out, and the Company's officials, confronted by the greatest losses any fire insurance company had ever been called upon to face, prepared to accept their heavy responsibilities.

On January 1, 1906, the Company's capital had been $1,250,000 and its surplus as to policyholders had been $6,400,696. But now, confronted by the burdensome task of paying losses that seemed certain to surpass eleven million, both capital and surplus had to be increased.

Having reached their conclusion as to the amount that would have to be raised, the Directors decided that the matter should be taken up with the New York firm of J. P. Morgan & Company, and on April 27th, only six days after the fire had ended, the needs of the Hartford Fire Insurance Company were explained in detail to J. P. Morgan personally.

Whether or not any suggestion was made in addition to the one that was followed does not appear in the Company's records. But as a result of that meeting it was agreed that the Company would issue 7,500 additional shares of stock. This was to be underwritten by J. P. Morgan & Company, and though the par value of each share was to be $100, the Company's reputation was such that even under the difficult conditions that confronted it, the stock was to be sold at $500 a share, and rights for the purchase of this were to go to the shareholders of record.

Thirty-five years earlier, at the time of the Chicago fire, a new issue of the Hartford's stock had sold at a premium of $85. Now the premium was $400, yet every share was promptly sold, and of the $3,750,000 that was raised, $750,000 was used to increase the Company's capital to $2,000,000 and the remaining $3,000,000 was added to the Company's surplus.

It was in this way that the Hartford was able to meet its San Francisco losses, but there were other losses during that year and, in addition to issuing the stock, the Company found it necessary to borrow a million and a half dollars. Within a year, however, this loan was repaid, largely because the "insurance public," confident of the Hartford's future, gave enough new business to the Company to increase its premium income by 10 per cent cent over what it had been the year before.

Undoubtedly, much of this confidence was earned through the Company's performance at San Francisco. It had not taken long for the country to hear about President Chase's message to Hartford agents, written at the height of the catastrophe.

"The appalling calamity at San Francisco has brought about conditions which may for some time prevent any definite statement as to the losses incurred by the various companies involved. Whatever losses may have been incurred by 'The Hartford' will be honorably adjusted and promptly paid, and the record established at Chicago, Boston and Baltimore will remain unbroken."

More important, America now knew and was impressed by how quickly and well that promise had been kept.

As a result of the earthquake and the fire some five hundred people had lost their lives in San Francisco, and buildings valued at $105,000,000 had been destroyed. Additional losses, though never completely reported, are usually said to have brought the total to $350,000,000 or more, and the 243 insurance institutions that were affected paid about $225,000,000 in claims. Of these institutions, 214 were foreign and American stock companies; 7 were underwriters' agencies whose policies were guaranteed by companies operating in California; 5 were inter-insurance associatons; 7 were Lloyd's associations; and 10 were mutual companies.

The great Chicago fire of 1871—the most destructive America had ever seen prior to the San Francisco disaster—had resulted in a total loss estimated at $196,000,000, only about half of which had been insured. At that time, 202 insurance companies had been involved: 68 of them failed and 83 paid their claims only in part. But in the intervening thirty-five years, big changes had occurred.

The insurance industry was far more soundly operated in 1906 that it had been a generation earlier, and financially it was much stronger. Where losses in Chicago had been less than $200,000,000, only half of which had been insured, losses in San Francisco had been the better part of twice as great, and some two thirds of this enormous total had been covered by insurance. Yet 68 companies had failed as a result of the Chicago fire, and only about fifty million dollars was ever paid in the settlement of claims. But only 20 companies failed as a result of the San Francisco disaster, and claims amounting to $225,000,000 were actually paid*—a

* *The Encyclopaedia Britannica*, 1957 edition, Vol. 19, p. 944, states that "insurance companies and San Francisco financial houses estimate the insurance paid at $300,000,000." The figures used above, however, are based on a detailed and carefully prepared report published in 1907 by the Alfred M. Best Company of New York.

giant sum only about ten per cent less than the total that might have been paid had every insurance company been willing and able to live up to its contract. Unfortunately a few companies failed to do as much as they could have done. For the most part, however, the record was an excellent one—one that proved beyond any shadow of a doubt that the capital-stock fire insurance companies had come of age.

The Hartford Fire Insurance Company, when its final San Francisco claim had been adjusted, had paid a total of $11,557,365†—the largest sum paid by any insurance company in connection with the California disaster. This had not been done easily. For a time the officers and Directors in Hartford had been hard pressed to strengthen the Company's financial position to the point at which the demands upon it could be met. In all, the losses for that year were $13,515,021—almost twice as much as the Company had ever been called upon to pay in any previous year. Yet this demand was met, and when that year finally ended, the Company's surplus to policyholders stood at $4,819,909—only about a million and a half less than it had been the year before. Furthermore, the premium income during 1906 showed a comfortable increase over that for 1905, and as the year ended, the Company's assets, almost a million dollars greater than they had been the year before, stood at the highest point they had ever reached in the ninety-six years of the Company's history.

"The Hartford Fire," said the *San Francisco Chronicle* on September 25, 1906, "is one of the companies spoken of very highly in the matter of adjustments. It had such a strong force of capable men to handle claims that although its losses were larger than those of any other company, it disposed of its obligations!"

And the special publication on losses in San Francisco, prepared by the Alfred M. Best Company, a New York firm specializing in the publication of insurance news and reports, concluded its report of the part the Hartford had played in San Francisco with the unadorned statement that "Its treatment of claimants was in every respect satisfactory."

Perhaps no other statement could more accurately reflect what the Company has always tried to do.

---

† This figure includes the sum of $1,280,865 paid by the Citizens Insurance Company of Missouri, a wholly owned subsidiary.

CHAPTER 16

THE

BROADENING FIELD

OF INSURANCE

THE FORMATIVE years of the business of fire insurance in America continued until the twentieth century was well begun. A century earlier the industry had been in its infancy; and its adolescence, which may be said to have begun about the time of the great New York fire of 1835, continued through and even somewhat beyond the remainder of that century. It is on that account that occasional pronouncements made in all seriousness by experienced insurance men late in the nineteenth century and early in the twentieth cannot now be read without a smile.

In 1882, for example, a General Agent in Cincinnati, a respected man to whom many agents brought their problems, received an inquiring letter from an agent in Osage City, Kansas. This woman—a rarity among insurance agents of that day—wrote to ask about the possibility of writing insurance against wind storms—a not unnatural inquiry from a state much given to tornadoes. Her letter, unfortunately, is not available, but the reply is; and the fact that it was written on a typewriter when such machines had only recently been introduced, plainly suggests that the General Agent, despite the attitude he assumed in his reply, was not averse to new ideas merely because they were new. His letter says, in part:

> In reply to your esteemed favor of the 23d inst. we beg
> to say that Wind Storms being entirely foreign to the busi-

ness of *fire insurance* in which we are engaged, we have
nothing to do therewith. Neither do we suppose that any
other reputable fire Co. does, but only such Companies as
must resort to some ludicrous method or worse in order
to get any business. One would hardly expect to find horse
shoes for sale at a Millinery store, yet such a commodity
would have as fit a place in such stock as wind storms would
have in the business of fire insurance. Now do we not speak
the truth?

This reply surely left small doubt as to the General Agent's beliefs
in the matter, but he seems to have been more than a little troubled by
the lady's inquiry. At any rate, having dictated and signed this letter,
he felt impelled to add the following postscript in his own bold handwriting:

If against Wind, why also not against Rain, Hail, Crushing
by snow, accidents caused by faulty construction of buildings, etc. etc. etc. The proposition, Mrs. Dodds, is too absurd
for any strictly legitimate fire insurance company to consider
for a moment.

In the year since this letter was written insurance has developed to
the point at which policies are regularly written not only on all of the
"absurd" ideas mentioned in the General Agent's letter but also on many
more that no one of that day had yet been able to envision. Automobile
insurance, for example, was undreamed of in the 1880's. It was not until
the 1890's that the first real automobiles were built, and insurance on
these new machines was slow in developing. Even after the twentieth
century had opened most underwriters were inclined to look upon the
idea very doubtfully, as the following letter clearly demonstrates:

NEW YORK UNDERWRITERS AGENCY

New York, July 7, 1903.

Mr. A. F. Prince, Agent,
   Hinckly, Illinois.
Dear Sir: Policy No. 5029—H. D. Wagner
We notice that the above policy covers on an automobile,
and regarding same, we would say that if, as we infer, it is
a gasoline machine, 10c should be added to the annual
rate, which would make the five year figure $1.50 instead

of $1.20, as you have it, and in addition, the enclosed clause should be attached to the contract. Will you please take this action and let us have a copy of the clause for attachment to daily report?

Replying to your inquiry as to whether policy may be written to cover the machine in any place where it may happen to be, would say that this is a kind of insurance which we prefer not to write, and we doubt if any company will write what amounts to a policy giving privilege for touring. We do occasionally write a policy on an automobile with a limited touring privilege, confining the scope to the county in which the automobile owner has his residence, and for a policy of this kind we charge a rate of not less than 2% per annum.

Yours very truly,
A. & J. H. Stoddart,
General Agents.

Though the policies to which this letter refers were written on automobiles, they bore little resemblance to automobile insurance policies of a later day. In fact, they were nothing more than fire insurance policies, and the policyholders were protected against nothing else—were not even protected against fire if they went touring. But at the very time this letter was written changes were under way. Theft coverage was introduced in that very year, and in 1905 collision insurance was first written. Few people, however, carried it until after World War I had come and gone. But it was not only automobile insurance that was developing. The entire field of insurance was broadening.

George L. Chase, from the time of his elevation to the Presidency of the Hartford in 1867, had been an outstanding figure in the field of fire insurance. From the moment of his arrival at the Home Office in Hartford he seems to have been determined to increase the number and efficiency of the Company's agents, and to enlarge and improve the activities of the Home Office as well. No record remains to tell us just what his reactions actually were when he first reached Hartford, but he had no sooner arrived than the Company began to feel the impact of his energy and his ideas. By 1876 the energetic, full-bearded Hartford President, who, on account of his beard, looked much older than he was, had come to be recognized as one of the nation's leading insurance executives. Because of that, he was elected president of the National Board of Fire Underwriters, and in the city of Hartford he was chosen as trustee and vice-president of the Society for Savings, a trustee of the Connecticut Trust and Safe Deposit Company, a director of the American National Bank, and a member of the Hartford Board of Trade.

It was under his direction that telephones were first installed in the Company's offices. It was he who ordered the Company's first typewriters and employed its first stenographers. And it was in the latter part of his administration that the Hartford so successfully overcame the very great difficulties that resulted from the San Francisco earthquake and fire.

January 8, 1908, had been chosen as the day for the Company's regular annual meeting, and the President's eightieth birthday was to be celebrated five days later. Some seven months earlier the Company had celebrated the fortieth anniversary of his election to the Presidency, but now, on the day before the annual meeting and six days before his own birthday, he died.

"Mr. Chase was remarkably endowed," a resolution of the Company's Directors truthfully pointed out. "He possessed to a very unusual degree the ability to choose men. . . . He possessed great energy, indomitable tenacity of purpose and a sanguine temperament. His courage and hopefulness were contagious and enabled those associated with him to accomplish results beyond their expectations. . . . He was . . . devoted . . . to the progress and success of the Hartford Fire Insurance Company. He delighted in its growth. His work and pleasure were combined in its service. This enthusiastic interest in his work, together with the qualities herein enumerated, resulted in a most remarkable and exceptional career, and made him one of the most important factors in the history of fire underwriting in this country."

As a partial measurement of Mr. Chase's success as President of the Hartford, it is worth recording that the Company's premium income for 1907, the final year of his Presidency, was more than three million dollars greater than it had been for *the ten years* of the decade in which he had first been elected. Where, in 1867, the Company's capital had been $1,000,000, its premium income $1,559,000, and its net surplus $26,744, in the year of President Chase's death the Company's capital was $2,000,-000, its premium income more than $14,000,000, and its net policyholders' surplus in excess of $5,000,000.

Though the Hartford Fire Insurance Company had felt no need for a Vice-President for the first twenty-six years of its existence, and—as mentioned earlier—even after establishing the office had failed for many years to attach any salary to it, the Company's expansion during the long administration of President Chase led to the selection of two salaried Vice-Presidents in 1903, each of whom, in the years ahead, was to become President of the Hartford. One of these was Charles E. Chase, a son of President George L. Chase and himself an experienced insurance executive who had served as the Company's Assistant Secretary for six years prior to his selection as First Vice-President. The Second Vice-President, who was also chosen at this time, was Richard M. Bissell, a son of the former General Agent of the Western Department and, at the time he was promoted and called to Hartford, Associate General Agent of the department his father had formerly headed.

It was Charles E. Chase who succeeded his father as President in 1908, and a year later Richard M. Bissell, having been promoted to First Vice-President, was also made Underwriting Manager. At the same time, John W. G. Cofran, General Agent of the Western Department, was called to Hartford as Second Vice-President.

Two years after Charles E. Chase succeeded his father as President of the Hartford, the Company celebrated the one-hundredth anniversary of its founding. This in itself was an event of real importance. Any organization that has continued in successful operation for a century has reason to pride itself on its accomplishments and, up to the time the Hartford passed that mark, not many American companies had done so. It was natural for the Company to take advantage of this opportunity in order to tell the story of its founding and development. In the accounts that were prepared, however, little space was given to events that were current at the time, and no reference was made to two major developments of that day, one of which played an important part in improving business ethics generally, while the other increased the scope of insurance in general and the business of the fire insurance companies in particular.

Even a superficial examination of business and political ethics in the United States for a generation or so following the Civil War makes it clear that higher standards were badly needed. As always, most men were honest and most businesses were, as well. On the other hand, unscrupulous financiers, politicians, and businessmen were not only numerous but were often dramatically successful. Little by little ethical standards improved, but many questionable practices continued into the early years of the twentieth century.

During these very years, several life insurance companies had developed into institutions of great size, and had become custodians of life insurance funds that ran into billions of dollars. One company alone had some six hundred thousand policyholders, a billion dollars of whose funds had been entrusted to the company.

Funds so enormous not unnaturally attracted the interested attention of certain financiers who, in their efforts to influence the investment of these funds, laid the groundwork for what has ever since been referred to as "the life insurance scandals of 1905."

For some time the struggle for control of one of these great companies was a silent one, waged by various directors behind closed doors. Little by little, however, some of the details reached the ears of newspapermen, and finally, after a powerful series of editorials in the New York *World* demanded official action, Governor F. W. Higgins of New York State called the legislature into session and a committee was appointed for the purpose of investigating the life insurance companies then operating in the state.

Charles E. Hughes was chosen to conduct the investigation, and in fifty-seven public hearings which continued from September 6 to December 30, 1905, he called to the witness stand a large number of New York's outstanding financiers, insurance executives, businessmen, and politicians. Cool, incisive, and unhurried in his questioning, Hughes succeeded in obtaining the information he wanted even from the most reluctant witnesses. More than a few national reputations shrank perceptibly under his attack, and in the end, as a result of his report, the New York Legislature adopted legislation which resulted in the needed reformation of the insurance business.

Important though the direct results of this investigation were, the indirect results were more important still. The particular life insurance companies that had been so thoroughly investigated were quick to eliminate such questionable practices as they had followed and, under the new laws and regulations that grew out of the investigation, they have come to occupy far greater places in the economy of America than they ever occupied before.

The Hughes investigation touched only a handful of the life insurance

CHARLES E. CHASE
President, 1908-1913

companies of the country, and no fire insurance companies entered it at all. But no other investigation in the country's history had ever cast so lurid a light on the ethics of so important a segment of the nation's leading financiers and businessmen. A later generation, unacquainted with the details of the Hughes investigation, sometimes assumes that insurance companies of all kinds were involved. Actually, as we have said, very few of the life insurance companies themselves were affected.

Everywhere, however—often even in the minds of those whose methods were above suspicion—business and financial ethics were re-examined and refurbished. It was not that the entire country instantly turned over a new leaf. Dishonesty was not completely routed. Sharp practices still continued. "Malefactors of great wealth," as Theodore Roosevelt called them, still continued along their selfish and self-centered ways. But, despite all this, it is clear that the ethical standards of the American people had improved; and, as a result of the life insurance investigation, that improvement was impressively dramatized—to the great advantage of the nation.

The Hartford Fire Insurance Company, by steps that seemed, at the time, to be only barely perceptible, was beginning to broaden its field of operation. A generation earlier, fire insurance companies were fire insurance companies and nothing else. Little by little, however, the public had come to be conscious of the need for protection against other risks—against tornadoes in the prairie states; against hail that so often ruins crops and even damages structures and equipment; against collision, defalcation, robbery, and unpredictable developments of many other kinds.

It was in England that thoughtful underwriters first came to recognize the potentialities of this development. There, as in America, the fire insurance companies continued well into the twentieth century to concern themselves primarily with fire, but ultimately what came to be called "allied fire lines" began to be added and, once this new idea began to take hold, it expanded most rapidly in America.

Because the charters of fire insurance companies usually confined them somewhat narrowly to their specific field, it was not easy for them to enter this new domain. Nevertheless, in many instances and perhaps in most, the new kinds of risks that ultimately came to be covered were suggested as possibilities very early in their history. "Many more kinds of insurance than are even now found useful," said the *Encyclopaedia Britannica* in its 11th Edition, published in 1910, "were attempted more than a century ago. But no statistical basis then existed for determining the probability of loss from various casualties, nor had the methods of canvassing, accounting, proving and checking losses, reached the perfection now recognized as necessary for efficiency and safety."

In its first hundred years the Hartford Fire Insurance Company had grown from its very small beginnings into an efficiently operated company with total assets of some twenty-three million dollars. It goes without saying that assets on such a scale would have been all but unbelievable to the group of Connecticut businessmen who founded the Company in 1810. But in all probability they would have been no more astonished had they known what the Company's first century was to bring, than President Charles E. Chase and his associates would have been in 1910 had they been able to foresee that in the next fifty years the total assets of the Company were to increase from twenty-three million dollars to more than a billion!

Having been limited by the Company's charter to fire insurance alone, it is understandable that during most of its history prior to this time, those in charge of the Hartford had given little thought to other categories of insurance. On one occasion, it will be remembered, the Directors had applied for an amendment to the charter that would have permitted the Company to enter the field of marine insurance. But the stockholders objected, and for many years no other attempt was made to broaden the Company's field of operations. By 1910, however, many fire insurance executives were broadening their outlook, and the Hartford, whose business in Canada had long since shown that the Company had no need to confine itself to the United States, had for some time had in mind the idea of operating in other lands. The records do not show just when the idea first began to assume important proportions, but at a meeting of the Directors held on December 6, 1910, it definitely took shape, as the following quotation from the minutes of the meetings shows:

> . . . President Chase stated that it was the unanimous
> opinion of the officers and managers that there were possi-
> bilities for the extension of the Company's business to certain
> localities outside the United States. Vice President Bissell
> submitted a report showing the result of investigations in
> connection with the subject and after discussion and on

motion duly made and seconded the following resolutions were passed.

Resolved, that the officers of this Company are hereby authorized to extend the business of the Company to Cuba, Porto Rico, Mexico, Panama, the Philippine Islands, and the larger ports in other countries in the Far East, where in their opinion it will be to the interest of the Company to do so.

Resolved further, that the officers of this Company are authorized to investigate conditions under which the business of fire insurance is conducted in Brazil, Argentine Republic, Uruguay and Paraguay in South America, and to extend the business of the Company to those countries in the event that their investigations indicate it will be to the interest of the Company to do so.

Resolved, that the officers of the Company are hereby authorized to make such deposits of securities and to execute such documents as may be required by the laws of the various places mentioned in the foregoing resolutions.

The Hartford Fire Insurance Company had long since lost all trace of insularity. Within a year of its founding it had entered New York State, and by 1836 its agents were established not only in nineteen states and territories but also in Canada. In 1885 Hawaii had been added to the list, while those islands were still an independent kingdom. Now, in 1910, the Company was pushing not only into Spanish America but also all the way across the Pacific to lands in the Far East.

Other developments were also under way. At a Directors' meeting held on February 8, 1911, a pension system for "all permanent salaried employees and officers" was inaugurated, and on May 2, 1911, the Directors adopted a resolution that marks the beginning of a decisive development in the Company's history—a resolution that reads as follows:

Resolved: that this Company, having been admitted or having applied for admission to transact business in the State of Illinois, in conformity with the laws thereof, does hereby authorize the President and Secretary, under the corporate seal of the Company, to make application for a license to transact business in the State of Illinois, and to make the following declaration on behalf of this Company: that it desires to do the business of Casualty Insurance in

said State, that it will accept a license therefor according
to the laws of said State, and that said license shall cease
and terminate in case and whenever it shall remove or make
application to remove, into any United States Court, any
action or proceeding commenced in any of the State Courts
of the State of Illinois, upon any claims or cause of action
arising out of any business transaction in fact done in the
said State of Illinois, any permission, consent, agreement,
condition or provision incorporated in any contract, mortgage, note, bond, obligation or policy of insurance, authorizing or consenting to such removal to the contrary notwithstanding.

Voted that the President of this Company be and he is
hereby authorized to deposit with the Treasurer of the State
of Connecticut One Hundred and Six Thousand Dollars
($106,000) par value of its holdings of City of Hartford,
Connecticut, Connecticut River Bridge 3½% Bonds, due
June, 1955, said bonds to be registered in the name of the
Treasurer of the State of Connecticut as Trustee for all the
policy holders of the Hartford Insurance Co. of Hartford,
Conn. The deposit of the above bonds being required by the
law of Illinois to enable the Company to write automobile
insurance in that State.

Changes were well under way by the time this move was made, but
even earlier another type of insurance had begun to develop when various states began to pass so-called "Workmen's Compensation Acts." The
idea of compensating workmen for injuries arising out of their employment had originated in Europe long before, but New York State, in 1909,
had passed the first such act in the United States. It is true that this particular piece of legislation was declared unconstitutional, but other states
were more successful, and employers found it necessary to protect themselves against the possibility of such claims. In looking for such protection they naturally turned to the insurance companies, which promptly
developed the necessary policies. This kind of insurance was a success
from the beginning. Within five years of the passage of the original New
York act, workmen's compensation insurance policies in the United States
called for the payment of premiums fully a quarter as great as all the fire
insurance premiums in the country.

By 1909 the Hartford, in addition to writing fire insurance, was writing tornado insurance as well. New forms of insurance were coming into use. "Rent policies" insured against the loss of rental income, and also insured against the loss of the use of property owned and occupied by the assured. Use and Occupancy insurance, now known as Business Interruption Insurance, was being written. A Special Risk Department devoted itself to insuring property equipped with automatic sprinklers, electricity, and power. The Company's automobile insurance had developed to the point at which insured cars were covered while they were on the road as well as while they were in their own garages. They were insured against fire, explosion, lightning, theft, and even collision.

There were "tourists' floater policies" on baggage, as well as "horse and wagon floater policies" which covered "horses, vehicles, and merchandise against risks by fire as well as while in transit." And, among the rest, policies were being written on salesmen's samples, on merchandise in transit, and "on inland marine craft, from the small private launch to the largest steamboat."

But even this was little more than a beginning in the new and broader field the Company had entered. In January 1913, the General Assembly of Connecticut was asked to amend the Company's charter so as to authorize it to increase its capital stock from time to time to an amount not to exceed ten million dollars, and at the same time the Company applied for a new charter that would permit the organization of a separate company, as required by law, for the writing of accident, liability, indemnity, and such other classes of insurance as were permitted by the various states.

The charter of this new company had no sooner been approved by the legislature than steps were taken to complete its organization. Known as the Hartford Accident and Indemnity Company, it proposed to write all kinds of accident, automobile liability, personal damage, and other lines of insurance. As the Company's magazine, *The Hartford Agent,* said at the time, "When the present plans get well under way, an agency representing the 'Hartford' will be in a position to write almost any kind of insurance desired by its patrons."

It was on August 5, 1913, that the first stockholders' meeting of the new company was held, and it was voted that the capital stock—5,000 shares, par value $100—be taken up at once at the rate of $200 a share. Thus the Hartford Accident and Indemnity Company was able to begin with $500,000 in capital stock, and with a surplus of the same amount, and "the Two Hartfords," as the closely related companies were immediately called, began to move in parallel fashion toward new accomplishments in their greatly broadened field.

In the long life of the Hartford Fire Insurance Company no other year had been marked by so many important changes as that eventful year of 1913. New horizons of many kinds were opened to the Company, and the groundwork was laid for new opportunities that were to lead to great successes in the future. But on the very day that had been chosen for the first stockholders' meeting of the new Hartford Accident and Indemnity Company, President Charles E. Chase, after only five years in office, felt compelled, because of his health, to offer his resignation with the request that it be permitted to take effect the following month.

The resignation did not come as a surprise, and in accepting it the Directors elected Mr. Chase to the chairmanship of the Board. Furthermore, they chose Vice-President Richard M. Bissell to be the seventh President of the Hartford Fire Insurance Company, and they elected him President of the new company as well.

Vice-President Cofran, who had come to Hartford from Chicago in 1909, had died three years later and, now that Richard Bissell had been elevated to the Presidency, it was necessary to choose two new Vice-Presidents. The first to be selected was Whitney Palache, the senior member of the firm of Palache & Hewitt, General Agents in charge of the Hartford's Pacific Department. The second was James Wyper, formerly Agency Secretary of the London & Lancashire Insurance Company's Hartford office and, at the time he was invited to join the staff of the Hartford, Manager of the combined Pacific Coast offices of the London & Lancashire Insurance Company and the Orient Insurance Company.

Having operated for a century exclusively as a fire insurance company, the Hartford now found itself at work in an immensely broader field. Only a few years earlier, fire insurance executives had shown very little interest in expanding beyond the narrow bounds set by their charters, but with the coming of the twentieth century most of them had been impressed by new ideas. Apparently with little in the way of preparation, ideas that had never been put into practice before began to appear in many unexpected places. Despite the enormous losses that had resulted from the San Francisco fire, most fire insurance companies that had survived had made real progress, and the Hartford, having made a wonderfully prompt recovery, now turned its attention very largely to the development of insurance in the new fields it had entered.

The Home Office in Hartford had greatly expanded, and the same was true of the long-established offices of the Western and Pacific Departments in Chicago and San Francisco. In addition to these, however, the Company had established the Southern Department with headquarters in Atlanta, and the Texas Department with headquarters in Dallas. The Marine and Transportation Department, as well as the Special Risk and Inspection Department, had been established in Hartford, while an agency had been opened in New York City for the insuring of craft operating on inland waters.

Merely the names of these various departments will show that the Company was already looking far beyond the fire insurance field. But when the Hartford Accident and Indemnity Company was organized "the Two Hartfords" had so enormously broadened their field of action that even the most imaginative of the Company's early executives would have found it difficult to visualize the extent of the changes that had taken place.

With new opportunities on so great a scale appearing wherever the Company's officers and agents cared to look, it is not surprising that 1914 opened with much promise. Conditions throughout the United States were good, and optimism was in the air. But five days before America celebrated the Fourth of July, an Austrian archduke and his morganatic wife, on an official visit to the Bosnian city of Sarajevo, were assassinated by a Serbian terrorist, and within a month most of Europe was at war— a war that was to engulf most of the nations of the world—that was to change the future of all mankind.

CHAPTER 17

THE FIELD

GROWS BROADER

STILL

As they read their afternoon papers on June 28, 1914, few Americans were conscious of the international significance of the assassination of the Austrian archduke in Sarajevo. They knew little of Bosnia or its mountainous neighbors. Though two Balkan wars had been fought in 1912 and 1913 and the nations of that peninsula had been much in the news at the time, the average American's ideas of that portion of Europe were based more on Anthony Hope's romantic novels, *The Prisoner of Zenda* and *Rupert of Hentzau,* than on anything closely related to the facts.

Throughout the spring and summer of 1914 newspaper headlines in the United States had dealt far more with American affairs than with European ones. Trouble with Mexico was prominent in the news, but aside from that, the headlines were largely dominated by President Wilson and Theodore Roosevelt, by heavyweight champion Jack Johnson and the activities of the suffragettes, by Republican criticism of the Underwood Tariff Act and Democratic defense of it.

In January, Henry Ford had astonished the nation by increasing basic wage rates at the Ford Motor Company from $2.40 for a 9-hour working day to $5 for an 8-hour day, and economists, financiers, employers, and working people were still wondering what the outcome of this

move would be. On January 28th, Germany and the United States had
been linked by wireless for the first time, and Kaiser Wilhelm, in the initial message, had sent his greetings to President Wilson. On April 21st
American marines and sailors had captured Vera Cruz only to withdraw
some three months later when Mexican revolutionists forced President
Huerta to resign.

During the spring, unemployment had been widespread, and serious
labor difficulties had developed. On April 21st the Cape Cod Canal had
been opened. On May 7th Congress had adopted a resolution establishing "Mother's Day," and before that month had ended the two largest
ships in the world—the German *Vaterland* and the British *Aquitania*—had
sailed on their first voyages across the Atlantic.

It was while reasonably normal activities such as these were in the
news that the assassin's fatal shots were fired at Sarajevo, and though a
month was to pass before war began, the fuse had been lighted. It was
not until July 28th that Austria declared war on Serbia, but in the week
that followed, Russia, Germany, France, Belgium, and Great Britain
were swept one by one into the struggle. And all the while the people
of the United States, busy with their own affairs but troubled by the
increasing boldness of the headlines, watched intently as war swept
across the continent of Europe.

Though no one seems to have understood it at the time, a funda-
mental change in the international scheme of things was under way.
Influenced by many developments, the old order that had controlled
Europe for a century—and through Europe, much of the world—had
broken down, and nothing, as yet, had been evolved to take its place.

Shocked though Americans were by Germany's heartless invasion of
Belgium, they almost unanimously supported President Wilson's proclamation of neutrality. But even before the President had acted, the United
States had begun to feel the impact of the war. Three days before Belgium was invaded, Germany declared war on Russia, and the New York
Stock Exchange, suddenly conscious of what war in the modern world
might mean, closed for the first time in four decades, and did not reopen
for more than four months.

The war had no more than begun than Germany found herself
blockaded. Still, a few German commerce raiders managed to reach the
high seas, and though the German battle fleet irresolutely remained in

port, a fast German squadron was in the South Pacific and, for a time, the threat to Allied merchant shipping was so great that the writing of marine insurance very nearly stopped. Lloyd's of London actually closed for a time, and when those important offices reopened, rates had been enormously increased.

In the United States a bill creating the Bureau of War Risk Insurance was promptly introduced. Passed by Congress, it went into effect early in September. Comparable action by the British Government aided the situation further, and insurance rates which, in the meantime, had soared to record heights, quickly declined. By the time the Bureau of War Risk Insurance opened for business, most rates were more or less normal again.

Though the sudden outbreak of the war had for a time confused the economy of every corner of the world, those nations not directly affected were quick to accustom themselves to the new conditions. For a few weeks, international trade was brought almost to a halt but the immense needs of the warring nations soon reversed that trend. Within a month or two trade was rising rapidly. This was especially true in the United States which, as the most productive nation not already at war, was called upon for supplies in such vast quantities that factories almost everywhere began to increase their output.

Employment rose. Factories grew in size. Wages increased and prices increased as well. Where unemployment had been a problem earlier in the year, labor was now in great demand. Cut off by the blockade from Germany and Austria, American trade, for the most part, was with Great Britain, France, and Russia; and the war had no sooner settled down into the stalemate that followed the critical Battle of the Marne than the United States, despite its announced neutrality, began to develop into the greatest single source of supply for the struggling Allies.

For a decade or more prior to the outbreak of the war, the Hartford Fire Insurance Company had been broadening its field of operations. In November 1916 a list of policies written by the Hartford Fire Insurance Company and the Hartford Accident and Indemnity Company was prefaced by an introductory statement which explained that they "write practically every form of insurance except life insurance. For over a century Hartford losses have been fairly and promptly paid. The Hartford has helped rebuild New York, Boston, Charleston, Chicago, San Francisco and all American cities that have been visited by conflagrations." And with this the following forms of insurance were listed:

Fire	Accident and Health
Rent	Burglary and Theft
Use and Occupancy	Plate Glass
Sprinkler Leakage	Workmen's Compensation
Explosion	Employers' Liability
Tornado	Elevator Liability
Hail	Teams Liability
Automobile	Doctors' Liability
Motor Cycle	Druggists' Liability
Tractor	Public Liability
Merchandise in Transit	Landlords' Liability
Mail Package	Fidelity and Surety Bonds
Registered Mail	Golfers'
Samples and Baggage	Live Stock
Art Exhibitors	Race and Show Horse
Marine Insurance	Dairy Herds

Unfortunately we do not know who was the first to suggest the organization of the Hartford Accident and Indemnity Company. However, Richard Bissell was not only a prime mover in the organization of the new company but, in addition to being elected President of the Hartford Fire Insurance Company at this very time, he also served as President of the new company during its formative years.

The "Two Hartfords," as the Hartford Fire Insurance Company and the Hartford Accident and Indemnity Company soon came to be known, were especially fortunate in having this particular man at the helm when, as a result of the war, the national economy was about to expand so greatly. With a favorable trade balance of almost seven hundred million dollars in 1913, the United States had entered upon a period of increasing prosperity even before World War I began. Under the impetus of war, however, the nation's exports expanded at an unprecedented rate. By 1915 they exceeded imports by a billion seven hundred million dollars, and a year later by almost three billion.

Financed by gold and securities that came to the United States from abroad, and by foreign war bonds worth additional billions of dollars, these vast purchases revolutionized the American economy. Industrial and commercial growth was apparent almost everywhere, and as a result of unparalleled profits, greatly increased wages, and a rapid increase in the purchasing power of the people, business of almost every kind expanded as never before.

The Hartford Accident and Indemnity Company, organized almost exactly one year before the outbreak of the war, was administered by the same officers who conducted the affairs of the Hartford Fire Insurance Company, and also had the same Directors. Because of the progress made by the new company from the first, the following resolution was unanimously adopted by the Directors who were acting for the Hartford Fire Insurance Company at a meeting held on December 22, 1914:

> *Whereas* the growth of the business of the Hartford Accident and Indemnity Co. renders an addition to its Surplus Funds desirable and in the opinion of this Board the addition thereto by this Company* of One Hundred and Fifty Thousand Dollars ($150,000.—) will increase the aggregate intrinsic value of the shares of its capital stock held by this Company as a shareholder
>
> *Voted* that upon the request of the said Hartford Accident and Indemnity Company this Company be and the Treasurer is hereby authorized to pay to said Hartford Accident and Indemnity Co. as an addition to its Surplus Fund the sum of One Hundred and Fifty Thousand Dollars ($150,000.—) in cash.

At the time of the organization of the new company, which was sixteen months before this particular action was taken, its combined capital and surplus had been one million dollars, and this additional sum had now been added to that total. On December 31, 1915, however, one year after this action was taken and only twenty-nine months after the original organization, the new company's progress had been so marked that its total admitted assets were only slightly less than three million dollars.

During these years the war in Europe had expanded far beyond the boundaries of the continent, and the United States had been affected in many unexpected ways. The command of the sea by the Allies had cut off almost all trade between the United States and Germany while commerce with Great Britain and France had increased sharply. Even before the end of 1914 the war on "the Western front" had settled into a deadlock, and during the spring of 1915 Germany not only initiated the use of poison gas but also sent her submarines into action as commerce destroyers. On May 1st the American ship *Gulflight* was sunk by a German submarine, and six days later the British liner *Lusitania* was

* i.e., The Hartford Fire Insurance Company.

torpedoed and sunk with the loss of 1,198 passengers and crewmen, 63 of whom were children and 114 of whom were Americans. And despite our notes of protest, this was only the beginning. During 1915 and 1916 the neutrality laws of the United States were violated by Germany and Austria so often and so callously that the Austrian ambassador to the United States, and both the military and naval attachés of the German embassy in Washington were ordered from the country. At length, on April 6, 1917, the United States entered the war.

For two and a half years the people of the United States had followed the news of the war with ever-growing interest. Little by little they had come to see that the struggle intimately affected not only the economic interests of their land but also the basic principles upon which it was founded, and now that they were actual participants they threw themselves wholeheartedly into the struggle.

A year earlier, encouraged, no doubt, by the success of the Hartford Accident and Indemnity Company, the Directors of the Hartford Fire Insurance Company decided to move into a relatively new field with another new company, and at a meeting held on May 3, 1916, they had taken the following action:

> *Voted:* That the Executive officers of this Company be and they are hereby authorized to take the necessary action for the organization of the Hartford Live Stock Insurance Company to be incorporated under the laws of the State of New York with a Capital of Two Hundred Thousand Dollars ($200,000.—) and a surplus of One Hundred Thousand Dollars ($100,000.—) and it was further
>
> *Voted:* That the Hartford Fire Insurance Company purchase and acquire nineteen hundred and eighty seven (1987) shares of the Capital Stock of said Hartford Live Stock Insurance Co. at a price not to exceed One Hundred and Fifty Dollars ($150.—) per share.

The Hartford Fire Insurance Company had instituted a Live Stock Mortality Division early in 1915 but it had been found that, owing to the insurance laws of some of the states, the Hartford itself was debarred from doing business in some areas of greatest potential. It was for this reason that it was decided in 1916 to incorporate the new company. However, the Connecticut Legislature was in recess and since it was deemed important to set up the Hartford Live Stock Insurance Company at the earliest moment possible, it was incorporated under the laws of the State of New York. The new company commenced operations in August and shortly thereafter reinsured the business of the Indiana and Ohio Live Stock Insurance Company. This then became, according to an article in *The Hartford Agent*, "a new line that is exclusively 'Hartford.' . . . Between the loading of live stock at the point of shipment," the article went on to explain, "and the unloading at the stock yards of the market lies a gap where neither shipper nor commission merchant has control, in which stupendous losses occur every year from the hazards of transportation."

It was this gap that the new insurance company was designed to fill. In the early days of the development of the United States, farmers had driven their cattle, sheep, and hogs to market. As the Middle West developed, however, and as the newly built railroads made possible the development of enormous meat-packing plants in Chicago, Omaha, Kansas City, and elsewhere, the shipment of livestock by rail came to be more and more important. It is not merely that livestock reach the packing plants by rail. In addition to that, range cattle from the ranch country are regularly purchased by farmers who feed and fatten them for the market, and the most important feeding areas are in the corn-belt states of the Middle West. For many years these movements—from ranch to corn-belt farm to market—were made almost exclusively by rail. More recently motor trucks have entered importantly into this business, though this has not changed the fact that the shipping of livestock is an important part of the production of meat in America, and whenever such shipments are under way, losses—sometimes very large losses—are possible. It is true that conditions have improved since the Hartford Live Stock Insurance Company was originally organized, but in that year—1916— almost 75,000 maimed or dead animals that had been valued at about $1,500,000 reached the Union Stock Yards in Chicago alone, and even more undoubtedly reached the stockyards in Omaha, Kansas City, and elsewhere. Furthermore, due to train wrecks and other accidents, many dead or crippled animals never reached these major markets at all.

Such losses are naturally serious to any producer, much of whose capital may be tied up in a single shipment. At every large market, instances can be cited to show how shippers have been ruined or forced out of business by losses suffered while their livestock was in transit.

But now, for the first time, the Hartford's "Live Stock Transit Policy" was available, and those protected by it were guaranteed against all such loss or damage.

Successful from the moment it was organized, this company is still in operation. But with the entrance of the United States into World War I, its organizers were instantly faced by a new problem, so on April 23rd, seventeen days after Congress officially declared that a state of war with Germany existed, a special meeting of the Hartford's Board of Directors was called "for the purpose of submitting to the members of the Board the question of writing war hazard insurance."

President Bissell presented the problem at some length, giving a list of the companies that were already writing insurance of this kind and, after long discussion, the following resolution was unanimously adopted:

> *Resolution:* That the officers of the Company be
> and they are hereby authorized to transact war hazard
> insurance under Standard form of policy, including
> explosion hazard.

Though the Hartford Fire Insurance Company had not written any such insurance prior to this time, it had long been conscious of the fact that some of the policies it had been regularly writing were subject to at least some of the hazards of war. From the time Germany's submarine campaign had been initiated, every ship that attempted to cross the Atlantic had been subject to attack, and as America's output of war supplies increased, sabotage increased as well. On occasion, the damage that was done and the losses that resulted were enormous.

Those who manufactured and shipped the products needed for the war naturally did their best to protect them, and insofar as possible everything was insured. The Hartford, along with other insurance companies, accepted large numbers of such risks.

Among the American ports that were busy with shipments to Great Britain and France, New York and its related ports across the Hudson in New Jersey stood first. Freight was piled high everywhere, but a Jersey City water-front area known as Black Tom was probably the nation's greatest transfer point for the shipment of ammunition and other explosives.

By the summer of 1916 German submarines were taking so heavy a toll of Allied merchant vessels that shipments were much delayed and vast quantities of supplies had begun to accumulate. This was true in Jersey City as it was elsewhere, and German sympathizers and saboteurs, conscious that millions of dollars worth of shells and other explosives were piling up at Black Tom, set themselves the task of destroying them.

The place was guarded, of course, and, insofar as possible, everything was insured, the risks being divided among many companies, one of which was the Hartford. Despite the care that was taken, however, a fire was somehow set during the night of July 30, 1916, and in the hours that followed, the people of Jersey City and many elsewhere in the Greater New York area were startled into wakefulness by a prolonged series of explosions that scattered shells and shell fragments over Jersey City and New York harbor, that broke windows in Manhattan as far north as Times Square, and that silhouetted the Statue of Liberty and any number of ships against the fires and the explosions of the Jersey City water front.

Black Tom was blasted into ruins and shells fell even on Governors Island two miles away. By great good fortune only two lives were lost, but the damage that resulted amounted to some $40,000,000.

Fortunately the losses were divided among so many insurance companies that no single one found its losses disproportionately high. Furthermore, many years later they all recovered what they had paid when Germany and Austria were conclusively shown to have planned this exceptional instance of sabotage while both countries were still at peace with the United States.

In September 1909, the Hartford Fire Insurance Company had established an agency "for writing insurance on inland marine craft." Originally managed for the Company by the Charles M. Hall Company of New York, this was succeeded in 1911 by The Vessel Agency. This continued until 1918 when the Hartford's Marine and Transportation Department became the Automobile and Transportation Department, and Chubb & Son, the long-established marine underwriting office of New York, was placed in charge of the Hartford's new Marine and Inland Marine Department.

The idea of marine insurance is fairly well understood even by laymen, but "inland marine" is quite another matter, though it originated when insurance in America was very young. Late in the 1700's when American insurance companies were few and inexperienced, marine insurance was somewhat more firmly established than fire insurance. No American company, however, was in a position to compete on equal terms with the English who, even then, led the world in insuring ocean-going ships and their cargoes. American companies, however, were successful in writing marine insurance on such ships and cargoes as played a part in our coastwise trade. Furthermore, as the nation's rivers and canals came into greater and greater use, American companies naturally wrote most of the policies that were required. Thus "ocean marine insurance" continued to be written, for the most part, by British underwriters while "inland marine insurance," so far as American waterways were concerned, was handled primarily by American companies.

Not infrequently, during this period in our history, shipments that traveled most of the way to their destinations by small craft on rivers, lakes, and canals, had to be transported for at least a part of the way by land. Sometimes this land travel amounted to nothing more than a short portage around some waterfall or series of rapids, though shipments sometimes were intended for destinations that lay at greater or lesser distances from usable waterways. On this account inland marine insurance, from the very first, found it necessary to accept responsibilities that, in part, were not marine at all. The problem was essentially a practical one, of course, and no one seems to have objected when, as roads improved and as railroads began to be built, inland marine insurance came more and more to cover anything insurable that was being transported by whatever means between two points in the same country, or even between points in adjacent countries if transportation by sea was not involved. By degrees, too, other risks of many unrelated kinds, finding no place for themselves in other insurance categories, gradually came to be accepted as a part of "inland marine." In fact, such risks, few of which were technically marine at all, ultimately came to dominate the inland marine field, and today inland marine insurance has so little connection with water that anyone unacquainted with insurance practice is likely to feel that the term is an inexcusable misnomer.

Despite this natural reaction on the part of laymen, the phrase "inland marine" has been used so long with no recognition whatever of its original meaning, that actual marine insurance policies, insofar as our rivers and lakes are concerned, are now referred to as "river risks" and "lake risks" in order to place them in a separate category, and "inland marine," in addition to providing coverage for scores of other diverse risks, does the same for bridges and tunnels, musical instruments and jewelry, *outboard* motors and motorboats but not *inboard* ones, motor trucks and their contents, motion picture film and cameras, cattle and horses, fine arts, morticians' equipment, electric signs, golfing equipment, personal effects, parcel post packages, radium, salesmen's samples, wedding presents, theatrical property, stamp collections, and any goods in transit (except trans-ocean), whether by mail, express, or freight, and in any quantity whatever. The essential condition in most of this—though not, it should be pointed out, in all—is that the insured property be movable.

Thus, merely by way of its inland marine policies the Hartford had again broadened the field in which it operated. Twenty years earlier much of this would have been all but unbelievable to insurance men in general. By the time World War I had ended, however, the Hartford Fire Insurance Company and its subsidiaries were in a position to cover risks of so many kinds that little besides life insurance was still excepted.

CHAPTER 18

THE EXPANSIVE

NINETEEN-TWENTIES

FOUR YEARS before World War I began, when the Hartford celebrated the hundredth anniversary of its founding, the Company was still a fire insurance company and very little more. If Nathaniel Terry, its first President, and Walter Mitchell, its first Secretary, had been able to spend a week or two in the Home Office in 1910, it is not unlikely that they would have gained a reasonably good idea of the Company's condition and that they would have come to understand its way of doing business. They would have been surprised to learn how greatly the Company had grown, but once they had grasped the fact that the population of the United States had increased from seven million to ninety-two million in the Hartford's hundred-year history, the Company's assets and income would surely have been understandable. It is quite possible, in fact, that they would have been much more impressed by typewriters, telephones, automobiles, and railroads than by the progress the Company had made, and it is not to be doubted that most of the Company's "stock in trade"— its fire insurance policies, that is—differed only in detail, and not in principle, from those with which President Terry and Secretary Mitchell had been familiar when the Company was new. It is true that a new department had been organized in 1909—the Marine and Transportation Department—and, as the centennial *History of the Hartford Fire Insurance Company** explains, "The contracts issued under the supervision of this department indicate the wide scope of insurance as developed since the

---

* Compiled by Charles W. Burpee and published in Hartford, 1910.

days of . . . Nathaniel Terry." But the "synopsis of them," which immediately followed this statement, plainly shows that what was thought to be "the wide scope of insurance" in 1910 was remarkably narrow by the measurements of even a few years later. In 1913, for example, when the Hartford Accident and Indemnity Company was organized, this list, "wide" though its scope had appeared, was greatly outmoded.

The fact is that all the changes that had taken place in the first hundred years of the Hartford's history had not brought about such significant alterations as materialized in the decade in which World War I was fought. In 1910, when the Hartford Fire Insurance Company's capital was $2,000,000, and its total assets were $23,000,000, it had only barely begun to look beyond the specific field in which it had operated for a century. But by 1920 its capital had increased to $4,000,000 and its total assets exceeded $55,000,000. Furthermore, the assets of its wholly owned subsidiary, the Hartford Accident and Indemnity Company, exceeded $11,500,000, while its newer subsidiary, the Hartford Live Stock Insurance Company, had already made a successful place for itself and was rapidly accumulating assets of its own.

Though most insurance companies had greatly increased their business during the war years, they had also been confronted with their full share of difficulties. In 1916, for example, the legislature of South Carolina had passed an act which made it illegal for "fire insurance companies or associations or partnerships doing a fire insurance business in the State to enter into any compact or combination with other fire insurance companies, associations, or partnerships."

Three years earlier, a similarly restrictive act had been passed in Missouri and, as a result, 120 fire insurance companies, of which the Hartford had been one, had withdrawn from the state. In the end, the act was held to be void and the companies returned, and now that a similar situation had arisen in South Carolina, practically all the insurance companies operating there withdrew as they had done in Missouri. It took some time to settle the argument, but in the end the legislature reconsidered its action and the various insurance companies returned. In the meantime, however, a year had passed and much harm had been done not only to the insurance companies but also to business in the state.

While this was going on, the Hartford was called upon to pay a small but very unusual claim in Texas. Under what is known as a "stock yards cover," the livestock in various stockyards in the country is automatically insured against fire. Such a policy, written by the Hartford, was in effect in 1916 at the Fort Worth stockyards. Frequently livestock received at these yards is sold to "feeders," who ship their animals to their fattening grounds; but in Texas, and elsewhere, cattle ticks may be troublesome, and each animal sold to a feeder must be "dipped" before being shipped.

In this particular case a small feeder bought seven cows at the Fort Worth stockyard. As a matter of course they were dipped in a solution composed, in part, of certain petroleum products. But the animals also had to be branded, and because their new owner was in a hurry, they were branded before they were dry. Branding irons, of course, must be red-hot, or very nearly so, for such a task; and the oil-saturated hair of the first cow, when the branding iron was applied, immediately ignited. Suddenly set on fire, the cow broke loose and ran in among the others that made up the little herd. They, too, were saturated with the same inflammable mixture, and before anything could be done to help them, all seven had burned to death.

The Hartford paid the loss at once; and the feeder, who probably bought seven other cows, either used some other solution when he dipped them, or waited until they were entirely dry and reasonably fire-resistant before using his branding iron again.

In 1917, the Transit Division of the Hartford's Live Stock Department covered more than fifty thousand carloads of cattle, sheep, and hogs which, in all, were valued at more than $150,000,000, and within two years of the time the Hartford's complete livestock policies were first written, some 15,000 shippers took advantage of the protection they offered.

In addition to policies such as these, the Hartford, shortly before the outbreak of World War I, had developed a very specialized policy designed to cover all the livestock in such stockyards as were insured, for the account of "whom it may concern." Usually such contracts are drawn in favor of the local livestock exchange or of the local company operating the stockyard, and all livestock received at the stockyard is covered though some of the animals may change ownership several times during their stay at the yards.

Serious fires in stockyards not infrequently result in the death of many animals, but other difficulties may also arise. Such animals as are saved, for example, may be so inextricably intermixed as to make it impossible to determine where their ownership lies. Under the Hartford contract, however, the Company itself immediately takes possession of all the rescued stock and sells it for the benefit of the owners. Every owner then presents his claim for the stock he had in the yard at the time of the fire, and receives payment whether his stock, or merely the *identity* of his stock, was destroyed or lost.

A Hartford policy of this nature was in effect at the stockyards in Kansas City when, in October 1917, a fire that was definitely incendiary in origin resulted in a conflagration that involved livestock valued at very nearly two million dollars. Large numbers of animals died but some twenty thousand head of cattle, belonging to nearly a thousand separate owners, were rescued. They were hopelessly mixed, however, and they ranged all the way from "scrub canners" whose value was low, to high-grade steers that should have topped the market.

It was no simple task to sort, grade, and dispose of these animals, and they had to be fed and cared for in the meantime. But despite this task, and within a month, the Hartford's Live Stock Department made out and delivered a draft for $1,733,779.99 payable to the Kansas City Live Stock Exchange "in full settlement, final satisfaction, and compromise of all claims against the Hartford Fire Insurance Company for loss and damage occasioned by Fire which occurred on the 16th day of Oct. 1917 to the property described in Policy No. 35821 of this Company."

Fortunately for the Hartford, this draft was not a fair measure of its loss. By the time the thousands of rescued cattle were disposed of, the major part of this "loss" had been recovered and, so far as the one-time owners of these animals were concerned, the Hartford's greatest contribution was to solve the otherwise unsolvable problem of that ownership.

Like most other fire insurance companies, the Hartford had greatly increased its premium income during the four years of World War I. During these same years, too, its "loss experience" had been definitely favorable. In 1918, for example, its premium income had somewhat surpassed thirty million dollars, and its losses had amounted to little more than fourteen million—46.2 per cent of the premium income for the year. Costs, it is true, had shown a great increase throughout the whole period of the war, and some among the Directors were troubled about the Com-

RICHARD M. BISSELL
President, 1913-1941

pany's future. For the most part, however, optimism prevailed and, following a recommendation by the Board, the stockholders, at a meeting held on June 25, 1909, increased the capital stock of the Company from $2,000,000 to $4,000,000. The Company's growth, and the growth of its subsidiaries, had naturally resulted in an increase in the number of employees in the Home Office—so great an increase, in fact, that additional space had been rented in an adjoining building. With still more growth ahead, the Directors saw that the Home Office was urgently in need of a new and larger building. With this in mind, the ten-acre tract which had long been occupied by the American School at Hartford for the Deaf on Asylum Avenue and Garden Street, was purchased in 1919, construction began the following year, and the first meeting of the Company's Board of Directors was held in the handsome new Hartford Fire Insurance Company Building on December 6, 1921.

In the two decades prior to the opening of the new building, the entire field of insurance had developed so rapidly that any insurance executive of 1901 would have found that greater changes had taken place in the succeeding twenty years than in most of the preceding century. Furthermore, changes were continuing. The American-Foreign Insurance Association is an example.

As a result of the war, American business interests in foreign lands had greatly increased, and fire insurance executives had begun to see that an opportunity existed for them to offer the services of their companies to such firms as had branches or connections abroad. American banks were already establishing themselves abroad with the idea of financing American enterprises doing business there, and it was clear that American insurance companies could do much the same thing. Thus, they would be able to protect the property and liability of American firms operating overseas.

The Hartford, interested in this idea from its inception, was one of the original members of the American-Foreign Insurance Association. In the years since then, Hartford agencies have been established in many countries and, by way of the Company's membership in the Association, it obtains a fixed percentage of all the business written by any member of the Association in the entire foreign field which, so far as the American Foreign Insurance Association is concerned, does not include Canada, Mexico, or Central America.

The idea on which this Association is based was not new even at the time it was organized. The Railroad Insurance Association is older—was, perhaps, the first such association to organize—and it, too, is made up of a number of companies which, from time to time, agree as to the share of all joint policies that each company is to accept. The Factory Insurance Association is a comparable organization, and others operate in other fields—grain and cotton, for example, and even in petroleum, aviation, and shipping.

Such associations usually write all standard types of insurance but, working together, as the member companies do, they spread the risk and find it much more economical, so far as inspection and servicing of policies are concerned. This is reflected not only in lower costs for policies but also in greater convenience to the assured.

Anyone who attempts to determine exactly when almost any of the new types of insurance came into use is likely to find a remarkable dearth of specific information. In 1882, for example, the very idea of wind insurance was fantastic to most insurance men of the day. By 1910, however, wind insurance had been widely accepted and when, in 1913, an especially disastrous tornado swept across Omaha, Nebraska, wind insurance—or tornado insurance, as it is commonly called in the prairie states—suddenly came into great demand. But just where or when, in the period between, the first such policy was sold does not appear.

Many new ideas for insurance seem to originate with agents of insurance companies. And it is not unlikely that some of the agents' ideas originate with individual clients who have ideas—or problems—of their own. Social, economic, and legislative developments also create demands for new coverages. In 1913, for example, the newly enacted workmen's compensation laws created so great a need that insurance companies everywhere saw what proved to be a great opportunity. The Hartford, impressed as others were by the new need, was founding the Hartford Accident and Indemnity Company at the time, and from the first it was authorized to write workmen's compensation and employers' liability policies as well.

Hail insurance, unknown not so long before, was widely in effect in 1914. By that time, in fact, the Hartford's "Hail Department" had been conducted for several years by Dugan & Carr, General Agents of the Company's Western Department in Chicago. Explosion insurance "except on bursting boilers and flywheels," was a natural outgrowth of

World War I when American munitions-makers, concerned not only by the hazards innate in the manufacture of explosives, were also troubled by the possibility of explosions caused by saboteurs.

Though the Hartford's business, as well as that of most other insurance companies, had been unusually good throughout the war, and had been almost equally good for the two years that followed, the reverse was true in 1921. The census of 1920 gave the United States a population of 105 million—a gain of 14 million in ten years, despite four years of war and a great decline in immigration. Yet business declined suddenly and seriously in 1921. Prices fell and the value of farm land, greatly inflated during the war, fell also. The cost of living, having very nearly doubled during the war, declined somewhat, but farm conditions in the Middle West were bad, the boll weevil was a serious menace to cotton throughout large portions of the South, and very widely throughout the country the farmers took a stand that firmly opposed not only the nation's manufacturers but also its distributors.

Prohibition, which brought "bootlegging" and "high-jacking" with it, encouraged other violations of the law. The labor unions, unwilling to accept any reduction in wages that had climbed to record heights during the war, attempted to gain their ends by strikes, one of which—a strike of the miners in 1925—lasted almost six months and even then was settled only with great difficulty.

"Almost everyone," President Bissell wrote in January 1922,* "thinks that 1921 has been an abnormal year businesswise, and everyone in the insurance business will agree that it has been a hard year, for it has been characterized by a combination of factors which have precluded any such results as those to which we have become accustomed in recent years.

"These factors were a decreasing income, stationary or increasing expenses, and a very largely increased burning ratio. On top of this . . . the so-called 'side lines,' notably marine insurance, hail insurance, and automobile insurance, have had a bad year. As a result . . . all fire insurance men have reached the : . . conclusion . . . that 1921 has been a hard year, one of the hardest, in fact."

He might have added that the Company's net premiums had declined, that its losses as well as its expenses had increased, plus the fact that the reserve for unearned premiums had gone up $1,600,000, which further tended to reduce the earnings for the year. Still it had been

* *The Hartford Agent*, Vol. XIII, No. 7, p. 193.

possible to add something more than $100,000 to net surplus.

Although the 1920's were marked by the sharp "recession" of 1921 and were later troubled by a vast economic collapse that brought about a world-wide depression, the years between these two difficult periods were marked by much activity and growth. For example, though the Directors of the Hartford Fire Insurance Company had voted, in 1919, to increase the Company's capital stock from two million dollars to four, and voted to double it again in 1922, they decided, at a meeting held on February 2, 1925, to recommend still another increase, as the following extract from the minutes shows:

> *Voted:* that a special meeting of the stockholders be held on Friday, March 6, 1925, to take action upon the following resolution, the adoption of which is recommended by the Directors:
>
> *Resolved:* that the Directors be authorized to increase the capital stock of the Company from Eight Million Dollars ($8,000,000.—) to Ten Million Dollars ($10,000,000.—) by the issue of twenty thousand (20,000) additional shares of the par value of One Hundred Dollars ($100.—) each, the right to subscribe therefor at Two Hundred Dollars ($200.—) per share to be offered to the stockholders of record as of close of business March 6, 1925, in the proportion of one (1) share of new stock to four (4) shares of stock held by them respectively; such rights to be exercised on or before April 15, 1925. . . .

At this same meeting, too, the Directors adopted another important resolution that appears in the minutes as follows:

> *Whereas* for over thirty years the Hartford Fire Insurance Co. has enjoyed a large income from one of its most important Departments known as the New York Underwriters Agency, and
>
> *Whereas* it now seems desirable that the New York Underwriters Agency be incorporated,
>
> *Therefore* be it resolved that the officers of the Hartford Fire Insurance Co. are hereby authorized and empowered to take any and all action that may be necessary to incorporate the New York Underwriters Agency with a

capital of $2,000,000.— representing 20,000 shares having a par value of $100.— per share and with a surplus of $3,000,000; and

Be it further resolved that the officers of the Hartford Fire Insurance Company be and they hereby are authorized and empowered to cause the Hartford Fire Insurance Company to subscribe and pay for the 20,000 shares of capital stock of the new corporation herein before mentioned at $250 per share.

This was the first of two important steps in the development of the New York Underwriters Agency that year. The second, which culminated at a meeting of the incorporators and subscribers to the capital stock of the new corporation which was held at 100 William Street, New York, on October 27th, not only organized the corporation but also authorized it to transact "any other business that may be lawfully considered" by the corporation acting as the New York Underwriters Insurance Company, which thus became the newest, as of that date, of the Hartford's family of subsidiaries.

It is interesting, in this connection, to note that Alexander Stoddart, who founded the New York Underwriters Agency, and George L. Chase, who later became President of the Hartford, had originally met when, as young Special Agents, both of them were traveling on a Mississippi steamboat on which, by chance, they had been assigned to the same stateroom. The record does not say what part that original meeting played in establishing the close relations that ultimately developed not only between the two men themselves but also between the companies they later headed. However, each of them was in a position of authority in 1894 when the Hartford made its original arrangement with the Agency—an arrangement that reached its culmination a generation later when these companies, after many years of association, expanded so greatly.

Despite the business recession of 1921 the Hartford continued to adopt new ideas. "Rain insurance," inaugurated only a little while before, had instantly caught on, and sponsors of all sorts of activities that could be adversely affected by bad weather accepted this new and novel form of protection. The very first rain policy ever issued by an American company covered a rodeo held at Dewey, Oklahoma, on July 3, 1920. Furthermore, it rained; and the Hartford paid a $2,000 loss. But thereafter all sorts of activities, ranging from church socials to outdoor athletic events and even to state fairs, turned to rain insurance in order to protect themselves. The American Legion Convention that was held in Kansas City in 1921, took out rain insurance on its auto races and its aviation meet, as well as its parade. It may be that the newspaper stories about this new type of insurance gave a Louisiana oilman the idea that caused him, about the time of the Legion Convention, to send the following telegram to the Home Office in Hartford.

> ADVISE IF YOU WILL GUARANTEE OIL IN COMMERCIAL
> QUANTITIES IN WELL BEING DRILLED NEAR PROVEN TERRITORY.
> IF YOU CAN COVER WILL FURNISH DETAILS. WIRE ANSWER.

At the time, the Hartford was full of new ideas, but "oil insurance" of the kind this inquirer had in mind was not among them. Still, race-horse insurance was, and in 1921, Man o' War, who was probably the greatest race horse the United States ever saw, was insured by the Hartford for $150,000.

One idea that was tried out during the latter 1920's is worthy of notice even though it proved a failure. As early as 1918 and 1919 the idea of crop insurance was under consideration, and several companies entered the field. The most extensive coverage, however, was written by the Hartford which, in 1920, assumed approximately $14,000,000 of liability under all risk crop forms. The risks were well diversified geographically, and the premiums for that year amounted to about $800,000, with average premium rates approximating 5.75 per cent.

The policies that were issued represented an attempt to insure the total cost of production, as that was based on reports made by the applicants.

Here, obviously, was an idea of great potential importance. If some practical method could be evolved whereby farmers could be insured at moderate rates against all the many risks that crops are heir to, much of the risk would be taken out of farming and the entire nation would benefit.

The problem was a complicated one, and, lacking any experience, the insurance companies that attempted to solve it had little on which to base their guesses of what the rates should be. Still, with its risks widely diversified, and with liabilities totaling a good many million dollars, the Hartford looked forward with much interest as it awaited the outcome.

But the outcome, unfortunately, was disastrous. Having collected premiums that totaled some $800,000, which is a tidy sum for an experiment, the Company learned, by the time the year was out, that its losses on those policies amounted, in round numbers, to $2,500,000.

The Hartford thoroughly understood, of course, that this first step into the field of crop insurance should be viewed as research. It seems apparent that Mr. Bissell, who was President at the time, took that point of view. On that account, even so great a loss during that first experimental year did not cause the Company to bring the experiment to an end. In fact, the Company continued to sell these policies throughout the 1920's, but always with little or no underwriting success. Consequently, after much thought and effort had been expended to make the idea work, the venture was ultimately abandoned about 1930.

The United States Department of Agriculture, which had learned that crop insurance was being introduced, was naturally disappointed when the companies that tried it felt compelled to halt their efforts, and during the 1930's the Government itself explored the possibility of entering this field. At Mr. Bissell's direction, the Hartford made available everything it had learned, and told those who were studying the matter all the Company knew about policy forms, applications, rates, and losses. Detailed reports covering the Company's experience were also provided.

Subsequently the Federal Crop Insurance Corporation was formed and in 1939, for the first time, it offered insurance on wheat. Unfortunately, its losses were enormous, and though the attempt was continued, Congress failed, in 1944, to appropriate funds except for the liquidation of the corporation. However, the act was amended a little later and the effort continued, luckily with somewhat better experience in later years.

In retrospect, it seems to be the general opinion among those Hartford officials who were closest to the Company's experiment that it had little chance of success because of the complexity and magnitude of the undertaking. Nevertheless, it characterized the spirit that brought success to the Hartford in other fields, and the mere fact that this idea failed so far as the Company is concerned, did not keep other experiments from being tried.

The economic recession of 1921 was much sharper and more discouraging than a later generation is apt to imagine. From an index figure of 231 in 1920, wholesale prices of commodities fell to 125 in April 1921. Buyers' strikes were widespread. Inventories depreciated immensely in value, and bankruptcies were numerous. Fortunately this difficult period was not prolonged, and business conditions—though not agricultural conditions—grew distinctly better in the years that followed. Every business naturally had its difficulties, and the Hartford was no exception. In 1927, for example, 140 tornadoes swept across widely scattered areas of the country, and the damage that was done was almost twice as great as that of any previous year. Property damage amounted to almost $50,000,000, and 469 lives were lost, with the city of St. Louis suffering the heaviest blow. On November 14th of that same year, too, a huge gas tank in Pittsburgh exploded, blasting the neighborhood into rubble and causing damage that was estimated at some ten million dollars.

Less destructive, except to Jack Dempsey's hopes for a comeback, was the Tunney-Dempsey fight at Soldiers' Field in Chicago. It was on September 22, 1927, that this heavyweight championship fight was held, and 104,943 fight fans paid to see the 10-round battle. But what very few of them saw or thought about was the part the Hartford played in the affair. Tex Rickard, the promoter, and George Getz, who represented a group of Chicago interests, insisted on having coverage for every conceivable contingency. The most important item was public liability on the fight itself, and the Hartford, which was the first company approached, wrote a policy with a top limit of one million dollars. Other policies were written as well—compensation insurance on those who performed the immense task of setting up more than a hundred thousand seats—a contingent policy to cover all the work that had to be sublet—a liability policy covering not only the various ticket offices but also such messengers as had to be employed. And it is interesting to note that among all these, it was not the million-dollar public liability policy that produced the greatest premium. It was the compensation insurance policy on the employees who arranged the seats. Still, those who saw the fight paid $2,658,660 to occupy those seats, and in doing so created the largest "gate" in the history of pugilism.

In 1924, Calvin Coolidge was re-elected President, and despite serious economic difficulties that troubled much of Europe, prosperity in the

United States developed on a scale so extraordinary that many business leaders and economists came to feel, as less experienced people also did, that business in the United States was operating in a "new era" in which the economic laws of an earlier day were clearly and definitely outmoded.

Superficially, at least, this viewpoint did not appear unreasonable. Earnings were high, and the stock market, to which large numbers of people turned despite their lack of information and experience, began to climb. In the five years ending in 1926 stock prices increased enormously. But along with the advanced stock prices, brokers' loans had risen, too. On January 1, 1925, they had totaled $1,750,000,000, but three years later the figure had risen to $4,400,000,000. In the summer of 1929, several hundred million shares were being carried on margin, and the more conservative financiers and publications were issuing serious warnings.

Optimism still continued, however, and thousands of people with small savings and no investment experience bought stocks on margin. Many such people, and others who should have known better as well, seemed to believe that the market could do nothing but rise. And rise it did, for the most part.

In 1928 Herbert Hoover, defeating Alfred E. Smith by a huge plurality, was elected to the Presidency and, as the time for his inauguration approached, stocks rose higher still. Warnings were more frequent now but they were little heeded. Even on October 25, 1929, when almost 13 million shares were sold in a wildly active market, Wall Street, according to the headlines, was "optimistic after stormy day" and the day's losses "recovered in part." Four days later, however, the market collapsed. More than 16 million shares changed hands. Values declined by billions. Many lifetime savings disappeared almost overnight, and before 1929 had ended the greatest economic depression in history was under way.

By this time President Richard M. Bissell had become widely recognized as one of the leading insurance executives in the United States. The organization and early success of the Hartford Accident and Indemnity Company must be largely credited to him, and the transformation of the New York Underwriters Agency into the New York Underwriters Insurance Company was largely his accomplishment. Furthermore, much credit must go to him for the developments that changed the London Mutual into the London-Canada Fire Insurance Company in 1922, and for the conversion of the Citizens of Missouri into the Citizens Insurance Company of New Jersey in 1929. It was also under his direction that the Hartford acquired a majority interest in the Twin City Fire Insurance Company in 1921 and made a management contract with the Northwestern Fire and Marine Insurance Company in 1925.

During World War I, he had performed important public services, especially when he was elected President of the National Board of Fire Underwriters in 1916. In this capacity he mobilized the skill, the resources, and the personnel of the Board for the national defense, thereby enabling the Government to obtain the data that were so urgently needed in the development of factories capable of producing enormous quantities of the vitally important munitions required during the war. It was during this period that tens of thousands of manufacturing plants were inspected by insurance experts, and some 50,000 specific recommendations were recorded. During these years, too, a huge and comprehensive fire prevention crusade was undertaken, with special attention being given to the nation's great military cantonments which, remarkably enough, were brought to completion with a fire loss of less than $3,000.

Following World War I, President Bissell had helped organize and had become the first President of the Eastern Underwriters Association. In addition, he was the first President of the Automobile Underwriters Association, and later was made Chairman of the Board of Trustees of the Insurance Executives Association.

Fortunately, this was the man—tall, distinguished-looking, quietly confident, and remarkably able—who was the Hartford's chief executive when in the autumn of 1929 the greatest economic crash in history abruptly changed the outlook, and even threatened the future, of the modern world.

CHAPTER 19

WORLD-WIDE DEPRESSION

AND

WORLD WAR II

MEASURED by generally accepted economic indices, the depression that burst upon the world in 1929 continued for six uninterrupted years. Even then the upturn that began proved weak, and the very moderate gains that were made in 1936 and 1937 were largely lost in 1938. So far as the average man had been able to see, almost nothing had foretold the coming of the crash, and during its initial phases many people felt that it would not be prolonged—that better times were "just around the corner."

As never before, practically everything felt the effects but, as had been apparent during earlier depressions, the Hartford Fire Insurance Company, along with other soundly operated companies in the same field, did not find conditions calamitous. Manufacturers, finding the demand for their products very sharply reduced, were compelled to lay off large numbers of employees. Retailers, with their shelves stocked with goods purchased at pre-depression prices, were seriously threatened or actually bankrupted by the sudden and widespread depreciation in values. Insurance companies, however, were confronted by no such sudden drop in the value of the "goods" they had for sale. They lost business, of course. President Richard Bissell, writing in *The Hartford Agent* in January 1930, frankly admitted as much. "When all industries and businesses are seriously depressed," he wrote, "and many become in-operative, unproductive, or unprofitable, it is inevitable that the business of insurance . . . should share in the misfortunes."

Troubled, as all thoughtful people were, he pointed out that "loud-voiced OPTIMISM alone can help very little. . . . What is needed is not merely to be sanguine but to make our own plans more wisely, to concentrate more intensely our efforts and thoughts upon the work that is now in hand, to acquire more skill in our business, to be more thrifty and more diligent, and especially to stiffen our determination so that it may shut the door on discouragement and impel us to keep our faces forward and our energies unimpaired. . . . Determination and hard work . . . are . . . the weapons which will make us helpful allies to the forces which are sooner or later going to bring us back to prosperous days."

"Historically," he wrote some three years later, "insurance has always lagged behind most other branches of business both in respect to entering and leaving depression periods."

He might have added, too, that the "highs" and "lows" of the business of insurance not only make their appearance a little later than the corresponding "highs" and "lows" of business generally, but also that they are noticeably less extreme. This was especially apparent during the 1930's, and it is interesting to note that while property values declined and the Hartford's premium income declined as well, arson was less frequent and the total number of fires was smaller, too. This was especially noticeable during the "bank holiday" that marked the beginning of President Franklin D. Roosevelt's first term in 1932, when the Hartford's losses were cut by almost a half. Exactly why this happened is even yet a subject for discussion among insurance men. Perhaps it was due to greater care at a time when everyone was troubled, but it may also be that many people were uncertain that the insurance companies would be permitted to pay any losses while the banks were closed and that this made them more careful.

It is apparent, after the passage of so many years, that the Great Depression was a dominant factor in the world at large from 1929 to the outbreak of World War II. In fact, even the war can be traced to it, for Adolph Hitler was very definitely a product of the economic conditions that were at their worst in Germany in the early 1930's. It is true that he and limited numbers of his Nazi supporters had been active for a decade before they gained control in 1933, but prior to 1929 the Nazi Party had been small, and in the election of 1928 its total strength had actually declined. But where, prior to the depression, some thirteen million Germans had been employed, by 1933 only nine million were at work, and Hitler, making endless promises, readily gained the support of hordes of frustrated people who followed him eagerly even into and during the war.

So far as the "Two Hartfords" were concerned, conditions had begun to change for the better by the end of 1935. A year earlier, President Bissell, writing in *The Hartford Agent,** had admitted that "we feel that we are still in the midst of a rapidly changing environment and that several years, at least, must elapse before settled conditions in industry, business or financial affairs can be re-established either as we formerly knew them or, as seems not unlikely, on some basis considerably removed from anything in our past experience."

"It seems to us," he added later in the same article, "the most helpful and perhaps the wisest thing we can do at the present juncture is to fall in line with those people who are hopeful."

The depression had begun a little more than five years before he put these thoughts on paper, and during that difficult period, he and his associates had been administering the affairs of the Hartford and its subsidiaries with the utmost care. The depression had hardly more than started when they reached the conclusion that a determined effort should be made to retain every possible employee, and in that the Company was remarkably successful. Except for a handful of married women whose pay was not vital to the welfare of their families, no Hartford employees were dismissed, and except for a ten-per-cent reduction in salaries which applied to everyone and which, in addition, was more than offset by the reduced cost of living, no pay cuts were effected.

On the other hand, few new ideas were initiated during these difficult years. Experiments too were kept at a minimum, and, in a statement that accompanied the publication of the annual report for 1935, *The Hartford Agent* was obviously confident in pointing out that "the year 1935 was a good year for us."

It must go without saying that the Hartford Fire Insurance Company and its subsidiaries were confronted with many difficulties throughout the 1930's. On the other hand, the Company itself—and the story of its

* January 1935, p. 109.

subsidiaries is somewhat comparable—was in a stronger position in 1939 than it had been before the depression had taken its economic toll. This is apparent from the following figures:

HARTFORD FIRE INSURANCE COMPANY

	1929	1939
Total assets	$96,794,000	$116,033,000
Surplus to policyholders	$43,185,000	$ 68,776,000
Premium income	$43,626,000	$ 37,956,000

It is true that these figures do not tell the whole story. Largely because losses had been moderate, both surplus and assets were greater in 1939 than they had been ten years before. The Company's premium income, however, was 13 per cent less. But, oddly enough, even the premium income for 1929 had been very greatly less than it had been earlier. Despite the unparalleled prosperity of the pre-depression years—years that showed a steady increase in business and a veritable boom on the stock market—the Hartford's premium income for 1929 was 18 million dollars less than it had been in 1925.

During the latter half of the 1930's terrible influences were at work in the world. Mussolini invaded Ethiopia; Hitler reoccupied the Rhineland; Japan renewed its attack on China; Hitler seized Austria; Great Britain and France, yielding to the German dictator's demands at Munich, made it possible for him to rob Czechoslovakia of the Sudetenland; and finally, in 1939, after signing a nonaggression pact with the Soviet Union, Hitler attacked Poland and World War II began.

Throughout the years of the depression many individuals and most business establishments had been confronted by the problem of survival. Many companies went by the board or, finding it impossible to continue their independent existence, combined with others in order to reduce their costs and otherwise improve their situations.

Because everyone was more than usually cost-conscious during the depression, the mutual insurance companies came to be more widely accepted. In addition to this, widespread efforts to reduce costs led to the emergence of "the direct writer"—a company, that is, that specializes in selling its policies directly to its clients without benefit of agents.

In time, the states began to adopt various financial responsibility laws, and enormously broadened the market for automobile insurance. Accident and health insurance spread rapidly when group insurance and the Blue Cross concept came to be widely accepted.

Many changes had taken place in the Hartford's manners and methods in the quarter of a century that separated the opening years of the two world wars. Before World War I the employees in the Home Office had been predominantly men. Green celluloid eyeshades were common among them, and most of them wore, almost as if it were a uniform, a gray cotton or alpaca coat. Office equipment, of course, was simple prior to 1914, and at least one old-fashioned article that disappeared in the years that followed was still widely in use throughout the Home Office. This was the lowly earthenware or polished metal receptacle known as the spittoon, or, to those of a more delicate turn of mind, the cuspidor. Many were in use, not only in the Home Office in Hartford but also in other offices of that day. Strategically placed, they were especially intended for the convenience of those who chewed tobacco. These modest utensils were often placed on small rubber mats that served as shields against occasional near misses, and they had a long history of usefulness. As World War I began, however, their future was limited. Along with other simple reminders of an earlier day, they were about to disappear.

By 1939 the Home Office bore little resemblance to what it had been in 1914. One of the most noticeable changes was that men were no longer in the majority, and green celluloid eyeshades, along with gray alpaca coats, had completely disappeared. Women—or, in the phraseology of the new day, girls—were in evidence everywhere. They were busy operating typewriters, adding machines, and other kinds of newly developed office equipment and, because of them, the atmosphere of the Home Office had lost much of the drabness that had been apparent twenty-five years before.

During the worst of the depression—let us say, from 1931 to 1935—people everywhere were seriously concerned for the future. Unemployment was widespread and many communities were burdened by those who were out of work. The city of Hartford was no exception. But for the most part the numerous insurance companies that play so important a part in the city's economy were little inclined to lay off many employees, and the Hartford, as we have noted, fared remarkably well in this regard throughout the depression.

It is easy to explain the Company's comparative good fortune during the difficult years of the depression. It had benefited from the great expansion of automobile insurance. It had also strengthened its position by entering a number of new fields on a mass basis; and especially, it had been a leader in developing new types of agricultural insurance. The Hartford had been the first company—or among the first—to develop rain insurance, crop insurance, and greenhouse insurance. The same was true of livestock transit insurance, livestock mortality insurance, 4-H Club animal insurance, and grain elevator insurance. As farmers more and more began to move their livestock to the great central markets by motor truck, the Company's Live Stock Transit Department broadened their policies to cover the risk inherent in this new method of transportation. This, in turn, gave Hartford agents the opportunity to acquaint farmers with other forms of insurance that were important to them.

It would be easy, in considering the developments that made it possible for the Hartford to weather the depression so well, to lose oneself among endless details. Many of these are important, it is true, but even more important is the significant but accidental fact that during the depression the Hartford and its subsidiaries were under the direction of a group of executives whose great ability was all the greater because of their many years of experience.

"Old men for counsel," the ancient saying goes, "young men for war."

And never before in the Hartford's history had long experience and sage counsel been more vital to its future. A generation later, another need came to be uppermost, and younger men were in demand; but the problems that arose during the greatest depression in history could be solved only by men of wisdom and long experience, and the Hartford had them.

President Bissell had begun his career as an insurance man in 1883.

Charles E. Chase, the Chairman of the Board, had made his beginning in 1887.

James Wyper, Vice-President not only of the Hartford Fire Insurance Company but also of the Hartford Accident and Indemnity Company and the Hartford Live Stock Insurance Company, had served as an insurance man since 1913.

F. C. White, Vice-President of the Hartford Fire Insurance Company and also of the Hartford Live Stock Insurance Company, had entered the insurance field in 1906. D. J. Glazier, Financial Vice-President of the Hartford Fire as well as of the Hartford Accident and Indemnity, and

Treasurer of the Hartford Live Stock Insurance Company, had first joined the Company in 1895. Charles S. Kremer, Secretary of the Hartford Fire Insurance Company, had joined the Company in 1900. James L. D. Kearney, Vice-President and General Manager of the Hartford Accident and Indemnity and Secretary of the Hartford Live Stock, had begun in 1914; and Paul Rutherford, Vice-President of the Hartford Accident and Indemnity, in 1900. There were other officials, of course, but in 1929 these were the most important and, at the time, their periods of service averaged twenty-eight years.

The Company's Departments, too, were under the direction of men of experience. A. G. Dugan of the Western Department had served the Company for thirty-four years. Joy Lichtenstein, Vice-President of the Hartford Accident and Indemnity and Manager of the Pacific Department, had been an insurance executive for twenty-three years. W. R. Prescott had been with the Southern Department for twenty-three years, and Peter A. McCallum had been Manager for Canada for thirty-seven.

Many members of the Board of Directors, too, were men of long experience. Charles E. Chase had been associated with the Company for forty-two years, had been President for five, and a member of the Board for twenty-one. Among the nine other Directors, only two—F. Spencer Goodwin and George S. Stevenson—were less than fifty years of age, and the remaining seven averaged sixty-two.

With men so mature and experienced as these counseling and directing affairs, it is understandable that, once the depression was under way, the Company was conservatively operated. In part, this was in keeping with the Company's past. However, many new ideas had been adopted during the two preceding decades, and these, almost without exception, were continued. In 1926, for example, the Company had given its support to a then new Northwestern University scholarship program which included a two-year course of study that specialized in property insurance. And, despite the depression, the Company's support of this program and of many other forward-looking ideas was continued.

While increasing profits during the expansive 1920's had provided the most acceptable measure of business success, mere survival often did so during the early 1930's. The Hartford, however, did far better than that and by 1940 the Company and its subsidiaries were well prepared to meet the problems that World War II had brought.

Throughout the difficult depression years the wisdom and experience of the Company's more elderly officials had been invaluable. Again it had been proved that

> " . . . age is opportunity no less
> Than youth, though in another dress."

But one by one, after having made their many contributions, these older men began to be taken from the Company. Peter A. McCallum, after forty years as Manager for Canada, died in 1932. Charles E. Chase, Chairman of the Board and former President, died in 1933. A. G. Dugan, General Agent of the Western Department, retired in 1938 and died five years later. Richard M. Bissell, for twenty-eight years President of the Hartford, and for even longer an outstanding figure in the development of insurance in America, died in 1941.

It is natural, in thinking of the passing of such men, to view their departure with a sense of loss. They had made many contributions. They had first contributed the energy and originality of youth to the welfare of the Hartford, and then, in their later years, had contributed even more importantly by way of their accumulated wisdom and experience.

The changes that followed the loss of these more elderly executives did not immediately catapult young men into positions of control. Charles S. Kremer, who had served for ten years as Secretary, and for six years as Vice-President, was chosen to succeed Richard M. Bissell as President. Owing to the pressure of international events, no abrupt changes in policy were apparent. Within three months of the time President Kremer assumed his new office, the Japanese struck their infamous blow at Pearl Harbor and instantly World War II spread all around the world.

Within thirteen days of his election, President Kremer celebrated his sixty-sixth birthday. Retirement, therefore, rather than election to a position of greater responsibility, might well have pleased him more. He began his term as President at a time when the international situation added enormously to the problems of the Company, and many years were to pass before he permitted himself to retire. Fortunately, he was aided from the moment he assumed his new office by James L. Thomson, who was Vice-President and Chairman of the Finance Committee. Mr. Thomson was a person of great executive capacity as well as unusual

CHARLES S. KREMER
President, 1941-1953

financial understanding, and important contributions that are traceable directly to him played an influential part in the Hartford's progress throughout President Kremer's administration.

Meanwhile, problems arising from the war influenced much of the thought and action of the entire world. The enormous and constantly increasing demand for war supplies resulted in a rapid increase in the cost of production of everything. Wages rose. Taxes climbed. Shortages became more and more apparent as factories that were normally engaged in the production of consumer goods suspended their usual activities and devoted their facilities to war production.

Even before Pearl Harbor the enlargement of manufacturing plants that were giving their attention to war needs, and the rapid increase in their value, had added greatly to the problems confronting the insurance companies of America. With the entrance of the nation into the war these problems grew. Even during World War I the problems that had arisen from developments such as these had been enormous, but early in World War II they far surpassed what had occurred during the earlier struggle.

Insurable values grew to immense size. Factories and other installations valued at fifty or seventy-five million dollars were reasonably common, and others reached or surpassed a hundred million. And all of these, potentially, were susceptible to "war damage" which normally is not covered by insurance. Even before Pearl Harbor the need for protection against war damage became apparent. So, after a series of conferences held by Government representatives and insurance leaders, the War Damage Corporation was organized. Though the Government assumed the greater share financially, the insurance companies played an important part in this organization and provided most of the "know-how" for its operation.

The part played by the insurance companies of the United States during World War II is a story in itself. Though all of them continued to administer their own affairs as best they could, and most were highly successful in doing so, they also collaborated most willingly and efficiently in protecting the interests of the nation. At a time when the uniformed forces required the services of millions of men and women, and every factory was confronted by serious shortages of labor, the insurance companies, despite the added duties they assumed, saw thousands of their employees, among whom many were of the very best, enter the various armed services in order to play their parts in the army, the navy, and the air force in every corner of the world.

Great though the contributions of the insurance companies were—and all of them, like the Hartford, are properly proud of what they were able to accomplish—it was their *collective* and not their *individual* effort that contributed most importantly to the nation's war effort and to victory. On that account, and in sincere admiration for the eager wartime collaboration of its peacetime competitors, the Hartford is inclined to view the part it played during the war more as a part of the industry's contribution than specifically as its own.

In a tangle as complicated as that created by World War II it was quite impossible for any portion of the troubled world to return to normal without an effort. Soldiers could stop fighting once the order to cease firing was given, but national activities long geared to war could be redirected into the activities of peace only after a long period of effort. Thus 1945, even after the surrender of the Germans in May and of the Japanese in August, contributed little to the actual reversion of the one-time belligerents to the activities of peace. By 1946, however, peace and the activities of peace were more apparent; and, so far as the Hartford was concerned, new plans—even a new atmosphere—were in evidence.

Indeed, the end of the war ushered in a new period in the economic development of the nation—and even, in a way, of a large portion of the world. From 1929 to 1945 little had been normal. It is true that despite the problems and difficulties that confronted the Hartford during these sixteen years, the progress that had been made was remarkable. Nevertheless, there had been difficulties of great magnitude, one of which threatened for a time to bring about so vast a change in long-established insurance methods as to threaten the future of the industry.

It will be remembered that the Supreme Court of the United States, in a decision handed down shortly after the Civil War, had unanimously held that insurance was *not* a part of interstate commerce and, therefore, that it was properly regulated by state and not by Federal law. As a result of this decision, which remained unquestioned for three quarters of a century, the entire insurance industry had developed with that decision in mind, and had assumed that that question had been answered for all time.

In 1944, however, in a case known as the United States of America vs. The Southeastern Underwriters Association, the Supreme Court handed down a decision that threw the insurance industry into a furor.

Justice Hugo Black wrote the opinion. Justices Reed and Roberts had disqualified themselves so, in effect, the case was heard by a Supreme Court made up of only seven members, two of whom—Justices Stone and Frankfurter—dissented, while Justice Jackson dissented in part.

Insofar as the decision is pertinent to the account given here, it read as follows:

> No commercial enterprise of any kind which conducts its activities across state lines has been held to be wholly beyond the regulatory power of Congress under the Commerce Clause. We cannot make an exception of the business of insurance.

But three quarters of a century earlier, in a decision handed down in the case of Paul vs. Virginia, this very court had expressed itself in these words:

> These contracts* are not articles of commerce in any proper meaning of the word. . . . They are not commodities to be shipped or forwarded from one State to another, and then put up for sale. They are like other personal contracts between parties which are completed by their signature and the transfer of the consideration. Such contracts are not inter-state transactions, though the parties may be domiciled in different states.

For seventy-five years every insurance company in the United States had accepted this earlier decision as the law of the land, and every conceivable angle of insurance, insofar as it was affected by law, was based on this interpretation. But under the 1944 decision the older concept, despite the many years during which it had never been seriously questioned, was suddenly—and most unexpectedly—reversed. As a result, legal difficulties that were beyond calculation potentially stared every insurance company in the face.

In an effort to eliminate the difficulty that had arisen, the insurance industry explained to Congress the complex problems that had been cre-

* i.e., insurance contracts.

ated by the decision, and sought an amendment to the antitrust laws that would grant an exemption from them and would permit a continuation of the concerted action which had for so long been permitted under the earlier decision. Congress seriously considered the matter, but instead of granting an outright exemption, the McCarran Act was written and adopted, thus permitting concerted action on the part of the insurance companies *to the extent that it was regulated by state law.*

With this much accomplished, the insurance industry, at the request and under the direction of the National Association of Insurance Commissioners, prepared what is known as the "All-Industry Bill," and recommended it to the various states as a model regulatory law under which regulation of the business would remain with the states. This has been pretty generally adopted by the states, either verbatim or in its essential parts, and under it the following is permissible:

RATING
    a. Official licensing of and rate-making by rating organizations.
    b. The use of uniform rates by companies.
ADVISORY SERVICE
    c. The creation and operation of organizations designed to furnish statistics or other information to rating organizations; namely, to advise them.
UNDERWRITING
    d. Joint underwriting and joint reinsurance pools.

For a time the insurance industry had been deeply concerned for its future. Fortunately, however, a solution had been found that enabled the industry to continue to play the important part for which, throughout its long existence, it had been trained—a part that was to become, in the years immediately ahead, far greater than it had ever been before.

CHAPTER 20

DEPARTMENTS,

AGENTS,

AND EXECUTIVES

UNLIKE many of its competitors the Hartford has never been inclined to concentrate control in its Home Office. Company policy has always emanated from there, of course, but for the most part the various departmental offices have always been remarkably independent. This very largely explains the ability of the departments to develop executives of unusual ability.

The first department, of course, was the Eastern Department though interestingly enough it did not receive that title until as recently as 1952, when it was formally organized under the management of Vice-President Arthur L. Polley.

Up until that time management of the Eastern states—New England, New York, New Jersey, Pennsylvania, Delaware, and the District of Columbia—was handled as an adjunct to Home Office affairs.

The history of the Eastern Department then is to a great degree interwoven with all Hartford history—from Nathaniel Terry to the present—wherever it was made.

The Western Department of the Hartford was established, as we have seen, in 1852 with headquarters in Columbus, Ohio. The Western Department office was moved to Chicago in 1863 with George F. Bissell as General Agent. Though Mr. Bissell, who served in that position until

1895, was never called upon to serve the Company in any higher capacity, he was an unusually able official and it was he who suggested his assistant, George L. Chase, for the Presidency in 1867. Furthermore, Richard M. Bissell, one of the outstanding insurance executives of America during and after World War I, was not only the son of General Agent Bissell but was also a product of the Chicago office where he obtained his early training and came to be Associate General Agent before being appointed Vice-President and called to Hartford in 1903.

George L. Chase was one of the most dramatic of those who, after having obtained their training and earliest promotions in the Western Department, were called upon to occupy higher positions with the Company, for he stepped directly into the Presidency from a secondary position in the Western Department. But there have been others. Philander C. Royce, for example, went from the Western Department to Hartford where he served as Secretary of the Company from 1886 to 1907. J. W. G. Cofran, too, after serving as Associate General Agent of the Western Department was called to Hartford in 1909. And there have been others, as will later appear.

A. G. Dugan and John H. Carr of the firm of Dugan & Carr were Associate General Agents from 1910 to 1923. Business grew rapidly and when the death of John Carr brought the firm of Dugan & Carr to an end in 1923, A. G. Dugan was appointed General Agent in charge of the Department.

During the 1920's the Western Department expanded its business and increased the number of its employees in much the same way that the Home Office and the other Departments did. Where General Agent Bissell and his immediate successors had had only a handful of clerks and assistants to aid them in the management of the Department's affairs, Dugan & Carr had 83 employees, and under General Agent Dugan's supervision during the expansive 1920's, the number greatly increased.

Like so many other Western Department executives, General Agent Dugan was an exceptionally competent insurance man, and his ability to choose and gain the enthusiastic support of able assistants was outstanding. Having served under R. M. Bissell and J. W. G. Cofran, both of whom had later been called to Hartford, he was thoroughly trained, and he was also a man of great understanding. It is true that sometimes he gave the impression of being distant and hard to approach, and he was inclined to be uncompromising when matters of principle were involved. Nevertheless, he knew the members of his office force better than many of them thought he did, and he was always willing to come to the support of agents and subordinates when he felt that they were right. It was this, perhaps, as much as anything, that made it possible for the Western Department to increase its premium income by some eight hundred per cent during the period of his management—an increase, incidentally, that benefited Mr. Dugan as well as the Company for, as General Agent, he participated in the profits. He was the last Department head to do so, and even the title he bore lapsed when he retired.

The loyalties that were apparent during his period of service in the Western Department were strong, and a story told by Philip S. Beebe, who not only served under Mr. Dugan but who also later became Manager of the Western Department, tells something of the character of the former General Agent and may also give the uninitiated a new idea of the deeply ingrained honesty and sense of responsibility of a great fire insurance company.

In 1920, shortly after Mr. Beebe joined the Service Department of the Hartford Fire Insurance Company in Columbus, Ohio, an elderly and obviously troubled agent from a small Ohio town came in to see him. The caller had been in Columbus for some time, so he said, in order to be near his wife who had been brought to a Columbus hospital for serious surgical treatment. Under the circumstances, he had paid no attention whatever to his business since he left home, but now he had learned that due to his absence from his office and his consequent oversight, the Hartford fire insurance policy on the Masonic Lodge in the town from which he came—a policy that he had always theretofore regularly renewed—had expired. And, worse still, subsequent to the expiration of the policy, the building had burned and was a total loss.

It was entirely natural for Mr. Beebe to sympathize with the deeply troubled agent, but he had been with the Company only a short time, his experience was limited, and he was far from confident that he knew how the Company would view such a situation. Consequently, Mr. Beebe decided to call Mr. Dugan in Chicago.

No record remains to tell just how he began his explanation when he finally got the General Agent of the Western Department on the phone, and Mr. Dugan's short questions and long silences gave the impression that he was unsympathetic. But after the situation was fully explained, Mr. Dugan spoke.

"I understand," he said, in effect. "Evidently you haven't been told what the attitude of the Company is in such cases. Tell your man not to worry. And tell him that there's only one thing to do. Have him make out a policy and date it back to the expiration date of the former policy. Once the loss has been settled, a draft must be issued for the amount of the loss—up to the amount of the expired policy. Then attach the policy to the proof, and the loss will be paid in the usual manner."

"It was an episode," Mr. Beebe remarked many years later, "that made a profound impression upon me, indicating as it did the attitude of the officials of our Company."

It must also have made a profound impression upon the elderly and troubled agent who, it can hardly be doubted, was a better and a more enthusiastic representative of the Hartford as a result.

C. H. Smith and C. E. Wheeler were made Associate General Agents of the Western Department in 1938 and L. G. Warder and James T. Leavitt were appointed Associate Managers at the same time.

In 1944, Associate General Agent C. H. Smith was elected Vice-President of the Hartford Fire Insurance Company and in 1945 he became sole Manager of the Western Department upon Mr. Wheeler's retirement.

C. H. Smith left a vivid and indelible impression on all who worked with him. His integrity and intelligence led him naturally and surely to the high honors and responsibilities which his Company and industry bestowed upon him. But to name the great number of official industry posts he held might be to detract from his most significant contribution—advisor and counselor to all who sought him out.

Mr. Smith was a man of varied interests. He was a keen student of the Civil War—even an authority—and made numerous pilgrimages to battlefields where he would plot out the course of a battle from his wide store of knowledge, his books and maps. On the purely recreational side, he was an avid baseball fan with a great fund of anecdotes and lore regarding the national pastime.

During his forty-three-year career with the Hartford, Mr. Smith saw the Western Department grow from a staff of less than a hundred in modest quarters on Chicago's La Salle Street to one with over eight hundred employees occupying the equivalent of five floors in the Wrigley Building.

In February 1953, C. H. Smith died. He was active to the last after a full day in the office.

Philip S. Beebe, having been made Associate Manager in the summer of 1947, succeeded Mr. Smith as Manager.

The department which Mr. Smith supervised and which Mr. Beebe inherited was a gigantic one covering twenty states stretching from Colorado to West Virginia, from North Dakota to Oklahoma. Taken by itself the Western Department of the Hartford constituted one of the largest insurance organizations in the country. It embraced over 9,000 agents when, in recent years, it became the foundation on which three new departments were built.

As has already been recorded, the Pacific Department was founded with headquarters in San Francisco in 1870 with Augustus P. Flint and Porter Heywood as General Agents. Mr. Heywood transferred to Chicago in 1872 and Augustus Flint remained in San Francisco as General Agent until 1885. At that point the firm of Belden & Cofran became the new General Agents of the Department and a great period of expansion took place. Mr. Cofran transferred to the Western Department in 1895 and a new partnership, this one of Henry Belden and Whitney Palache, was formed and they served the Company as Associate General Agents. A year later Mr. Belden died and Dixwell Hewitt joined Mr. Palache to form the firm of Palache and Hewitt, which then handled Pacific Department business for the Hartford.

In 1913 Mr. Palache was called to the Hartford as Vice-President of the Company and Mr. Hewitt continued as head of the Pacific Department until his retirement in 1924.

Joy Lichtenstein, a graduate of the University of California who had been Assistant City Librarian in San Francisco at the time of the earthquake and fire of 1906, joined the Pacific Department as Pacific Coast Manager of the Hartford Accident and Indemnity Company in 1914. Because of the destruction of the library in 1906 he had been forced to look about for other work and had entered the insurance business, holding various positions prior to his association with the Hartford. Now, following the retirement of Dixwell Hewitt, Mr. Lichtenstein succeeded him as General Manager of the Pacific Department in which both the

Hartford Fire Insurance Company and the Hartford Accident and Indemnity Company were represented.

Though the Pacific Department had only thirty-eight employees during the difficult period that followed the earthquake and fire of 1906, it had grown so greatly by the time Joy Lichtenstein became General Manager that new and larger offices were necessary. Consequently, at a meeting of the Company's Board of Directors in Hartford on June 12, 1925, a resolution was adopted authorizing the expenditure of $76,000 for a plot of ground on California Street in San Francisco and the Directors also agreed to the erection there of a new Pacific Department office building, the cost of which was not to exceed $300,000. Erected the following year, this building was later enlarged and, within twenty-five years of the time its cornerstone was laid, the Pacific Department had grown far more than in all the previous years of its existence.

Joy Lichtenstein retired on January 1, 1946. Addison C. Posey, Vice-President of the Hartford Accident and Indemnity Company, was chosen to succeed Mr. Lichtenstein and on the day of his predecessor's retirement he assumed his duties as Manager of the Pacific Department. Having been with the department for twenty-one years, he was well acquainted with its problems, and the development of this territory—California, Oregon, Washington, Arizona, Utah, Idaho, Montana, Nevada, Alaska, and Hawaii—from the close of the war to the current date of writing has taken place under his direction.

The Southern Department of the Hartford was organized in Atlanta, Georgia, in 1906 with the firm of Egleston & Prescott as Associate General Agents. The states included in the department were Georgia, North Carolina, South Carolina, Virginia, Florida, Alabama, Mississippi, and Louisiana. Following the death in 1916 of John B. Herford, General Agent of the Hartford for Texas, that department was transferred and consolidated with the Southern Department. When Thomas Egleston passed away in February 1916, Mr. Prescott was appointed General Agent—a position he retained (though his title was changed to Manager) until his death in 1953.

During his career with the Hartford, Mr. Prescott became a towering figure in the insurance industry in the Southeast and a respected leader. With his hand at the Hartford Fire tiller, the Southern Department experienced its greatest growth.

Few men in the insurance business have been as admired by competitors and beloved by associates.

Hartford staff members and their families in the South still enjoy, during week ends and vacations, the facilities of Prescott Lodge, a lakeside retreat in the mountains of northeast Georgia. Mr. Prescott gave the lodge for the use of Southern Department employees and their families.

In his will, Thomas Egleston had left funds to establish the Henrietta Egleston Hospital for Children in Atlanta, in memory of his mother. As executor under the will, Mr. Prescott was instrumental in bringing his partner's wish to fruition. After the hospital was built in 1928, Mr. Prescott was chairman of its board of trustees for more than twenty years.

It is worth recording that when the first "fireproof" building to be built in Atlanta was completed in 1891, the Hartford Fire Insurance Company and the local agency of Perdue & Egleston were its first tenants. In fact, they moved into Room No. 201 before the building was quite completed. This was long before the Hartford's Southern Department was organized, and Thomas Egleston was then the General Agent for the Hartford, though his office, which also housed the Hartford Fire Insurance Company and the Perdue & Egleston Agency, consisted of only a single room—an electric-lighted room, it is true, for this was an up-to-date building. But otherwise the office was a simple one which contained a centrally located table, three roll-top desks, five chairs, and a couple of closets, one of which, built of paneled wood and standing some seven or eight feet high, contained the office files, though it looked more like a mid-Victorian wardrobe than anything else.

Soon the Hartford came to need much more space than that first room provided. This was especially true after the organization of the Southern Department. But the Equitable Building into which the Company had moved in 1891 had somehow succeeded in becoming a kind of center for insurance headquarters in Atlanta and, in addition, it had successfully withstood the structural and architectural deterioration that causes many buildings to decline. It changed its name, it is true, and came to be known as The Trust Company of Georgia Building, but otherwise, by way of frequent rearrangements, renewals, refurbishings, and even redesign and reconstruction, it kept pace with the times. Even after the passage of more than threescore years, during which the Hartford's office expanded from a single room to two full floors, the building retained its up-to-the-minute atmosphere; and when the Southern Department was organized it remained at the same address.

If mention is made of "conscience money," with which all insurance companies are familiar, someone in the Atlanta office is likely to tell how Charles Briscoe, the trusted and likeable man who formerly handled the incoming and outgoing mail, came hurrying up to the Office Manager one pleasant January morning in 1945 and, obviously much perturbed, thrust an envelope into his hand. It had been postmarked at Orlando, Florida, the day before but bore no return address, and when the Office Manager glanced inside, he was surprised to see, in addition to a couple of lines of writing on a plain piece of paper, a Federal note for $500.00 and two others for $1,000.000 each.

"What's this, Charley?" he asked.

"I don't know, sir," Charley replied. "I just opened it and saw that money, and I was in a hurry to turn it over to somebody else. I never *did* have that much money in my hands before."

It was only then that the Office Manager read the concise communication that was enclosed.

"Gentlemen:" it read. "Please accept the enclosed as restitution of funds paid out by you unjustly.

(*Signed*) "Thanks"

Such incidents not infrequently occur in the departments of the Company and, as is very often the case when "conscience money" is concerned, the office never learned whose conscience had been at work. Thus it was impossible to connect the amount that had been refunded with any specific payment the Company had made. Obviously, some "loss" had been paid when it had not really been due, and it had been returned because someone's conscience hurt him. But Charley Briscoe's didn't, for he, trustworthy person that he was, had no sooner seen all that money than he had been "in a hurry to turn it over to somebody else."

W. R. Prescott, Manager of the Southern Department since 1916, had celebrated his fiftieth anniversary with the Hartford in 1951. Two years later, still Manager of the Department, he died.

John H. Ledbetter, who had been with the department since 1915 and Associate Manager since 1939, was appointed Manager shortly after Mr. Prescott's death. Mr. Ledbetter had been extremely active in the development of the Southern Department during the years that he served as Associate Manager and played an important part in the department's progress during that period.

As the war reached its end, Mr. Prescott passed his 78th birthday and, though he continued as Manager until his death at 86, it was natural that Mr. Ledbetter should assume an increasing share of departmental responsibilities. When he finally became Manager, therefore, his responsibilities changed far less than did his title.

The Hartford Fire Insurance Company established its first Canadian agency in 1836. However, no Chief Agent was appointed for the Dominion until 1876. It was then that the Canadian Insurance Department issued what appears to have been its first published report, and in it Robert Wood of Montreal is listed as the Hartford's Chief Agent. The Company's income from premiums in Canada that year was $78,207, and its total assets, in Canada and the United States, were reported as being somewhat in excess of three million. In 1880 Chief Agent Wood became a member of the firm of Wood & Evans and the two partners acted as Chief Agents for the Company until late in 1891 when the Hartford's Head Office for Canada was moved to Toronto and Peter A. McCallum was appointed Chief Agent and Manager.

So far as is known, Peter McCallum was connected with the Company only as an independent agent prior to this appointment, and the record he established remains unique. From the moment he first came to be directly associated with the Company he held the Hartford's highest post in Canada, and he retained that position throughout forty busy years.

In the four decades during which he served the Company, Chief Agent McCallum became an outstanding figure in the field of Canadian insurance. During his long connection with the Company the whole business of insurance underwent great changes. Beginning when the Government's statistical requirements were of the simplest, and when the office he headed was engaged only in a straight fire insurance business that brought in an annual premium income of less than a hundred and fifty thousand dollars, he saw the Company develop into an important group of companies, whose multiple lines of insurance brought about a great expansion of income under constantly increasing governmental requirements.

As the Hartford's Chief Agent for all of Canada, Peter McCallum had certain Company responsibilities for all the Provinces, but in the matter of annual statements and other Federal and Provincial requirements, his responsibilities were originally limited to the Provinces of Ontario and Quebec. In the late 1920's, however, the Provinces of Manitoba, Saskatchewan, and Alberta which, up to that time, had reported through the W. W. Scrimes Agency to the Western Department in Chicago, were taken over by the Toronto office, as were also New Brunswick, Prince Edward Island, Nova Scotia, Newfoundland, and British Columbia.

In 1904, following the great fire that devastated Toronto in that year, it was Peter McCallum who was chosen to act as chairman of the committee of underwriters that handled the adjustment of the losses. It was a heavy task and he carried it to successful completion, but his health suffered as a result. He recovered, fortunately, and continued as Chief Agent for the Hartford in Canada until 1932 when he died suddenly in his 74th year while on a vacation at Virginia Beach.

Those who knew him remember him not only as one of the outstanding figures in the field of Canadian insurance, but also as an executive far ahead of his time, especially in staff relations.

"It was typical of him," a former associate has written, "that he provided in his will the sum of $100 for each member of his staff."

For many years the Hartford's Head Office for Canada was at 27 Wellington Street, East, in Toronto, but in 1916 it was moved to the London Mutual Building at 24 Wellington, East. In January 1923 the Hartford acquired the London Mutual Fire Insurance Company.

Following this purchase, the London Mutual ceased writing under the mutual system and on June 12, 1925, as the result of a petition, "His Majesty, by and with the advice and consent of the Senate and House of Commons of Canada," changed the name of the London Mutual to London-Canada Insurance Company.

Peter McCallum was still Chief Agent when the London Mutual became a subsidiary of the Hartford, and he continued in that position until his death in 1932. B. W. Ballard, who succeeded him, had served not only as Assistant Chief Agent since 1920, but also as Assistant General Agent for Canada of the Hartford Accident and Indemnity Company.

For the next eighteen years—from 1932 to 1950—Chief Agent Ballard was not only in charge of the Hartford Head Office in Toronto but was also responsible for the Company's other Canadian interests, including the London-Canada Insurance Company. In 1950, H. Douglas Coo, after eight years as Assistant Manager of the Toronto Office, succeeded Mr. Ballard as Chief Agent, and was also elected President and Managing Director of the London-Canada.

In the many years since the Hartford appointed its first agent in Canada, its Canadian representatives have been fully as active in the development of new ideas as their counterparts south of the border. When automatic sprinkler systems were first introduced sometime in the 1880's, for example, Canadians, like many of their neighbors in the United States, were slow to install them; and the Toronto office, in urging their use, played a part in acquainting their clients with them and, as a result, in reducing the cost of fire insurance. Unfortunately, however, sprinklers, which are not proof against accidents, sometimes go into action when they shouldn't and damage property they otherwise effectively protect. On that account it is wise for those who have protected their property and reduced their fire insurance premiums by the installation of this type of automatic equipment, to go a step further and take out insurance, the cost of which is small, against the improper action of the sprinklers themselves.

At the turn of the century, before this kind of insurance had been developed, E. L. McLean, an especially well-informed Hartford agent in Toronto, saw the need for it. He gave the matter much thought but was uncertain as to how such policies might be written or what the rates should be.

With this in mind, he decided to visit Hartford and, as a result, the Sprinkler Leakage Policy was evolved. Furthermore, when Mr. McLean retired many years later, he liked to recall that when the first such policy was issued at the Home Office in Hartford, it "covered on a risk" in Toronto.

The Hartford's growth in Canada has been significant. Today there are 2700 Hartford agents and 300 Company employees serving the insurance needs of Canadian citizens.

Space does not permit us to cover all the skills necessary to operate a present-day insurance company or departmental office. There are representatives of practically every vocation: engineers, accountants, actuaries, lawyers, writers, doctors, teachers, artists, printers, and many more. These numerous professions and the parts they play in the operation of a company would make a book within itself. However, there is one job unique to the insurance industry that is worthy of mention especially since it played a great part in the establishing of an agent of the Hartford in practically every town and village in the United States. This is the job of Special Agent.

When the Hartford was young and small, Company officers traveled to various parts of the country appointing agents for the Company. However, as the Company and the country both grew, this proved too great a task for the few officers, especially since their duties in the Home Office were demanding more and more of their time. As we have seen, this led to the establishment of departmental offices—at first under the supervision of a General Agent or Chief Agent as he was sometimes called. Usually these departmental offices consisted of the General Agent and a few clerks. The General Agents were granted the authority to appoint agents and they traveled throughout their territory appointing agents and conducting the affairs of the Company. Here again, as the departmental offices grew the General Agents found, as the officers of the Company had, that their time was more and more taken up with important duties in the office and that therefore they must further delegate the authority given them. Thus the job of Special Agent was created. The Special Agent's primary duty was to travel the territory assigned him, appointing and closing agencies and conducting the affairs of the Company on the local scene. For many agents this was the only personal contact they had with the Company.

The first Special Agents for the Company traveled very sizable territories and their travels often kept them away from home for months at a time. Travel was by railroad or a rented horse and buggy from the local livery stable. Dress in those days was not so informal as today. Old-time Special Agents tell of shipping their trunks on ahead with practically all their clothing, including full dress, for they never knew when they would be required to attend formal functions. They would usually establish their headquarters in a town which provided hotel facilities, visiting the surrounding villages in a rented rig. When it was necessary to remain overnight in a village without other accommodations they would stay at the home of the local agent for the Company.

In those days the Special Agent would rate the various risks on which the local agent desired to write insurance and often adjust losses. It was not uncommon, therefore, for him to remain in one town for a week or two before packing up his trunk and moving on to the next town and there again establish his headquarters. These men over the years created a close personal relationship between the Company and its agents.

With today's excellent highways, Special Agents travel mainly by automobile. Their territories are much smaller since agents are more numerous and the complexities of the business require more frequent visits than the annual or semiannual visits of years ago. No longer are Special Agents required to rate individual risks, as this is done by the Rating Bureaus. However, they continue to inspect and evaluate properties insured by the local agent. Losses are now handled through Company and Bureau adjusters located in the immediate vicinity so that they can provide prompt adjustment of claims. With the development of casualty insurance and surety bonds it has been necessary for the Special Agents to specialize, as no one individual could expect to be an expert technician in all types of insurance. Today there are Fire Special Agents, Casualty Special Agents, Bond Special Agents, Inland Marine Special Agents, and more besides. However, even though his job has changed, the Special Agent still serves, as he always has, as a close personal contact between the Company and its far-flung system of local agencies.

There are, in all, about 34,000 of these local agents, and all of them are independent businessmen. Their success is based, at least in part, on the Hartford's long-time recognition of the fact that "expirations belong to the agents." The New York Underwriters Agency was one of the first to insist that this right be recognized, and the Hartford was quick to follow, with other companies rapidly falling into line. From the point of view of the agents, this "ownership of expirations" is vital. Though these 34,000 agents represent the Hartford and its subsidiaries, most of them also represent other insurance companies as well. Many of these agencies have been in operation for generations, and some for a century or more. They are not only highly successful businesses, but more than a few have fascinating histories of their own. Among these agencies some have played important parts not only in the development of the Hartford and other insurance companies, but also in the development of the communities in which they operate and the nation of which they are a part.

The story of the Hartford would be incomplete without an acknowledgment of the invaluable contributions that agents and agencies have made to the Company's development and growth. And it is not the Hartford alone, or even just the insurance industry, that has benefited. To a greater extent than most of us are apt to realize, insurance agents, as they go their daily round, step well outside the specific field in which they operate and contribute to the general welfare in ways that bring them much satisfaction.

The many years—even the many generations—through which large numbers of agencies have served, is proof of the fact that worth-while opportunities are available to those who enter this field. Furthermore, the fact that such large numbers of men find both economic opportunities and personal satisfaction in agency work, is demonstrated by the number who serve as agents throughout all their working years. In this connection it should be noted that Richard M. Bissell, while still a Vice-President of the Hartford in 1910, succeeded in establishing the Hartford Distinguished Service Medal, which is given to those who have served the Hartford with distinction for fifty consecutive years.

CHAPTER 21

CONSOLIDATION

AND

BUILDING FOR THE FUTURE

THE SUSPENSION of hostilities in 1945 marked the beginning of a promising new era. For sixteen years every corner of the globe had been confronted by difficulties, many of which had been without parallel in the history of the modern world, and the return of peace brought with it a confident belief that better times lay ahead.

So far as the story of the Hartford is concerned, the fifteen years between the end of World War II and the one-hundred-and-fiftieth anniversary of the Company's founding may be divided into two almost equal parts. The first of these covers the last eight years of President Kremer's administration. The second covers the first seven years of the administration of his successor.

At the time the Japanese surrendered in 1945, President Kremer came face to face with the different but often equally difficult problems of the postwar period. The Company had lost a number of its more important elders and, entering upon a period of great expansion, it began to elevate many of its younger executives to positions of greater importance.

Writing in 1945 just after the war had been concluded, President Kremer had this to say:

> It will take the best abilities we can muster to solve the new problems successfully. . . . The business is in good standing with the public.

In general it has done its duty by its policyholders and it will continue
to do so. . . . We feel, therefore, that we can all look forward now
with hope of even greater accomplishment . . . than ever before.

Written by a man who had just seen his Company through four years
of the greatest and most costly war in the history of the world, this had
a little of the ring of prophecy about it—prophecy that even he was to
see fulfilled before passing his responsibilities on to his successor.

With the return of peace, business confidence returned as well, and
business conditions in the United States improved so greatly as actually
to surpass the formerly unequaled predepression days. Although President Kremer's administration was marked by few outstanding innova-
tions in the industry, the growth in the Company's business and that of
its subsidiaries was remarkable. As has already been pointed out, the
premium income of the Hartford Fire Insurance Company for 1939, the
year the war began, was almost 38 million dollars. In 1953, however,
premiums surpassed 149 million—an increase of about 338 per cent. During this period, the Company's total assets had more than doubled and
its surplus as regards policyholders had increased by more than eighty
per cent.

Throughout these years the Company's subsidiaries were still growing. Of these, the Hartford Accident and Indemnity had made by far the
most significant progress. Founded in 1913, it was a comparative young-
ster in the industry but its rapid strides—attributable at least in part to
the reputation of its parent—had already brought it to a position of major
importance in the industry.

In 1934, recognizing that the Hartford Accident and Indemnity
Company had "come of age" and seeing "the need for an executive group
that would collaborate constantly in the work of maintaining the administration and operation of the Company on a plane of high efficiency," R.
M. Bissell moved into the position of Chairman of that Company's Board
of Directors. Mr. James L. D. Kearney became President of the Casualty
Company with Paul Rutherford, Vice-President and General Manager.
In 1937, when Mr. Kearney's health forced him to resign, Mr. Rutherford succeeded him. By 1953, when Wilson C. Jainsen became President,
the assets of the Hartford Accident and Indemnity Company stood at
$304,000,000. Come of age, indeed! With the Hartford Fire it formed a
formidable well-balanced combination that few other insurance organizations could match.

During a period that was marked by so great an increase in business, it goes almost without saying that the number of the Company's employees grew by leaps and bounds. The Home Office in Hartford was enlarged in 1948 by the addition of a wing that alone accommodated some seven hundred employees.

In Chicago, the great increase in the business of the Western Department of the Fire Companies also necessitated an increase in staff. In 1944 the Department's premium income had been about $16,000,000 and ten years later, when the figure stood at $43,000,000, only a handful of competing insurance companies in the United States were doing more business than the Hartford's Western Department alone. With some 9,400 agents in the area it controlled, it is not surprising that within a decade of the end of the war the Western Department of the Fire Companies alone required the services of over a thousand employees.

The Pacific Department was also growing. As 1950 approached there were more than a thousand Fire and Casualty employees, and a little later the Department employed 1,040 merely in the State of California. Though a new headquarters building in San Francisco had been completed just before the depression, the number of employees grew so rapidly in the years that immediately followed the war that in 1950 the structure had to be almost doubled in size.

The business of the Canadian Department was similarly expanding. By 1950, new and larger offices were opened in Toronto, and branch offices in Montreal, Quebec, and Winnipeg, as well as service offices in Ottawa and Calgary, were also growing.

In Atlanta, where W. R. Prescott was about to celebrate his fiftieth year with the Company, the Southern Department was enlarging its business, keeping pace with its sister Departments.

Growth on such a scale naturally necessitated an increase in the number of executives. This was true not only of the Hartford itself, but of its subsidiaries, and at almost every executive level. Throughout the 1930's, age rather than youth had been apparent among the Company's Directors and most important officials. But these Company elders were a sturdy lot and they remained at their posts during the war. When the nation's military needs had called millions of young men from their normal activities, large numbers of the nation's older citizens willingly stepped into the breach. In the Hartford as well as other companies, once the war was over, the toll among the older ones was heavy and younger men began to be called upon to step into new and higher posts or to take over posts from which older men had been removed by the remorseless passage of time.

President Kremer continued as the Company's chief executive officer for eight more years after the war. During his administration difficult problems had faced the industry and, as President of one of the nation's greatest insurance companies, he was called upon to lead in the solution of many of them. The Supreme Court decision which, for a time, had threatened the position of the insurance companies, had had to be considered. Inflation, manpower shortages, difficulties that had arisen in the field of automobile insurance, and more besides had created an almost endless series of problems to which he had had to give his attention. As the Company's chief executive, he had also been called upon to play an important part in the selection and promotion of younger men, numbers of whom throughout the postwar years had to be added to the Company's executive staff.

In 1944 James C. Hullett, a young man from the Western Department, had been brought to Hartford as a Vice-President. A Kentuckian by birth, his first experience in the field of insurance had been as a part-time office boy, working during the summers and after school for the insurance agency of Herdman & Stout in his home town of Bowling Green. This agency, which, incidentally, represented the Hartford Fire Insurance Company, is now known as the Charles M. Moore Agency though it still bore its original name while James Hullett was its office boy.

After several years of part-time work in this office, the boy completed high school and then attended Western Kentucky State Teachers College for two years. Insurance, however, still interested him and, after learning of the newly developed insurance course that had been introduced at Northwestern University and was supported by stock fire insurance companies, he was offered a scholarship by the Hartford Fire Insurance Company in 1929. The appointment also provided part-time work at the headquarters of the Hartford's Western Department.

For the following fifteen years he continued with the Western Department. Having completed the insurance course at Northwestern University he was able to make good progress with the Company. After starting with the underwriting department, where he remained four years, he next went to Oklahoma as Special Agent. Serving there from

J. C. HULLETT
President, 1953

1933 to 1936, he was married in the latter year to Patricia O'Sullivan of Oklahoma City and was transferred to Ohio where he supervised the Company's field activities in the northwestern section of the State until 1940. While engaged in this work he set an exceptional record as Special Agent, and was consequently called back to Chicago where he was made Assistant Manager of the Western Department in 1941—a somewhat exceptional position for a young man of 31. There, however, he succeeded so well in solving the problems that came to his desk that three years later—in 1944—he was elected Vice-President of the Hartford Fire Insurance Company and was called to the Home Office in Hartford.

In the nine years that followed, Vice-President Hullett's responsibilities constantly grew broader. How much of this was of his own seeking, and how much was due to the willingness of his seniors to thrust new tasks upon him, does not appear. Though he is apt at demonstrating his ability in many different ways, he usually does so by accomplishing the tasks that are set before him, and not by *promising* to do so.

Though only thirty-four when he was made Vice-President, he was soon representing the Company on many important committees. He became Chairman of the Committee on Laws of the National Board of Fire Underwriters, and Chairman of the Executive Committee of the Factory Insurance Association. He was made a member of the Board of Directors of the General Adjustment Bureau, Vice-Chairman of the Executive Committee of the National Insurance Service and Advisory Organization, a member of the Executive Committee of the Interbureau Insurance Advisory Group, a member of the Actuarial Bureau Committee of the National Board of Fire Underwriters, and of other organizations as well. Furthermore, he served from time to time as a member, and often as chairman, of special committees of many kinds.

On February 26, 1953, Charles D. Kremer, after twelve years as President of the Hartford, was elected Chairman of the Board of Directors. But the Directors were not content with this one move. Once Mr. Kremer had been elected Chairman of the Board, they were faced with the necessity of electing someone to succeed him as President. Whatever discussion took place is not a matter of public record, but whatever was said obviously met no opposition, and Vice-President James C. Hullett at the age of 43 and after only nine years as a Home Office executive, was elected President of the Hartford Fire Insurance Company. At the same time he also succeeded his predecessor as President of four of the

Hartford subsidiaries—the Citizens Insurance Company of New Jersey, the New York Underwriters Company, the Hartford Live Stock Insurance Company, and the Twin City Fire Insurance Company—and was elected a member of the Board of Directors of the Hartford Fire Insurance Company and the Hartford Accident and Indemnity Company.

On July 19, Mr. Hullett was elected Chairman of the Finance Committees of the Hartford Fire Insurance Company and the Hartford Accident and Indemnity Company. Six years later, on July 14, 1959, he became President of the latter Company when Wilson C. Jainsen requested retirement.

As the business of insurance had begun to broaden, and as the Company's subsidiaries materialized, they had continued to operate with considerable independence. In New York, for example, the offices of the Hartford Fire Insurance Company were at 104 John Street for many years though those of the Hartford Accident and Indemnity Company were at 110 William Street and another subsidiary—the New York Underwriters Agency—had its offices at 90 John Street. These offices were entirely independent of each other and even when the Hartford Fire Insurance Company decided to move to 90 John Street, the offices it established there were still separated from those of the New York Underwriters.

In Chicago, where the consolidated offices of the Western Department headquarters are soon to occupy a handsome new office building across the Chicago River from the Union Station, a similar situation has long been in evidence. Though the Western Department's offices of the Hartford Fire Insurance Company have for years been in the Wrigley Building at 410 North Michigan Avenue, the Hartford Accident and Indemnity offices, under the direction of W. H. Rutherford, have long been the better part of two miles away in the Insurance Exchange Building at 175 West Jackson Boulevard.

It is true that the smaller subsidiaries—the Citizens Insurance Company of New Jersey and the Twin City Fire Insurance Company, for instance—have always been housed with the Hartford Fire, but until recently the Hartford Accident and Indemnity Company has maintained separate offices.

Early in its development the Hartford Accident and Indemnity Company had no reason to compete with Hartford Fire. Little by little, however, opportunities for competition arose. During the 1940's "multiple line underwriting laws" began to be enacted and insurance companies that had formerly been restricted to narrower fields were permitted to write both fire and casualty insurance.

Under these conditions, the two great Hartford Companies began to overlap in many areas. So when President Hullett first sat down at his new desk this was one of the problems that confronted him. Entirely convinced that geographic decentralization should be continued, he was equally certain that within the Hartford family competition and the separation of interests should give way to closer collaboration and even to consolidation. In the relationship between the Hartford's various associated companies, President Hullett believed that a change was necessary and, during his administration, a change has come. From coast to coast, he felt, they should work together and come to be known as the "Hartford Fire Insurance Company Group."

In this connection he expressed himself as follows in February 1957:

Until a few years ago the laws of the several states were such that a fire insurance company could only engage in the business of fire and allied lines insurance and, likewise, a casualty company was not permitted to do other than a casualty and surety business. Therefore, until the enactment of the so-called multiple line statutes it was necessary that a fire company which wished to engage in the casualty and surety business (or vice versa) organize a separate company in order to provide these additional facilities. It was this now removed legal barrier which in 1913 required that the Hartford Fire Insurance Company establish the Hartford Accident and Indemnity Company— in order to enter the casualty field. That it was a wise and timely action is amply attested by the success of the H. A. & I.—today one of the leading casualty companies in the industry. Its record, growth and pre-eminent position have more than proven the vision and wisdom of those who not only formed this new company, but also encouraged it to pursue a co-operative but, at the same time, somewhat independent course within the Group's sphere of activity. Over the years this method of operation has served us well and, therefore, we have been reluctant to change it. However, the broadened underwriting scope now available to fire, casualty and surety companies alike has brought about the intermingling of the traditional fire, casualty and surety perils under single contracts, and this development, in turn, makes necessary an internal adjustment if we are efficiently and effectively to cope with the problems that flow from these new trends. In other words—these changes in the structure of our business now compel a closer relationship between our several companies—not only as respects the production and servicing of the business, but also in order that we might keep ourselves fully competitive on the expense side of the ledger—where, in the opinion of many, the battle of the business will be won or lost.

While consolidation of the Companies was proceeding, the plan of geographic decentralization for greater local autonomy was also being pursued.

On February 6, 1957, announcement was made that a new Northwestern Department, with headquarters in Minneapolis, would supervise the business of all Companies in Iowa, Minnesota, Nebraska, North Dakota, South Dakota, and certain counties in northwest Wisconsin. Later, Colorado and Wyoming were to be added to this list of states all formerly under control of the immense Western Department. The new regional headquarters was set up under the management of C. W. Hall.

More developments followed in rapid succession. On April 11 of the same year, it was announced that offices of member companies of the Group in New York City would move together that autumn into a new building at 123 William Street. This office was organized as the New York Department, under the management of Benjamin F. Gates.

On March 1, 1958, the states of Texas, New Mexico, Oklahoma, Arkansas, and Louisiana were grouped into a new Southwestern Department, under the management of Paul A. Dow. These states were formerly under the supervision of the Western and Southern Departments. On January 25, 1960, the department formally opened headquarters in a new fourteen-story Hartford Building in Dallas, a distinctive newcomer to the Texas city's skyline.

The Western Department business was still large enough to justify further decentralization. On August 25, 1959, Mr. Hullett announced a new departmental office at Cincinnati, later named the Central Department. The new department was organized to provide group services for agents and policyholders in Ohio, Kentucky, Tennessee, West Virginia, and part of Indiana. Earle S. Whitcombe was named as the first manager.

At the time of Hartford's one-hundred-fiftieth anniversary, President Hullett had been in office for seven years, but so much of his career lies in the future that his full impact on the Companies he heads cannot yet be estimated. Nevertheless, the success he has already attained in the consolidation of the Companies and the establishment of new departmental offices is certain to stand to his credit throughout his future years of service.

In addition to this, other major accomplishments must also be credited to these early years of his administration. One of these is the acquisition by the Hartford Fire Insurance Company of The Columbian National Life Insurance Company.

Many years ago the Hartford's Directors became aware of the possibility that someone might sometime apply for a charter in the name of the "Hartford *Life* Insurance Company." At the time, the Hartford had no immediate plans for entering the life insurance field, but it was clear that the use of that name by anyone who had no connection with the Hartford Fire Insurance Company would be certain to lead to difficulties. On that account an application for a charter was made under that name and, when it was granted by the Connecticut legislature, the document was carefully renewed and reviewed regularly.

President Hullett, of course, knew of that old and unused charter and, shortly after his elevation to the Presidency, he began to discuss the possibility of adding a life insurance company to the Hartford Group. He did not favor the organization of a new company but, under his urging, the Directors began to feel that an established and well-regarded company could be acquired.

In 1902 The Columbian National Life Insurance Company had been organized in Boston. Its reputation was good but its agencies were limited in number and its volume of written business was modest.

President Hullett succeeded in gaining the support he needed in order to acquire the Company. Negotiations were consequently opened and on January 6, 1959, the stockholders of the Hartford Fire Insurance Company voted to increase the Company's capital by issuing up to 175,000 shares to be exchanged for outstanding shares of the capital stock of The Columbian National Life Insurance Company. In this way a new, important company became a member of the Hartford Fire Insurance Company Group, and under President Hullett's leadership a vast insurance field hitherto unexplored by any company of the Hartford Group was entered.

On June 27, 1960, the one-hundred-fiftieth anniversary of the founding of the Hartford Fire Insurance Company, the name of the new life insurance affiliate was changed to the Hartford Life Insurance Company.

It is appropriate that in this sesquicentennial year of the Hartford organization, there is another major company to bear the name Hartford, and that the Group is now in position to write virtually every form of insurance in the three major classifications: fire, casualty and life.

A versatile top management team had been developed to meet the diversified needs of the new organization. Active in administrative duties was Roland H. Lange, Assistant to the President, and Vice-President, another product of Northwestern University's fire insurance course and the Western Department, who had risen from Special Agent ranks. Manning W. Heard was elected Executive Vice-President of the Hartford Accident and Indemnity Company to head the casualty operations of the Group. He continued as Vice-President and General Counsel of the Hartford Fire Insurance Company. These two executives have also constituted a liaison committee under Mr. Hullett's guidance which has directed the consolidation and reorganization program of the Group. Julian D. Anthony, who had been President of The Columbian National Life Insurance Company prior to its acquisition, remained as President of the new subsidiary. Barnard Flaxman, Vice-President, functions as head of the important Investment Department of the Group. Philip S. Brown, Vice-President, widely experienced in accounting and allied procedures, administers the dramatic changes now being instituted in this area.

Recent years have seen many new developments in the business of insurance. Inflation has increased the dollar cost of everything. Income levels have changed. Home ownership has increased. Suburbs are growing, and almost every city is troubled by the deterioration of certain areas. Because of these and other influences, insurance practices have changed and are continuing to do so. "Package policies," which combine several coverages of both fire and casualty nature in single contracts, have made an important place for themselves in recent years. In 1959 the homeowners package contracts alone exceeded twenty-five million dollars in premiums written for the Group. The "retrospective rating principle" now sometimes permits adjustment of the final premium for a given risk to be determined on the basis of its own loss experience, subject to maximum and minimum limits. And so many new ideas and new applications are a part of insurance today that the wisest layman is he who chooses an expert agent and follows his advice.

An invaluable new organization, recently established, is the Insurance Information Institute, in which, as its first President, Hartford's Assistant to the President, and Vice-President Roland H. Lange played a leading role. Its purpose is to represent some three hundred stock fire and casualty companies in attaining better public understanding and acceptance of the insurance business through more effective public relations activities. And the Hartford, following what might be called the orderly channels of the industry, sincerely co-operates with and is a member of the many bureaus, associations, and other organizations that the industry has brought into existence. Many of its officers are active in them and have, through the years, assumed places of leadership in them.

In insurance, as in other fields of endeavor, the influence of government grows ever more apparent. Withholding taxes, social security payments, city and state taxes, complex and never-ending reports—all these and much more must be added to the intricate recording and accounting that have always played so great a part in the business of insurance. Merely the keeping of an insurance company's records has attained such almost unbelievable proportions that without electronic machines and other aids to automation much of the task would be impractical. And as it is, the Hartford's experience has shown that it takes annual premiums of $35,000,000 in a department to justify the installation of well-designed electronic equipment.

The changes that have come to the Hartford in a hundred and fifty years could never have been imagined by the little group of Connecticut businessmen who first discussed the founding of the Company. Insurance against fire was all they had in mind, and even that seemed hedged about with difficulties. Nowadays, of course, any layman would be lost among the intricacies with which the Hartford Group now finds it necessary to deal. In fact, the Company has long since learned—and its competitors have learned as well—that insurance agents themselves are much better able to serve both the insurance companies and the insured if they are adequately trained. Time was when agents picked up—or made up—such methods as they used, learning—or failing to learn—as they went along. But insurance in our day is a complicated subject in which the better agents have come to be remarkably expert. And the Hartford Fire Insurance Company together with the Hartford Accident and Indemnity have long maintained the Hartford Training Center, which alternately provides courses of four weeks' duration, first in Fire and Inland Marine lines, and second in Casualty and Bonding lines.

Maintained for the training of Hartford agents and their employees, the Training Center is conveniently located in its own building across the street from the Home Office, and the alternate courses are given at regular intervals throughout the year. The teaching staff is composed of able and experienced men who have worked both in the Company and producer ranks. Classrooms are well equipped and comfortable. Classes are divided into small discussion groups. Those who attend are given individual and personal as well as class instruction, and the hundreds who complete the course each year not only increase their own efficiency but also the efficiency of the agencies with which they are connected.

For years, fire insurance companies have been periodically asked by schoolteachers, or even by schools, to provide material that might prove useful in the schoolroom for fire prevention instruction. Some states make such instruction mandatory but fail to provide any aids to instruction, and in 1947 it became apparent at the Home Office of the Hartford that in order to be really effective in the classroom, such material as was provided should be designed so as to catch and hold the interest of the children.

With this idea as a beginning, a program was evolved to provide a simple blank form that would help the pupils—and their parents—in eliminating such fire hazards as are commonly or occasionally found in dwellings. And, in order to encourage action, each child who brought back to school the inspection form properly filled out and signed by a parent, would be named a "Junior Fire Marshal" and would be awarded a well-designed certificate to prove that the title was "real" and had been earned. Later, badges and red firemen's hats were also awarded, and millions of these have long been in the hands of children all across the country.

From the first, this program was successful. Within a few years more than fifteen million Junior Fire Marshals had earned their title. Originated and still sponsored by the Hartford Fire Insurance Company, the program has been enthusiastically furthered by fire departments in many parts of the country. A "Hartford Gold Medal" is awarded to youngsters in the third, fourth, and fifth grades of the country's schools who have performed some outstanding fire prevention service or have played effective parts in fire emergencies. The selection of those to whom the medals are to be awarded has been left, from the first, in the hands of nationally known school and fire authorities.

The program also includes the Junior Fire Marshal Magazine which is printed quarterly and distributed free by the Company. Though the whole idea was originally promotional in intent, the Company has never tried to commercialize or monopolize it. Instead, it welcomes progress from any source that encourages children and parents alike to aid in the reduction of fire hazards and loss of life in the nation's homes.

Any search of the Hartford's records is certain to turn up innumerable accounts of startling losses—of enormously important surety bonds—of interesting and unusual policies.

In the early 1890's, Colonel William F. Cody—whom the whole world knows much better as Buffalo Bill—collected $2,000 from the Hartford when a structure of some sort—the only remaining record does not describe it—was destroyed by fire in North Platte, Nebraska.

On April 7, 1926, a stroke of lightning set fire to the tank farm of the Union Oil Company near San Luis Obispo, California. For two days the enormous blaze continued, and when it finally subsided, the loss payment that was made by the Hartford was $2,709,163.47—the largest loss ever paid to one assured by the Company's Pacific Department.

After the loss adjuster wrote the enormous check, he found that the office Protectograph was not capable of covering a check so large. But, more than that, a search of San Francisco failed to find any other Protectograph that was capable of going beyond $999,999.99. Thus the check went through "unprotected," a happening so rare as to be newsworthy.

In 1939, the first Soviet-manufactured automobile ever to reach the United States was insured in the Hartford Accident and Indemnity Company.

In 1945, when the first meeting of the United Nations was held in San Francisco, the Hartford Accident and Indemnity Company wrote Comprehensive Liability Insurance on the War Memorial Opera House and the Veterans Memorial Building in which the sessions of the Conference were held, the insured being the City and County of San Francisco and the Trustees of the War Memorial.

Because tragic possibilities might follow the injury of any of the delegates, Hartford engineers and others examined the two buildings with meticulous care. The elevators were taken apart and every part was inspected. Extra elevator operators were trained. Electric facilities were thoroughly checked. Lighting was tested so that partitions and other temporary installations would not cast shadows that might contribute to an accident.

About 160 large buses, trucks, jeeps, and sedans were used in connection with the Conference and all of these were also insured by the Hartford. The drivers, most of whom were women, were carefully selected and trained for the work they were to do by Hartford engineers.

And, owing to the careful preparations, the Conference ended with no accidents, no injuries, no claims.

In 1955, when the 1,600-year-old *Yonan Codex* was to be transferred from a bank vault in Washington to the Library of Congress, the Hartford Accident and Indemnity Company was asked to insure it for an hour and a half. Scholars say that the ancient Codex is the only complete New Testament in the original Aramaic-Syriac language used by Christ and his disciples, and thus is an invaluable document. Covered by a Hartford Bankers' Blanket Bond even while it was in the vault of the National Savings and Trust Company, it had to be covered by a Valuable Papers Policy while it was being moved.

The policy, issued after consultation with the Home Office, was for $1,500,000 and was to remain in effect for an hour and a half! The time included an allowance for a side trip to the White House so that President Eisenhower could view the document.

No one connected with the Hartford had ever considered the idea of insuring any German submarines—not, that is, until the Chicago Museum of Science and Industry and some public-spirited Chicagoans raised $175,000 for the purpose of preserving an 840-ton U-boat that the Navy had captured during World War II.

Getting the U-boat to Chicago was not difficult, but getting it out of Lake Michigan and across Lake Shore Drive and another busy street on an 800-foot land journey to the Museum grounds was quite another matter. And that is where the Hartford came into the picture. An Indiana engineering firm had the contract to transfer the submarine from its native element to its final resting place, and the Hartford Accident and Indemnity Company wrote the liability policy providing a maximum of $50,000 for Bodily Injury, and $1,000 for Property Damage. But at the last minute the engineering firm reached the conclusion that higher limits were necessary. Cruising across the Lake Shore Drive in a submarine, they felt, would be safer if the liability policy were larger—providing a maximum of $300,000 Bodily Injury and up to $50,000 Property Damage.

The Pittsburgh Underwriting Department reviewed the situation. The Chicago office hurried to make a physical inspection, and the Home Office approved the change.

It had taken U-505 ten years to get to Chicago from near the coast of Africa where she was captured, but she crossed Lake Shore Drive in short order and without incident. Nothing was hurt on the way except the feelings of impatient motorists who had to be re-routed for a little while, but the Hartford liability policy has yet to be written for coverage such as that.

And so the stories go . . . thousands of important events, interesting anecdotes, human interest situations chronicled by the insurance written in the Hartford.

One dictionary definition of insurance reads as follows: "Act of insuring, or assuring, against loss or damage by a contingent event." As far as it goes, that is quite true, and the average person, little informed about other phases of insurance, is apt to give them very little thought. When a house burns down, insurance is apt to come to anybody's mind. But when a giant dam goes up, or a magnificent new bridge is being flung across a mighty river or a strait, few people think of the part the great insurance companies play in aiding the contractors.

Through its Surety Department, the Hartford has contributed very significantly over the years to the construction "miracles" which have meant so much to our country's progress. This contribution has been made through the writing of contract bonds for the builders of such projects as the Hoover Dam, the St. Lawrence Seaway, the San Francisco-Oakland Bay Bridge, the "Texas Towers" anchored in the Atlantic as outposts for detecting an oncoming enemy attack.

Let us imagine that the visions of our engineers for another great seaway, a bridge, a water conservation or flood control project have been translated into blueprints. Contractors, operating individually or in co-venturing groups, must be found if such a project is to become a reality. The engineers and authorities who envisioned the project and are responsible for its completion must be certain that those contractors to whom they award the contract, most probably after receiving competitive bids, have in adequate measure all of those qualities necessary to perform the contract as it has been envisioned and planned.

Before the contractor submits his bid, he must consult with his bonding company—in this case, the Hartford Accident and Indemnity Company. The Hartford operates importantly as a bonding company as well as an insurance company. Here, every pertinent detail of the proposed project is considered by the Hartford's underwriters: the contractor's financial stability, his experience, organization, equipment, and bank credit. If, after the bonding company has made a rigid examination, it is concluded that the contractor has these qualities in sufficient measure, he is given a "bid bond." The "bid bond" guarantees that in the event the contractor is the successful bidder he will enter into a contract for the construction of the project and deliver a final bond (or bonds) guaranteeing that he will perform the contract as called for by the plans within the time limit specified and that he will pay all labor and material bills. This guarantees to the owner a completed contract built to specifications and delivered free of liens. Many such projects run into tens of millions of dollars—in fact, frequently they are of such size that no single bonding company could or would undertake the entire risk. In such a situation it arranges to bring in other bonding companies, as reinsurers or co-sureties, to participate in the risk.

In addition to the bonds that the contractor files with the authorities, guaranteeing his contract obligation, he also arranges for the various types of insurance that will protect him against the numerous insurable hazards involved in any great construction project.

Other contributions have been made by the Hartford's fidelity and surety departments, among the most important of these being the collaborative use, with other companies, of Blanket Bond Forms in financial institutions, in government, and in the vast mercantile field. It has long been obvious that man's ingenuity for malfeasance is virtually boundless, and the only certain way for an owner or a governing body to protect its goods and property against loss through employee dishonesty is the fidelity bond, which, while affording indemnification on the one hand, acts as a certificate of good character to the great majority of honest employees or public servants on the other.

With new scientific developments forever in the news, it is important for the nation's insurance companies to keep up with the times. The

Nuclear Age has already arrived, and the Hartford, along with other insurance companies, is already prepared to sell "nuclear insurance."

This type of protection will not insure you against atomic bombs. It has been developed in connection with peacetime uses of atomic energy, and such policies as may be written cover risks that are inherent in the construction, installation, operation, and maintenance of such complicated equipment as nuclear reactors, whether they are for industrial use or for research.

Installations of this nature are fantastically expensive—so expensive, in fact, as to be beyond the limits that individual insurance companies find it prudent to assume on single risks. Still, these installations must be insured and the Hartford Fire Insurance Company, in collaboration with about 180 other capital stock insurance companies, has formed the Nuclear Energy Property Insurance Association—NEPIA—to underwrite physical damage coverage on nuclear risks and provide such inspection engineering and loss prevention services as are needed for commercial nuclear operations. Furthermore, the Nuclear Energy Liability Insurance Association—NELIA—has been formed by the Hartford Accident and Indemnity Company in association with about 130 other stock casualty companies and is prepared to write liability insurance up to limits of $46,500,000 on any given reactor.

Seven years after President Hullett's elevation to the Presidency then, enormous changes have taken place under his direction. Still decentralized, and decentralizing even more as new departments are created, the various Companies that make up the Hartford Group are more cooperative among themselves.

Three conspicuous programs—Group consolidation, the establishment of new departmental offices, and the acquisition of The Columbian Life— already stand to the credit of President Hullett and his associates. But, along with many lesser accomplishments, another highly important one should be included.

For a century and a half, growth has marked the progress of the Hartford. Its premium income, increasing with each decade from the time of its founding, totaled almost $227 million at the end of its first century. In that year, too, the Company's assets stood at almost $23 million, an increase in ten years of a hundred per cent.

But on the Company's one-hundred-fiftieth anniversary of its founding, every measurement is on a vastly greater scale. For 1959 alone the premium income of the Hartford Group was twice as great as the total had been for the whole of the Company's first century. Furthermore, where assets stood at $23 million in 1910, they exceeded $600 million at the end of 1952 and surpassed a billion as 1960 opened. This then is the record.

The value of looking back, of course, is in the guidance it affords those who must progress further along the path of history.

The men who today bear the great responsibility of leading the Hartford Fire Insurance Company Group through the challenging years ahead can take strength and direction from the tradition they have inherited.

Men of character and vision did more than found a Company in 1810. They established the Hartford way of doing business. They regarded their insurance contracts as being promises to be kept at all cost. And, as we have seen, they and their successors kept their promises to the letter even amid the discouraging days of our nation's greatest tribulations. On this tradition of trust has grown a billion-dollar organization. More important, a priceless reputation has been built . . . a public acceptance which has led hundreds of thousands of men and women confidently to entrust to the Hartford the protection of all they possess.

It would be out of character for today's Hartford officials to prophesy about the years ahead. But that their organization will perform in such a way as to bring added luster to the Hartford heritage is their devout wish for the future.

APPENDIX

AN ACT

TO INCORPORATE THE HARTFORD FIRE INSURANCE COMPANY

Passed at a General Assembly of the State of Connecticut,
Holden at NEW HAVEN, *in said state,*
on the second Thursday of May, in the year of our Lord
One Thousand Eight Hundred and Ten:

¶ 1.   Be it enacted by the Governor and Council, and House of Representatives in General Court assembled, That the subscribers to the Hartford Fire Insurance Company, their successors and assigns, shall be and are hereby created and made a corporation and body politic, by the name and title of the Hartford Fire Insurance Company, and by that name shall be and are hereby made capable in law to have, purchase, receive, possess, and enjoy, to them and their successors, lands, rents, tenements, hereditaments, goods, chattels, and effects of whatever kind or quality. Also, bank stock of any bank within the United States, and the same to sell, grant, alien, and dispose of, and to sue and be sued, to plead and be impleaded, defend and be defended, in all courts in this State and other places whatsoever. Also, to have and use a common seal, the same to break and renew at pleasure. Also, to ordain and put in execution such by-laws and regulations as shall be deemed necessary and convenient for the well ordering and governing said corporation, not being contrary to this charter, or the laws of this State or of the United States. To do and execute all and singular the matters and things which to them shall or may appertain: subject to the rules, restrictions, and provisions hereinafter provided.

¶ 2.   The capital stock of said company shall be one hundred and fifty thousand dollars, to be divided into shares of fifty dollars each, which shall be paid in the following manner, viz.: five per centum shall be paid in thirty days after the passing of this act, and five per centum more shall be paid within sixty days after the passing of this act; and the remainder shall be secured by mortgage on real estate, or by indorsed notes payable thirty days after demanded by the president and directors; and all notes given for the payment of the installment aforesaid, shall be payable to order, and indorsed to the satisfaction of the president and directors.

¶ 3.   That for the well ordering the affairs of said corporation, there shall be nine directors chosen on the first Thursday of June annually (after the first election), by the greatest number of votes given by the stockholders of said company, at a general meeting. And those who shall be duly chosen at any election shall be capable of serving as directors until the expiration of the first Thursday of June next ensuing such election. And the directors, at their first meeting after such election, shall choose one of their number for a president.

¶ 4.   The number of votes each stockholder shall be entitled to in the choice of directors, or any other business respecting the interest or concerns of said company, shall be equal to the number of shares he shall hold.

¶ 5.   All stockholders shall be entitled to vote, by themselves, or their agents duly appointed. None but stockholders shall be eligible as directors. Public notice shall be given by order of the directors, twenty days previous to holding an election or general meeting of the stockholders, in a newspaper published in the city of Hartford, and in such other places as the directors shall judge necessary.

¶ 6.   In case of the death or resignation

of a director, his place may be filled by a new choice for the remainder of the year, provided a majority of the directors judge it necessary. All elections for directors shall be by ballot, and the nine persons who shall have at any election the greatest number of votes shall be declared to be duly chosen.

¶ 7. The directors for the time being shall have power to appoint such officers, secretaries, and servants, as they shall judge necessary; and shall be capable of executing such other powers for the well ordering and governing the affairs of the company as shall be deemed for the best interest of the same. No director shall be entitled to any emolument, unless the same shall be ordered by the stockholders at a general meeting.

¶ 8. Not less than three directors shall constitute a board for transacting business of the company, of whom the president shall always be one, except in case of sickness or necessary absence, in which case the directors present shall supply his place by electing one of their number as president for the occasion.

¶ 9. Said corporation shall keep their office in the city of Hartford, and may make insurance on dwelling houses, or other buildings, on ships and vessels of every description, while in port and on the stocks, also on goods, chattels, wares and merchandise, and other personal estate, of every name, nature, and description, and shall be liable to make good and pay to the several persons who shall be insured by the said corporation for all losses they may sustain by fire in their houses or other buildings, ships, or vessels, goods, chattels, wares, merchandise, or other personal estate, as aforesaid,— provided always, that no stockholder shall be liable for any loss or damage, or be responsible in their person or property other than the property vested in the capital and fund of the corporation.

¶ 10. The stock of said corporation shall be transferable according to such rules as the directors shall institute, and every subscriber of any share or shares in said stock who shall neglect to pay according to the installments aforesaid, or secure the payment of the residue of said share or shares as aforesaid, shall forfeit to the corporation such share or shares, and all payments made thereon, and all profits which may have arisen therefrom.

¶ 11. All notes or policies of insurance signed by the president, and counter-signed by the secretary, shall be binding and obligatory on said corporation, according to the terms and tenor thereof; and all notes made by any subscriber, for the payment of their installments, and all notes in writing which shall be made and signed by any person or persons, his, her, or their agent or servant, who is usually intrusted by him, her, or them, said notes being given for the payment of money only, and made payable to any person or persons, his, her, or their order, or to the bearer, and indorsed over to the corporation, shall be assignable, or indorsable over in the same manner as inland bills of exchange are or may be according to the custom of merchants; and said corporation to which the same shall be indorsed shall and may maintain their action thereupon for the money promised in said note against the person who, or whose agent as aforesaid, shall sign the same, or any of the persons who shall indorse the same, in like manner as in case of inland bills of exchange; and the directors may loan the money of the company upon such security as they shall think fit, and may purchase for the company any of the funded debt of the United States, or bank stock, or dispose of the same at their discretion, and shall once in six months make such dividend of the profits as they shall think proper.

¶ 12. The stockholders in a general meeting may hereafter, if they judge expedient, enlarge the capital of said company to the sum of two hundred and fifty thousand dollars.

¶ 13. If it should happen for any cause whatsoever that the election of directors should not take place in any year on the day herein for that purpose mentioned, said corporation shall not for that reason be dissolved, but such election may thereafter be held on such convenient day as may for that purpose be fixed on by the directors, they causing such public notice thereof to be given as hereinbefore required for an election on the days hereby dsignated for that purpose.

¶ 14.   In case any insured, named in any policy or contract of insurance made by the said corporation hereby created, shall sell and convey or assign the subject insured, during the period of time for which it is insured, it shall be lawful for such insured to assign and deliver to the purchaser such policy or contract of insurance, and such assignee shall have all the benefit of such policy or contract of insurance, and may bring and maintain a suit thereon in his own name. Provided, that before any loss happens he shall obtain the consent of the assurer to such assignment, and have the same indorsed or annexed to the said policy or contract of insurance, executed and signed as a new policy or contract ought to be, according to the rules hereafter to be prescribed by said directors for that purpose, and not otherwise.

¶ 15.   Daniel Wadsworth, Daniel Buck, and David Watkinson are authorized to call a meeting of the stockholders, at such time and place as they shall appoint; to notify the time and place of the first meeting. And at such first meetings, the stockholders shall have power to choose directors in the same manner as is provided for at their annual meeting, and the directors so chosen shall hold their offices, with all the powers given to directors by this act, until the first Thursday in June next ensuing said election. Provided, that this act may at any time be altered, amended, or revoked by the General Assembly.

General Assembly, May Session, 1810.

LYMAN LAW, *Speaker of the House of Representatives.*

JOHN TREADWELL, *Governor.*
Attest, THOMAS DAY, *Secretary.*

LIST OF ORIGINAL HARTFORD FIRE INSURANCE COMPANY STOCKHOLDERS WITH SIZE OF THEIR SHAREHOLDINGS

Hudson & Goodwin	100	William Moseley	40
David Daggett	100	Nathaniel Patten	100
Shipman Denison & Co.	60	James H. Wells	40
Nathan Smith	20	James R. Woodbridge	20
Charles Denison	20	Frederick Wolcott	40
Edward Watkinson	40	John R. Landon	20
James B. Hosmer & Co.	20	Seth Terry	10
Luther Savage & Co.	50	Eliphalet Terry, Jr.	20
Harry Pratt	10	Caleb Moore	10
Andrew Kingsbury	20	George W. Bolles	10
Daniel Wadsworth	80	Lewis Strong	43
Mehitable Wadsworth	50	Joseph Lyman	44
Jacob Sargeant	20	Theodore Strong	43
Ebenezer Barnard	50	Isaac D. Bull & Co.	25
John Russ	40	Thomas Chester	30
Nathaniel Terry	100	David Porter	40
Horace Burr	10	Joseph Perkins	40
Chauncey Goodrich	20	Peter Lanman	60
William H. Imlay	25	John W. Holley	25
Kimberly & Brace	100	Isaac Thompson	50
Henry Terry	75	Joseph Skinner	50
Ward & Bartholomew	50	Joseph Trumbull	10
Ward Woodbridge	50	Philo Hillyer	10
Samuel Tudor, Jr.	25	Peter W. Gallaudet	10
Jonathan Brace	50	Joseph Rogers	10
Isaac Bull	25	Elisha Colt	10
John Sargeant	50	Normand Knox	20
Thomas Glover	50	Michael Olcott	10
Roland Lee	40	Jonathan W. Edwards	60
Henry Newberry	20	Moses Tryon, Jr.	50
Nehemiah Hubbard, Jr.	40	Daniel Lombard	20
Joseph Hubbard, 2nd.	40	Eli Ely	10
David Watkinson	85	Joseph Pratt, Jr.	10
Jeremiah Brown	40	Charles B. King	10
Samuel Watkinson	40	Hitchcock & Wolcott	15
Abigail Hubbard	40	Williams & Perkins	20
John R. Watkinson	40	Elisha Dodd	10
Walter Mitchell	25	Daniel Bunce, Jr.	10
Enoch Perkins	20	Ephraim Root	35
Daniel Buck & Co.	100	Dwell Morgan	20
Caleb Pond	10	Samuel Ledlie	10
Spencer Whiting	30		

SIGNIFICANT DATES IN HARTFORD HISTORY

1810   Founding of Hartford Fire Insurance Company, June 27. Nathaniel Terry elected first president; Walter Mitchell, secretary. Jonathan Trumbull of Norwich, Connecticut, appointed first Hartford agent, December 27.

1811   Appointment of first Hartford agent outside of Connecticut—Ebenezer F. Norton of Canandaigua, New York.

1819   First record of payment of agent commission (5%) to Hartford agent Hooker Leavitt of Greenfield, Massachusetts. Up until then, flat fee of 50¢ a policy had been paid.

1822   Hartford reinsures the New Haven Fire Insurance Company . . . one of the first instances of reinsurance in America.

1825   First fire insurance policy for an American college written for Yale University by the Hartford.

1829   Conflagrations in Augusta and Savannah, Georgia. Lewis Bliss becomes the Hartford's first full-time employee.

1835   Eliphalet Terry succeeds his cousin Nathaniel as president of the Hartford, June 4. The new president sleighs one hundred and eight miles to the New York City conflagration of December 16, to pay all claims in full.

1836   Hezekiah Huntington, Jr., becomes first vice-president of the Hartford. First Canadian agent appointed.

1845   Major fires in New York City; St. John's, Newfoundland; and Nantucket bring Hartford losses of $208,227.

1848   Albany, New York, fire on August 27. Hartford pays losses of $57,673.

1849   St. Louis fire of May 18. Hartford pays $58,676 in losses. Eliphalet Terry resigns presidency because of ill health. Hezekiah Huntington, Jr., succeeds him.

1852   Hartford's Western Department established with headquarters in Columbus, Ohio.

1857   Fowler and McLean in San Francisco appointed first Hartford agents in California.

1859   Robert E. Lee applies on October 17 for a Hartford fire insurance policy on his Virginia home, "Arlington."

1860   Abraham Lincoln insures his Springfield, Illinois, home—the only home he ever owned—with the Hartford on February 8, prior to leaving for Washington to be inaugurated as President of the United States.

1861   Hartford agent A. H. Hayden, cut off from contact with Hartford by the Civil War, buries his clients' proofs of loss following the Charleston, South Carolina, fire of December 13. (After the war, his faith in the Hartford is substantiated as the Company honors all claims.)

1863   Hartford's Western Department headquarters moved to Chicago.

1864   President Huntington retires, is succeeded by Timothy C. Allyn.

1866 Portland, Maine, fire. Hartford pays losses of $151,000. Hartford plays major role in founding of National Board of Fire Underwriters.

1867 George L. Chase elected president.

1870 Hartford's Pacific Department organized with headquarters in San Francisco.

1871 The Great Chicago Fire of October 8–9. 250 dead, 17,450 buildings destroyed. Hartford pays losses totaling $1,968,225.

1872 Conflagration in Boston. Hartford pays $485,000 in losses.

1885 Hartford begins writing business in Hawaii.

1891 Hartford's Head Office for Canada established in Toronto.

1900 Ottawa, Ontario, fire brings Hartford losses of $177,785. Year's losses total $4,260,475, a new high.

1901 Jacksonville, Florida, fire. Hartford losses—$215,900.

1902 Hartford one-year fire losses exceed $5 million.

1904 Great Baltimore fire of February 7. Hartford pays losses of $1,213,843.

1906 Great San Francisco earthquake and fire of April 18–21. Hundreds killed, 28,188 buildings destroyed. Hartford pays losses totaling $11,557,365. Establishment of Hartford's Southern Department with headquarters in Atlanta.

1908 George L. Chase, president of the Hartford for over forty years, dies on January 7. His son, Charles E. Chase, is elected president.

1909 First edition of Company publication, *The Hartford Agent*.

1910 Hartford celebrates its one hundredth anniversary.

1913 Hartford Accident and Indemnity Company founded on August 5. Charles E. Chase resigns as president of the Hartford Fire, becomes chairman of the board of directors. Richard M. Bissell becomes president of the Hartford Fire and the new casualty company as well.

1916 Hartford Live Stock Insurance Company organized.

1920 Hartford issues first rain insurance policy by an American company on a rodeo in Dewey, Oklahoma, on July 3.

1922 Hartford acquires London-Canada Fire Insurance Company.

1925 New York Underwriters Insurance Company acquired.

1929 Citizens Insurance Company of New Jersey becomes another Hartford subsidiary.

1931 Hartford writes contract bond on great Hoover Dam.

1934 Chicago Stockyard Fire, May 19. Hartford losses, $1,140,345. James L. D. Kearney elected president of Hartford Accident and Indemnity Company as Richard M. Bissell becomes that company's chairman of the board.

1936 Golden Gate Bridge in San Francisco opens. Construction had been bonded by the Hartford.

1937 Paul Rutherford becomes president of the Hartford Accident and Indemnity Company.

1941   Charles S. Kremer becomes president of the Hartford Fire upon death of Richard M. Bissell.

1944   Atlantic coast windstorm, September 14. Hartford pays $708,000.

1945   Hartford Accident and Indemnity Company writes liability coverage on first sessions of the United Nations in San Francisco.

1947   Texas City, Texas, disaster, April 16. Hartford losses, $1,460,440. Florida and Gulf Coast windstorms, September 18–20. Hartford losses, $872,933. Beginning of Hartford's Junior Fire Marshal Program, October 8.

1948   Windstorm in Midwest, March 18. Hartford pays $1,322,834.

1949   Windstorm in North Central States, October 9. Hartford pays $1,304,991.

1950   Windstorm in North Central States, May 5. Hartford pays $2,262,945. Windstorm in Northeast, November 25. Hartford pays $6,984,231.

1953   James C. Hullett elected ninth president of the Hartford Fire, February 26. Wilson C. Jainsen elected president of Hartford Accident and Indemnity Company. General Motors Fire at Livonia, Michigan. Hartford pays $1,008,000.

1954   Hurricane "Carol," August 31. Hartford pays $4,245,582. Hurricane "Hazel," October 15. Hartford pays $5,667,748.

1957   Hartford's Group Consolidation Program begun by establishment of the Hartford Group Northwestern Department with headquarters in Minneapolis, February 6. Establishment of New York Department in New York City, April 11.

1958   Establishment of Hartford's Southwestern Department with headquarters in Dallas, March 1.

1959   Acquisition of required number of shares of Columbian National Life Insurance Company of Boston to lead to that company's becoming a member of the Hartford Insurance Group, January 8. James C. Hullett elected president of Hartford Accident and Indemnity Company upon resignation of Wilson C. Jainsen, July 14. Establishment of Hartford's Central Department with headquarters in Cincinnati, August 25.

1960   On June 27, the one hundred-fiftieth anniversary of the Hartford organization, The Columbian National Life becomes the Hartford Life Insurance Company.

No 2

Wm Imlay.

Sum Insured £ 800

Prem 7 ⅌⅌ℳ ———— A ——

Premium received
S & W

WHEREAS *William Imlay Esqr of Hartford*

or whom else it may concern, wholly or partly, Friend or Foe, doth make Assurance *on His House*

against Fire, and all Dangers of Fire; moreover against all Damage which on Account of Fire may happen, either by Tempest, Fire, Wind, own Fire, Negligence and Fault of own Servants, or of Neighbours, whether those nearest or furthest off; all external Accidents and Misfortunes; thought of and not thought of, in what Manner foever the damage by Fire might happen: *for the space of one Year commencing on the eighth day of February 1794 and ending on the eighth* day of February 1795, both at twelve O'clock at Noon *valuing specially and voluntarily the said*

House at the Sum Insured ——

And the Assured, or whom it may concern, in case of Damage, or Hurt, shall need to give no Proof nor Account of the Value; but the producing this Policy shall suffice. And in case it should happen that the said *House* ———— the Whole or Part, are burnt and suffer Damage, on that Account, we do hereby promise punctually to pay and ratify, within the space of three Months after the Fire shall have happened, due Notice having been given to us, and no Deduction to be made from the Sum assured except Two and an Half per Cent. provided said Loss amounts to Five per Cent. under which no Loss or Damage will be paid. And in case of a partial Loss, all that shall be found to be saved and preserved, shall be deducted, after the Deduction of the Charges paid for the saving and preserving; and concerning which the Assured shall be believed on his Oath, without our alledging any thing against it. And so we the Assurers are contented, and bind Ourselves and Goods present and to come, renouncing all Cavils and Exceptions contrary to these Presents, for the true Performance of the Premises, the Consideration due unto us for this Assurance by the Assured, at and after the Rate *of one half per Cent*

Reciprocally submitting all Differences to two Persons, One to be chosen by the Assured out of Three to be named by the Assurer, the other by the Assurer or Assurers, out of Three to be named by the Assured, who shall have full Power to adjust the same; but in case they cannot agree, then such two Persons shall choose a Third, and any Two of them agreeing, shall be obligatory to both Parties.

IN WITNESS WHEREOF, We the Assurers have subscribed our Names and Sums assured in *Hartford* the — 8th Day of *February* One Thousand Seven Hundred and *Ninety four*

£800, Sanford & Wadsworth *Eight hundred Pounds*
for the Hartford Fire Insurance Company

HARTFORD FIRE INSURANCE COMPANY.

P R O P O S A L S

FOR INSURING

HOUSES, BUILDINGS, STORES, SHIPS IN HARBOUR, AND ON THE

STOCKS, GOODS, WARES, AND MERCHANDIZE,

FROM LOSS OR DAMAGE BY FIRE.

THE HARTFORD FIRE INSURANCE COMPANY having been incorporated by the Legislature of the State of Connecticut with a capital of One Hundred and Fifty Thousand Dollars—with a power of enlarging the Capital to Two hundred and Fifty Thousand Dollars ; and the Capital of One Hundred and Fifty Thousand Dollars being already paid and secured, to be paid according to law, the Directors now offer to the public the following terms upon which they propose to conduct the business of the Company

As all classes of Citizens are exposed to great calamities from fire, we presume that prudence will induce them to pay the small premium which is required for an Indemnity against such accidents. The practice of procuring Insurance against losses from fire, has already become very general through this country, and the Company are confident that the extent and solidity of their funds, and the fairness, liberality and promptitude with which they shall adjust the claims of sufferers, will ensure the confidence and patronage of this, and the neighbouring States.

** No Insured Person will be liable to make good the Losses of others ; but in case of Fire, the Sufferer will be fully indemnified to the amount insured.—The Company also make good Losses on Property burnt by Lightning.

CLASSES of HAZARDS, and RATES of ANNUAL PREMIUMS for INSURANCE against FIRE.

No. I.	No. II.	No. III.	No. IV.
Hazards of the First Class. Brick or Stone Buildings, covered with Slate, Tiles, or Metal.	*Hazards of the Second Class.* Brick or stone Buildings, covered with wood.	*Hazards of the Third Class.* Buildings the sides of which are part of Brick or stone, and part of Wood.	*Hazards of the Fourth Class.* Buildings, the sides of which are entirely of Wood.
Goods not hazardous contained in such Buildings.	Goods not hazardous, contained in such Buildings.	Goods not hazardous, contained in such buildings.	Goods not hazardous, contained in such Buildings.
	Hazardous Goods, contained in Buildings of the First Class.	Hazardous Goods, contained in Buildings of the Second Class.	Hazardous Goods, contained in Buildings of the Third Class.
For sums not exceeding 10,000 Dollars in one Risk, 25 Cents per 100 Dollars per Annum.	*For sums not exceeding* 10,000 Dollars in one Risk, 37¼ Cents per 100 Dollars per Annum.	*For sums not exceeding* 10,000 Dollars in one Risk, 50 Cents per 100 Dollars per Annum.	*For sums not exceeding* 10,000 Dollars in one Risk, 75 to 100 Cts. per 100 Dls. per Ann.

** Ships in Port, or their Cargoes, Ships Repairing or Building, may be Insured against Fire.

†‡† This manner of Classing Hazards will give a general idea of the Rates of Insurance, but there will necessarily be an increase of Premium in all cases where the local situation, and other circumstances, increase the Risk : such as joining, or being contiguous to Wooden Buildings, or Buildings occupied in carrying on hazardous Business—distance from Water—no Engines or Firemen in the town or Place, &c. &c.—The premiums may also, in some cases, be reduced on Wooden Buildings in the country, when standing single or detached, or attended with circumstances of peculiar security.—Larger sums than 10,000 Dollars may be insured by special agreement.

☞ Soap Boilers, Tallow Chandlers, Brewers, Maltsters, Bakers, Rope Makers, Sugar Refiners, Distillers, Chemists, Varnish Makers, Stable Keepers, Tavern Keepers, China, Glass, or Earthenware Sellers, Oil and Colourmen, Turpentine Works, Paper Mills, Printing Houses, Coopers, Carpenters, Cabinet Makers, Coach Makers, Boat Builders, Ship Chandlers, Apothecaries, Theatres, Mills and Machinery, and all Manufactories that use Fire Heat, are deemed extra hazardous, and must be particularly described in the Policy ; and for all such Risks an additional Premium will be required.

CONDITIONS OF INSURANCE.

I. ALL Applications for Insurance must be made at the office of the Company, in writing ; and the Subject offered for Insurance accurately described.

II. If the property offered for Insurance is within the District of a Surveyor of this Company, he will examine and report thereon ; but if not within any such District, then the Applicant must himself furnish an accurate and just description thereof ; viz. of what Materials each Building is constructed ; whether occupied as Private Dwellings, or how otherwise ; where situated ; the Name of the present Occupiers ; how situated with respect to other buildings —And in the Insurance of Goods, Wares and Merchandize, the Place where the same are deposited, is to be described ; also, whether such goods are of the kind denominated Hazardous, and whether any Manufactory is carried on in the Premises, all which is to be certified and attested in such manner as the nature of the case may admit. And if any Person or Persons shall insure his or their Buildings or Goods, and shall cause them to be described in the Policy otherwise than they really are, so as the same be charged at a lower Premium than is herein proposed ; or if such Description be false or fraudulent, such Insurance will be void and of no effect.

III. Goods held in Trust, or on Commission, are to be declared as such , otherwise the Policy will not extend to cover such Property.

IV. Every Policy of Insurance, made by this Company, shall be sealed with its Seal, and signed by the President and Secretary ; and the person for whose Interest the Insurance is made, must be declared and named therein ; nor can any Policy, or Interest therein, be assigned, but by consent of the Company, expressed by Endorsement made thereon.

V. No Insurance will be considered as made or binding, until the Premium is paid.

VI. Persons insuring Property with this Company, and who have already made other Insurance on the same Property, shall give notice thereof in writing at the Company's Office, before, or at the time of the execution of the Policy ; and Persons who, after insuring Property with this Company, have insurance made on the same Property elsewhere, shall, with all reasonable Diligence, notify the same in writing at the office of the Company, and have the same endorsed on the Policy, or otherwise acknowledged in writing ; in default whereof, the Policy shall cease, and be of no effect : and in case of Loss, each Party insuring shall be liable to the Payment of a Rateable Proportion only of the Loss or Damage which may be sustained.

VII. No Loss or Damage by Fire will be paid, that may happen or take place in consequence of any Earthquake, Invasion, Civil Commotion, Riot, or Military or Usurped Power whatever.

VIII. Books of Accounts, Written Securities, Notes, Bills, Bonds, Deeds, Ready Money, or Bullion, cannot be insured.

IX. Jewels, Plate, Medals, or other Curiosities, Paintings and sculptures, are not included in any Insurance, unless such Articles are specified in the Policy.

X. All Persons insured by this company, sustaining any Loss or Damage by Fire, are forthwith to give Notice to the company, and as soon as possible, to deliver in as particular an account of their Loss or Damage, signed with their own Hands, as the Nature of the Case will admit, and make Proof of the same by their Oath or Affirmation, and by their Books of Accounts, and other proper Vouchers, as shall be reasonably required : and shall make Oath, whether any and what other Insurance is made on the same Property ; and shall procure a Certificate, under the Hand of a Magistrate, Notary Public, or Clergyman, most contiguous to the Spot where the Fire happened, and not concerned in such Loss, that they are acquainted with the Character and Circumstances of the Person or Persons insured ; and do know, or verily believe, that he, she, or they, really, and by Misfortune, and without Fraud or evil Practice, have sustained by such Fire, Loss and Damage to the Amount therein mentioned ; and, until such Affidavits and Certificates are produced, the Loss shall not be payable —Also, if there appears any Fraud, or false Swearing, the Claimant shall forfeit his Claim to Restitution or Payment, by Virtue of his Policy.

XI. In case any Difference shall arise, touching any Loss or Damage, it may be submitted to the Judgment of Arbitrators, indifferently chosen, whose Award in writing shall be binding on the Parties. And when any Loss or Damage shall happen, the Company shall pay for the same in Sixty Days after the Loss shall have been ascertained and proved, without allowance of Discount, Fees, or any Deduction whatever

XII. Insurance may be made for seven Years, by paying the Premium for Six Years, and for a less number of Years than Seven, a reasonable Discount will be allowed.

Hartford, July 27, 1810.

N. B. The company will commence business on the sixth day of August next.

Hartford Fire Insurance Company, of Hartford, Conn.

THE estimated value of Personal Property, and of each Building to be insured, and the sum to be insured on each, must be stated separately. When Personal Property is situated in two or more Buildings, the value and amount to be insured in each must be stated separately. When insurance is wanted on Personal Property, the same description should be given of the Building containing the property, as if Insurance is wanted on the Building.

Application of *R. E. Lee, U, S, A,*

for Insurance against loss or damage by fire by the **HARTFORD FIRE INSURANCE COMPANY**, in the sum of *Five Thousand, Eight Hundred* Dollars on the property specified : the value of the property being estimated by the Applicant.

	SUM TO BE INSURED.	VALUATION.
On *Dwelling House*	$5000	$20,000,
On *Barn*	$800	$1200
On	$	$
On	$	$

The Applicant will answer the following questions, and sign the same, as a description of the premises on which the Insurance will be predicated.

1. BUILDING—Is it stone, brick, or wood? How many stories high? Where situated? When built? Which part occupied by Applicant?

2. WALLS—Are the division walls of brick? Are they entire? Do they rise above the roof?

3. ROOF—What is it covered with? Are the gutters stone, metal or wood? Is there a scuttle and stairs to it?

4. Are the stoves and apparatus for using fire properly secured, and will you engage to keep them so?

5. Do the pipes enter a chimney? And is it built from the ground? Do pipes pass one or more wood partitions or floors? If so, how secured?

6. What fuel is used? And how are ashes disposed of?

7. What material is used for lighting?

8. For what purpose is the building used? How many tenants?

9. Distance and materials of other buildings, within 100 feet of the one to be insured? And how occupied?

10. What other insurance is there upon the property, and at what office? Has this Company any other Insurance within 100 feet of this risk?

11. Is the property mortgaged? And to what amount? Is there any insurance by the mortgagee?

12. Is there any other party interested in the property?

13. Has the building a lightning rod? If so, is it on the old or new plan?

"Arlington"

¹Dwelling of Brick, main building two stories high, and wings one story, In Alexᵃ Co, Va, built about the year 1820 – All occupied by applicant. ¹The Barn is of brick, one story high, with a stone basement. ³The main building of the Mansion House is covered with Slate and the wings with gravel – ³The Barn is covᵈ with gravel. ³The gutters are metal. ²The division walls are of brick – ³There is not a scuttle in the roof of the dwelling – ³The Barn has a Cupola from wh. access to the roof is easy. ⁵Pipes enter chimney – ⁵Chimnies built from the ground. ⁵No wood partitions – ⁴Stoves and warming apparatus well secured ⁶Wood & Coal are used for fuel. ⁶ashes are put out a safe distance – ⁷Burning fluids, or candles, or Kerosene Oil, or Gas are permitted. ⁸Dwelling House – one Tenant – ⁹A one story brick Kitchen & a one story brick Store House, both covᵈ with wood – ⁹The one standing West of the Dwelling on a line with the north line thereof, & the other on a line with the south line thereof, both distant 44 feet – ¹⁰$5000 by the "Home" Insᵒ, ¹⁰No other risk within 100 feet. ¹⁰No other Ins. on the Barn – ¹¹Property unencumbered. ¹³Barn has a lightning rod. ¹³Dwelling has one on new plan. Barn has a cattle shed about 40 feet south east, and a waggon shed about 100 feet south, otherwise detached.

And the said applicant hereby covenants and agrees to and with said Company, that the foregoing is a just, full and true exposition of all the facts and circumstances in regard to the condition, situation, value and risk of the property to be insured, so far as the same are known to the applicant and are material to the risk.

Dated *October 17ᵗ* 185*9*.

R E Lee .... Applicant.

For *1* year at *40* cents.

" *1* " at *80* " [☞ *Make a diagram of the premises on the other side of this sheet.*]

Facsimile of fire insurance policy issued to Abraham Lincoln in 1861 to cover his home in Springfield, Illinois.

Hartford Fire Insurance Company
HARTFORD, CONN.
Incorporated 1810   Charter perpetual

No 253 $3200

By this Policy of Insurance,
THE HARTFORD FIRE INSURANCE COMPANY.

In consideration of _____ Twenty and Four _____ Dollars, to them paid by the Assured hereinafter named, the receipt whereof is hereby acknowledged,

DO INSURE,

Abraham Lincoln of _Springfield Illinois_

AGAINST LOSS OR DAMAGE BY FIRE TO THE AMOUNT OF

Three Thousand and Two Hundred Dollars

3000 $ On his frame two story dwelling House to Rent. Front Part being 20 by 39 feet. Rear 22 by 24 feet. Porch South Side of Rear Part 7 by 24 feet. Front Part Covered with Shingle Rear Covered with Metal

75 $ On his frame Carriage House 18 by 20 feet. 6 feet East of Dwelling

125 $ On his frame wood House and Privy 13 by 50 feet. adjoining Carriage House and 78 feet East of Dwelling. All situated on South 10 feet of Lot 7. and Lot 8. Block 14. E. Iles addition to Springfield Illinois

For a more particular description reference is had to application and Survey No. 253. on file in this Office hereby made a Part of this Policy and a Guaranty on the Part of the Assured.

3200 $ @ 3/4 $24.00

And the Hartford Fire Insurance Company above named, for the consideration aforesaid, doth hereby promise and agree to make good unto the said Assured, ...his..... Executors, Administrators and Assigns, all such immediate loss or damage, not exceeding in amount the sum insured, as shall happen by fire to the property, as above specified, from the ....Eighth.... day of ....February.... one thousand eight hundred and ....Sixty One.... (at noon,) unto the ....Eighth.... day of ....February.... one thousand eight hundred and ....Sixty Two.... (at noon,) the said loss or damage to be estimated according to the true and actual cash value of the property, at the time the same shall happen; and to be paid within sixty days after notice and proof thereof made, by the assured, and received at this office, in conformity to the conditions annexed to this Policy. PROVIDED ALWAYS, AND IT IS HEREBY DECLARED, that this Company shall not be liable to make good any loss or damage by fire, which may happen or take place by means of any invasion, insurrection, riot, or civil commotion, or of any military or usurped power, or any loss by theft at or after a fire. AND PROVIDED FURTHER, that in case the assured shall have already any other insurance against loss by fire, on the property hereby insured, and not notified to this Company and mentioned in or endorsed upon this Policy, then this insurance shall be void and of no effect. And if the said assured, or....this.... assigns, shall hereafter make any other insurance on the same property, and shall not with all reasonable diligence, give notice thereof to this Company, and have the same endorsed on this instrument, or otherwise acknowledged by them in writing, this Policy shall cease and be of no further effect. And if any subsequent insurance should be made upon the property hereby insured which, with the sum or sums already insured, should, in the opinion of the said Hartford Fire Insurance Company, amount to an over insurance, said Company reserve to themselves the right of cancelling this Policy, by paying to the Assured the unexpired premium pro rata. And in case of any other insurance upon the property hereby insured, whether prior or subsequent to the date of this Policy, the Assured shall not, in case of loss or damage, be entitled to demand or recover of this Company, any greater portion of the loss or damage sustained, than the amount hereby insured shall bear to the whole amount insured on the said property. AND IT IS AGREED AND DECLARED, to be the true intent and meaning of the parties hereto, that in case the above mentioned premises shall at any time after the making, and during the continuance of this Insurance, be appropriated, applied, or used to or for the purpose of carrying on, or exercising therein, any trade, business or vocation denominated hazardous or extra-hazardous, or specified in the memorandum of special hazards to the terms and conditions annexed to this Policy, or for the purpose of storing, using, or vending therein any of the articles, goods, or merchandise, in the terms and conditions aforesaid denominated hazardous or extra-hazardous, or included in the memorandum of special hazards, unless herein otherwise specially provided for, or hereafter agreed to by this Company, in writing, and added to or endorsed upon this Policy, then, and from thenceforth, so long as the same shall be so appropriated, applied, used, or occupied, these presents shall cease, and be of no force or effect. AND IT IS MOREOVER DECLARED, that this Insurance is not intended to apply to, or cover any books of account, written securities, deeds, or other evidences of title to lands, nor to bonds, bills, notes, or other evidences of debt, nor to money or bullion. And that this Policy is made and accepted in reference to the conditions hereto annexed, which are to be used and resorted to in order to explain the rights and obligations of the parties hereto, in all cases not herein otherwise specially provided for.

This Policy shall not be valid until countersigned by the duly authorized Agent of said HARTFORD FIRE INSURANCE COMPANY, at _Springfield Ill_

In witness whereof, The Hartford Fire Insurance Company have caused these presents to be signed by their President, and attested by their Secretary, in the City of Hartford, and State of Connecticut.

Attested,

Timo C Allyn Secretary.   _H Huntington_ President.

Countersigned at _Springfield_ this _8th_ day of _February_ 1861

James L Hill & Co Agents

DIRECTORS AND OFFICERS
HARTFORD FIRE INSURANCE COMPANY GROUP
through June 27, 1960

———••———

HARTFORD FIRE INSURANCE COMPANY

DIRECTORS

Nathaniel Terry .	1810–1835	George Putnam .	1836–1840
Nathaniel Patten .	1810–1831	Junius S. Morgan .	1836–1841
David Watkinson .	1810–1817		1843–1852
	1824–1830	Henry Waterman .	1837–1838
Daniel Buck .	1810–1818	Ezra White, Jr. .	1838–1843
Thomas Glover .	1810–1815	John D. Russ .	1838–1840
Thomas K. Brace .	1810–1817	James Goodwin, Jr. .	1840–1878
James H. Wells .	1810–1836	John P. Brace .	1841–1846
Ward Woodbridge .	1810–1817		1852–1864
Henry Hudson .	1810–1824	George C. Collins .	1841–1842
Spencer Whiting .	1815–1816	Charles Boswell .	1842–1885
	1820–1823	Henry Keney .	1842–1895
Elisha Colt .	1816–1820	William T. Lee .	1846–1847
	1825–1828	Calvin Day .	1847–1885
	1832–1833	Daniel Buck, Jr. .	1848–1849
	1835–1836		1851–1852
Edward Watkinson .	1817–1829	David F. Robinson .	1849–1851
Roswell Bartholomew .	1817–1830	Charles J. Russ .	1852–1861
Eliphalet Terry .	1817–1849	Enoch C. Roberts .	1861–1876
John Russ .	1818–1819	Timothy C. Allyn .	1864–1867
Jesse Savage .	1819–1820	Christopher C. Lyman .	1865–1884
Thomas Day .	1820–1822	George L. Chase .	1867–1908
Seth Terry .	1822–1835	Henry J. Johnson .	1867–1875
Thomas Chester .	1823–1825	Jonathan B. Bunce .	1868–1912
Harvey Seymour .	1827–1835	E. B. Watkinson .	1868–1885
	1837–1838	Olcott Allen .	1869–1870
Edward P. Cook .	1828–1834	John H. Goodwin .	1869–1873
Anson G. Phelps .	1830–1834	H. W. Conklin .	1869–1881
Luther P. Sargeant .	1830–1834	G. Wells Root .	1873–1881
Henry Shepard .	1831–1832	George Sexton .	1874–1881
Isaac Thompson .	1833–1834	James J. Goodwin .	1878–1915
Fontienne Raphel .	1834–1835	Jacob L. Greene .	1879–1905
Isaac D. Bull .	1834–1835	Theodore Lyman .	1884–1920
Hezekiah Huntington, Jr.	1834–1865	George Roberts .	1884–1921
Roswell B. Ward .	1834–1836	John C. Day .	1885–1900
Samuel H. Huntington .	1835–1842	William C. Skinner .	1885–1922
	1843–1848	Meigs H. Whaples .	1893–1928
Albert Day .	1835–1874	James M. Thomson .	1900–1913
Samuel Williams .	1835–1837	Charles E. Chase .	1905–1933
Frank J. Huntington .	1835–1836	Richard M. Bissell .	1908–1944
Edwin D. Morgan .	1836–1837	Henry S. Robinson .	1912–1926
	1840–1841	C. L. F. Robinson .	1913–1916
Job Allyn .	1836–1843	Walter L. Goodwin .	1915–1952
	1849–1867	Samuel Ferguson .	1917–1950

Philip L. Gale 1917–1945	Raymond E. Baldwin . . . 1945–1949
George S. Stevenson . . . 1922–	Henry R. Mallory 1949–1955
Joseph R. Ensign 1923–1941	George F. B. Smith . . . 1952–1956
F. Spencer Goodwin . . . 1923–1953	Sherman R. Knapp . . . 1952–
William Maxwell 1927–1939	J. C. Hullett 1953–
Porter B. Chase 1928–1944	Jonathan Goodwin . . . 1953–
James L. Thomson 1931–1959	Philip S. Brown 1955–
H. Bissell Carey 1938–	Isaac B. Grainger 1956–
John B. Byrne 1940–	Barnard Flaxman 1959–
Paul Rutherford 1941–1959	Julian D. Anthony . . . 1959–
Charles S. Kremer 1941–1959	James W. Foley 1959–
James Wyper 1942–1945	
Pomeroy Day 1942–1956	
1956–	

HARTFORD ACCIDENT AND INDEMNITY COMPANY

DIRECTORS

James J. Goodwin 1913–1915	Paul Rutherford 1936–1959
Theodore Lyman 1913–1920	H. Bissell Carey 1938–
George Roberts 1913–1921	John B. Byrne 1940–
William C. Skinner . . . 1913–1922	Charles S. Kremer 1941–1959
Meigs H. Whaples 1913–1928	James Wyper 1942–1945
Charles E. Chase 1913–1933	Pomeroy Day 1942–1956
Richard M. Bissell . . . 1913–1941	1956–
Henry S. Robinson 1913–1926	Raymond E. Baldwin . . . 1945–1949
C. L. F. Robinson 1913–1916	Henry R. Mallory 1949–1955
Walter L. Goodwin . . . 1915–1952	George F. B. Smith . . . 1952–1956
Norman R. Moray 1916–1929	Sherman R. Knapp . . . 1953–
Samuel Ferguson 1917–1950	J. C. Hullett 1953–
Philip L. Gale 1917–1945	Wilson C. Jainsen 1953–1959
George S. Stevenson . . . 1922–	Jonathan Goodwin . . . 1953–
Joseph R. Ensign 1923–1941	Philip S. Brown 1955–
F. Spencer Goodwin . . . 1923–1953	Isaac B. Grainger 1956–
William Maxwell 1927–1939	Barnard Flaxman 1959–
Porter B. Chase 1928–1944	James W. Foley 1959–
James L. D. Kearney . . . 1929–1940	Manning W. Heard . . . 1959–
James L. Thomson 1931–1959	

HARTFORD LIFE INSURANCE COMPANY
formerly
THE COLUMBIAN NATIONAL LIFE INSURANCE COMPANY
(*Acquired 1959*)

DIRECTORS

Julian D. Anthony 1959–	Philip M. Childs 1959–
Frederick Ayer 1959–	Barnard Flaxman 1959–
Philip S. Brown 1959–	Harry K. Haag 1959–
C. Rodgers Burgin 1959–	Manning W. Heard . . . 1959–
J. C. Hullett 1959–	Francis P. Sears 1959–
Joseph A. Kelly 1959–	Francis P. Sears, Jr. . . . 1959–
Lothrop Withington . . . 1959–	Fred S. Sibley 1959–
Roland H. Lange 1959–	Theodore L. Storer . . . 1959–

HARTFORD LIVE STOCK INSURANCE COMPANY
(*Incorporated July, 1916*)

DIRECTORS

James L. D. Kearney . . . 1916–1937	Robert S. Stoddart 1926–
Richard M. Bissell 1916–1941	Morgan E. Harris 1928–1959
James Wyper 1916–1945	Clyde P. Smith 1929–1938
Norman R. Moray 1916–1929	George W. Graham . . . 1932–
Charles E. Chase 1916–1933	John H. Ray 1933–1954
Whitney Palache 1916–1920	George T. Merrick 1934–1959
Alonzo A. La Duke . . . 1916–1924	Ferdinand W. Richter . . 1936–
William P. Cavanaugh . . 1916–1918	James L. Thomson 1938–1959
George W. Kear 1916–1928	Arthur R. Johnson 1939–
Howard Hampton 1916–1932	Charles S. Kremer 1941–1959
Thomas J. Lasher 1916–1918	Arthur L. Polley 1945–
Wallace Stevens 1916–1920	Alfred W. Tyrol 1945–1950
1937–1955	J. C. Hullett 1950–
Walter J. Higenbotham . . 1916–1925	Philip S. Brown 1954–
Arthur D. Pollock 1918–1922	Roland H. Lange 1955–
Curtis C. Wayland 1918–1926	Barnard Flaxman 1956–
N. H. Moore 1920–1936	Harold C. Davis 1959–
Frederick C. White . . . 1921–1945	Benjamin F. Gates 1959–
Henry J. O'Kane 1922–1934	Hale Anderson, Jr. . . . 1959–
W. A. Earl 1924–1939	Brice M. Draper 1960–
H. C. Klein 1925–	

CITIZENS INSURANCE COMPANY OF NEW JERSEY

(*Incorporated 1929*)

DIRECTORS

Charles E. Chase	1929–1934	G. S. Atkinson	1941–
Richard M. Bissell	1929–1941	A. W. Tyrol	1945–1950
F. C. White	1929–1945	J. C. Hullett	1945–
James Wyper	1929–1945	Malcolm G. Wight	1945–1952
D. J. Glazier	1929–1936	Francis T. Fenn	1947–1956
Clyde P. Smith	1929–1947	Philip S. Brown	1952–
C. S. Timberlake	1929–1945	Roland H. Lange	1954–
J. C. Stoddart	1929–1941	Sidney G. Behlmer	1956–
James L. Thomson	1935–1959	R. E. Young	1956–
Charles S. Kremer	1936–1959	Barnard Flaxman	1958–
A. L. Polley	1941–1960	M. R. Bigham	1960–

NEW YORK UNDERWRITERS INSURANCE COMPANY

(*Acquired 1925*)

DIRECTORS

Charles E. Chase	1925–1933	R. L. Tanner	1938–
Richard M. Bissell	1925–1941	W. J. Purcell	1939–1954
F. C. White	1925–1945	T. C. Taliaferro	1941–1951
T. D. Richardson	1925–1953	Charles S. Kremer	1942–1959
R. M. Bennett	1925–1928	J. C. Hullett	1945–
A. R. Stoddart	1925–1938	H. C. Davis	1949–
George W. Kear	1925–1928	C. H. Plath	1949–1956
Curtis C. Wayland	1925–1926	Albert Rowland	1949–1956
Howard Hampton	1925–1932	G. W. Owens	1951–
W. B. Cooley	1925–1927	A. J. McDavid	1952–1958
H. C. Klein	1925–	E. G. Bock	1954–
R. S. Stoddart	1925–	C. H. Avery	1954–1955
N. H. Moore	1925–1935	Philip S. Brown	1954–
M. H. Simpson	1926–1939	D. A. Kretschman	1955–
Arthur H. Smith	1927–1954	F. R. Scott	1956–
Morgan E. Harris	1928–1957	Barnard Flaxman	1956–
J. C. Stoddart	1928–1941	Roland H. Lange	1958–
Chandler Seymour	1932–1953	L. D. Ulrich	1959–1960
James L. Thomson	1934–1959	Benjamin F. Gates	1960–
Joseph Nelson	1935–1949 1952–1958		

TWIN CITY FIRE INSURANCE COMPANY
(*Acquired 1921*)

DIRECTORS

Sewall D. Andrews	. . .	1921–1948
Richard M. Bissell .	. . .	1921–1941
G. W. Buffington .	. . .	1921–1922
		1926–1934
Charles E. Chase .	. . .	1921–1932
D. Draper Dayton .	. . .	1921–1923
John H. Griffin .	. . .	1921–1944
F. W. Hilger	. . . .	1921–1944
C. T. Jaffray .	. . . .	1921–1956
F. A. Krehla .	. . . .	1921–1960
P. J. Leeman .	. . . .	1921–1934
J. J. Reichert	. . . .	1921–1925
W. J. Vonder-Weyer .	. .	1921–1941
William Walsh .	. . .	1921–1928
Fred C. White .	. . . .	1921–1945
E. H. Sherwin .	. . . .	1922–1933
R. W. Webb .	. . . .	1923–1948
John W. Black .	. . . .	1923–1956
E. C. Warner .	. . . .	1928–1942
D. J. Glazier .	. . . .	1932–1936
William Collins .	. . . .	1933–1934
C. W. Hall .	. . . .	1934–
L. B. Van de Wall .	. . .	1934–1949
James L. Thomson .	. . .	1936–1959
Charles S. Kremer .	. . .	1941–1959
Allan J. Hill .	. . . .	1942–1959
George C. Holmberg .	. .	1945–1953
J. C. Hullett .	. . . .	1945–
A. E. Wilson	. . . .	1945–1952
Sewall D. Andrews, Jr.	. .	1949–1960
Michael Schweihs .	. . .	1949–
Walther H. Feldmann	.	1949–1950
Frederic D. Weld .	. . .	1952–
Paul Reyerson .	. . .	1952–1958
Robert E. MacGregor .	. .	1952–1960
Roland H. Lange .	. . .	1953–
Charles P. Clifford .	. .	1955–1960
C. Palmer Jaffray .	. .	1957–1960
John A. Moorhead .	. .	1957–1960
Rufus W. Hanson .	. .	1959–1960
Barnard Flaxman .	. .	1959–
Philip S. Brown .	. . .	1960–
Brice M. Draper .	. .	1960–
M. R. Bigham .	. .	1960–

LONDON-CANADA INSURANCE COMPANY
(*Acquired December, 1921*)

DIRECTORS

Peter A. McCallum	. . .	1922–1932
B. W. Ballard .	. . . .	1922–1951
H. A. Fromings .	. . .	1924–1934
A. R. Knight .	. . . .	1924–1933
A. G. Cruickshank .	. . .	1924–1934
W. J. Scrimes	. . .	1931–1935
John R. Cartwright	. .	1932–1950
Alexander R. Martin .	. .	1932–1954
William A. Clarke .	. .	1933–1948
John G. Moore .	. . .	1934–1952
Harold Fry .	. . . .	1934–
Dr. V. F. Stock .	. . . .	1934–1954
George E. Watson .	. .	1935–1949
George N. Molesworth	.	1938–1953
William C. Terry .	. .	1949–
H. Douglas Coo .	. .	1950–
Gordon D. Watson .	. .	1950–
Arthur V. Stamper .	. .	1951–
R. Leopold Jones .	. .	1953–
Arthur C. Thompson .	. .	1953–
Philip S. Brown .	. . .	1954–
J. C. Hullett .	. . . .	1955–

HARTFORD FIRE INSURANCE COMPANY

OFFICERS

Chairmen of the Board

Charles E. Chase 1913–1932
   Honorary 1932–1933
Charles S. Kremer 1953–1956

Presidents

Nathaniel Terry 1810–1835
Eliphalet Terry 1835–1849
Hezekiah Huntington, Jr. . 1849–1864
Timothy C. Allyn 1864–1867
George L. Chase 1867–1908
Charles E. Chase 1908–1913
Richard M. Bissell . . . 1913–1941
Charles S. Kremer . . . 1941–1953
J. C. Hullett 1953–
   (and Chairman of Finance Committee)

Chairmen of Finance Committee

James L. Thomson 1935–1939
   (and Vice President) . 1939–1953
   Honorary 1953–1959
J. C. Hullett 1953–
   (and President)

Vice Chairman of Finance Committee

James L. Thomson 1934–1935

Assistant to the President, and Vice President

Roland H. Lange 1958–

Honorary Vice Presidents

Hezekiah Huntington, Jr. .   1836
   (temporary)
Charles Boswell   1849
Albert Day 1856–1857
              1867–1874
James Goodwin 1874–1877
Calvin Day 1878–1884
Henry Keney   1885
              1887–1895
Jonathan B. Bunce . . . 1895–1903

Vice Presidents

Charles E. Chase 1903–1908
Richard M. Bissell . . . 1903–1913
John W. G. Cofran . . . 1909–1912
Whitney Palache 1913–1920

James Wyper 1913–1944
S. E. Locke 1920–1925
F. C. White 1920–1944
D. J. Glazier 1928–1936
James L. D. Kearney . . . 1931–1937
Charles S. Kremer 1935–1941
G. A. Russell 1935–1936
C. S. Timberlake 1936–1944
James L. Thomson 1939–1953
   (and Chairman of Finance Committee)
A. L. Polley 1944–1959
A. W. Tyrol 1944–1950
J. C. Hullett 1944–1953
C. H. Smith 1944–1953
J. S. Gilbertson 1945–1952
William A. Forrester, Jr. . 1948–1953
Barnard Flaxman 1952–
Philip S. Brown 1953–
Roland H. Lange 1954–1958
Frank C. McVicar 1959–
M. R. Bigham 1959–
Harry V. Williams . . . 1960–

Vice President and General Counsel

Manning W. Heard . . . 1955–

Vice Presidents, Secretaries and Treasurers

Francis T. Fenn 1952–1956
R. E. Young 1956–

Vice President and Comptroller

Harry K. Haag 1958–

Vice Presidents and Secretaries

G. S. Atkinson 1953–
W. S. Vanderbilt 1953–
Burton B. Gracey 1953–1960
Roland H. Lange 1953–1954
Sidney G. Behlmer . . . 1955–
Brice M. Draper 1957–
Arthur W. Gregory, Jr. . . 1958–
James F. Keating 1959–
J. Stewart Johnston . . . 1960–
James Wyper, Jr. 1960–

Assistant Vice Presidents

Barnard Flaxman 1948–1952

Malcolm G. Wight	1950–1952
G. S. Atkinson	1950–1953
Philip S. Brown	1950–1953
Burton B. Gracey	1950–1953
W. S. Vanderbilt	1950–1953
Arthur W. Gregory, Jr. . .	1952–1958
James C. Parr	1956–
Charles F. Nettleship, Jr. . .	1959–

Secretaries and Treasurers
D. J. Glazier	1920–1928
Francis T. Fenn	1948–1952

Recording Secretary and Treasurer
D. J. Glazier	1913–1920

Executive Secretary
Clyde P. Smith	1942–1946

Secretaries
Walter Mitchell	1810–1835
James G. Bolles . . .	1835–1851
Charles Taylor	1851–1852
A. F. Wilmarth	1852–1853
Caleb B. Bowers . . .	1853–1858
Timothy C. Allyn . . .	1858–1864
George M. Coit	1864–1870
John D. Browne . . .	1870–1880
Charles B. Whiting . .	1880–1886
Philander C. Royce . .	1886–1907
Thomas Turnbull . . .	1908–1910
Frederick Samson . . .	1910–1920
Sidney E. Locke . . .	1910–1920
G. A. Russell	1925–1935
Charles S. Kremer . . .	1925–1935
C. S. Timberlake . . .	1925–1936
Clyde P. Smith (Recording)	1928–1935
	1935–1942
J. S. Gilbertson	1931–1945
C. L. Goldby . . .	1931–1936
John M. Holmes . . .	1935–1946
A. W. Tyrol	1935–1944
Malcolm G. Wight . . .	1935–1950
Robert D. Morse . . .	1940–1946
Philip S. Brown . . .	1940–1950
Francis T. Fenn . . .	1940–1948
A. L. Polley	1940–1944
W. S. Vanderbilt . . .	1940–1950
G. S. Atkinson	1940–1950
R. C. Chapin . . .	1944–1947
Burton B. Gracey . . .	1944–1950
Barnard Flaxman . . .	1944–1948

Arthur W. Gregory, Jr. . .	1951–1952
Roland H. Lange . . .	1951–1953
Francis E. Mann . . .	1953–
E. M. Kelley	1953–
R. E. Young	1953–1956
Harry K. Haag . . .	1954–1958
James Wyper, Jr. . .	1956–1960
James F. Keating . . .	1956–1959
J. Stewart Johnston . .	1956–1960
James F. Wyatt . . .	1956–
John F. Gilmore . . .	1957–
R. Channing Barlow . .	1959–
Robert C. Hannah . . .	1960–
Robert B. DeVore . . .	1960–
Edward B. Stout, Jr. . .	1960–

Recording Secretary
D. J. Glazier	1910–1913

Secretary and Actuary
Harold C. Grossman . . .	1953–

Assistant Secretary and Actuary
Harold C. Grossman . . .	1951–1953

Actuary
W. N. Bowers	1855–1862

Comptroller
E. R. Belmont	1920–1921

Assistant General Counsels
Hale Anderson, Jr. . . .	1959–
Herbert P. Schoen	1959–

Assistant Secretaries
Christopher C. Lyman . .	1835–1878
Philander C. Royce . . .	1881–1886
Thomas Turnbull	1886–1908
Charles E. Chase . . .	1894–1903
Frederick Samson . . .	1908–1910
Sidney E. Locke . . .	1908–1910
E. A. Bolmar	1913–1915
Thos. H. Scotland . . .	1914–1928
Gilbert A. Russell . . .	1920–1925
Charles S. Kremer . . .	1920–1925
Frederick C. Moore . . .	1920–1928
C. S. Timberlake . . .	1923–1925
John M. Holmes . . .	1923–1935
A. W. Tyrol	1925–1935
Clyde P. Smith	1926–1928
Francis T. Fenn	1928–1940
Hinton J. Hopkins . . .	1930–1934

Malcolm G. Wight	1932–1935	R. E. Young	1950–1953
G. S. Atkinson	1935–1940	Harry K. Haag	1953–1954
Philip S. Brown	1935–1940	James Wyper, Jr. . . .	1954–1956
E. M. Malmquist . . .	1935–1954	Gertrude M. Schroeder . .	1957–
R. D. Morse	1935–1940	Albert J. Hall	1957–
A. L. Polley	1935–1940	Alan D. Phillips . . .	1958–
W. S. Vanderbilt . . .	1935–1940	Robert B. Dwyer . . .	1958–
M. M. Pease	1937–1943	Gordon W. Shand . . .	1958–1959
Barnard Flaxman . . .	1937–1944	Philip C. Loomis . . .	1958–
C. Bernard Edwards . .	1940–1952	Martin W. Davenport . .	1958–
Raymond C. Chapin . .	1940–1944	George C. Munterich . .	1958–
Burton B. Gracey . . .	1940–1944	Robert C. Hannah . . .	1959–1960
Charles F. C. Hutt . . .	1940–1959	R. H. Kutteruf	1959–
George A. Robinson . .	1940–1947	J. Kenneth Cagney . . .	1959–
Benjamin L. Whorf . .	1940–1941	Breckinridge T. E. Stoddart .	1960–
William T. Bissell . . .	1940–1953		
Arthur W. Gregory, Jr. .	1947–1951	*Assistant Treasurers*	
Russell P. Barton . . .	1950–1953	Wilfrid Platt	1951–
Barton M. Douglas . .	1950–1958	Thomas A. Shannon . . .	1960–
E. M. Kelley	1950–1953	Edward F. Lindeman . . .	1960–
Francis E. Mann . . .	1950–1953	A. Edmund Tuller	1960–
Harold Wilkinson . . .	1950–1960		

HARTFORD ACCIDENT AND INDEMNITY COMPANY

OFFICERS

Chairmen of the Board

Charles E. Chase . . .	1913–1932
Honorary	1932–1933
Richard M. Bissell . . .	1934–1941
Paul Rutherford . . .	1953–1955

Presidents

Richard M. Bissell . . .	1913–1934
James L. D. Kearney . .	1934–1937
Paul Rutherford . . .	1937–1953
Wilson C. Jainsen . . .	1953–1959
J. C. Hullett	1959–
(and Chairman of Finance Committee)	

Chairmen of Finance Committee

James L. Thomson . . .	1935–1939
(and Vice President) . .	1939–1953
Honorary	1953–1959
J. C. Hullett	1953–

Vice Chairman of Finance Committee

James L. Thomson	1934–1935

Executive Vice President

Manning W. Heard . . .	1959–

First Vice President and General Counsel

Manning W. Heard . . .	1953–1959

Vice President and General Counsel

Manning W. Heard . . .	1946–1953

Vice Presidents

Charles E. Chase	1913
Norman P. Moray . . .	1914–1915
(and Manager)	
(and General Manager) .	1915–1928
Whitney Palache . . .	1917–1920
James Wyper	1917–1944
James L. D. Kearney . . .	1920–1928
(and General Manager) .	1928–1934
Paul Rutherford	1925–1934
(and General Manager) .	1934–1937
Joy Lichtenstein . . .	1928–1945
George H. Moloney . . .	1933–1956
Wallace Stevens . . .	1934–1955
Wilson C. Jainsen . . .	1935–1953
James L. Thomson	1939–1953
(and Chairman of Finance Committee)	

Edmund G. Armstrong	. .	1939	Frank C. McVicar . .	. . . 1939–1945
Manning W. Heard	. . . 1939–1946		A. W. Spaulding	 1939–1945
Addison C. Posey .	. . . 1939–		John L. Barter . .	. . . 1939–1945
John L. Barter . .	. . . 1945–		Francis T. Fenn . .	. . . 1946–1948
Frank C. McVicar .	. . . 1945–		Barnard Flaxman .	. . . 1947–1948
A. W. Spaulding .	. . . 1945–1950		Frank R. Aikin . .	. . . 1948–1949
Harry A. Kearney .	. . . 1945–1948		Robert V. Ahern .	. . . 1948–1956
George T. Merrick .	. . . 1945–1956		R. H. Dexter . .	. . . 1948–1957
William H. Wallace	. . . 1945–		Francis P. Handley	. . . 1948–1955
William A. Forrester, Jr.	. 1948–1953		C. W. Collins . .	. . . 1948–1958
Barnard Flaxman .	. . . 1952–		C. M. O'Dowd . .	. . . 1948–
E. A. Cowie . .	. . . 1953–		E. A. Cowie . .	. . . 1950–1953
Francis P. Handley	. . . 1955–		A. P. Sigmans . .	. . . 1950–
H. V. Williams .	. . . 1955–		R. V. Sinnott . .	. . . 1950–1952
M. R. Bigham .	. . . 1959–		H. V. Williams . .	. . . 1950–1955

Vice Presidents, Secretaries and Treasurers

		Daniel H. Quigg	. . . 1950–
Francis T. Fenn	. . . 1952–1956	James F. Keating	. . . 1950–1959
R. E. Young .	 1956–	Arthur W. Gregory, Jr.	. . 1951–1952

Vice Presidents and Comptrollers

		R. E. Young . .	 1955–1956
		Robert B. DeVore .	. . . 1955–
Joseph Broucek .	. . . 1946–1958	J. Stewart Johnston	. . 1956–1960
Harry K. Haag .	. . . 1958–	John F. Gilmore .	. . . 1956–

Vice Presidents and Secretaries

		John F. Beardsley .	. . . 1957–
J. Collins Lee .	. . . 1928–1934	Harry K. Haag . .	. . . 1957–1958
Arthur W. Gregory, Jr.	. . 1958–	Charles T. Johnson	. . . 1957–
James F. Keating .	. . 1959–	Jere J. Flynn . .	. . . 1958–
J. Stewart Johnston	. . . 1960–	Donald Day . .	. . . 1958–

Vice President and Treasurer

		Henry G. Mildrum .	. . . 1958–
		Arthur A. Hansen .	. . . 1958–
D. J. Glazier .	 1928–1936	R. Channing Barlow	. . . 1959–

Assistant Vice Presidents

		Edward B. Stout, Jr.	. . . 1959–
Barnard Flaxman .	. . . 1948–1952	Robert C. Hannah .	. . . 1960–
Arthur W. Gregory, Jr.	. . 1952–1958		
James C. Parr . .	. . . 1956–		

Recording Secretary

Charles F. Nettleship, Jr.	. 1959–	Clyde P. Smith .	 1928–1936

Recording Secretary and Treasurer

Comptrollers

		R. C. L. Hamilton	. . . 1916–1938
D. J. Glazier .	. . . 1913–1928	Joseph L. Broucek .	. . . 1940–1946

Secretaries and Treasurers

Actuary

Clyde P. Smith .	. . . 1936–1946	Joseph L. Broucek .	. . . 1933–1940
Francis T. Fenn .	. . 1948–1952		

Associate General Counsels

		Hale Anderson, Jr.	. . . 1959–
		Herbert P. Schoen .	. . . 1959–

Secretaries

James L. D. Kearney .	. . 1914–1920		
J. Collins Lee . .	. . . 1920–1928		

Assistant General Counsels

Edmund G. Armstrong	. 1936–1939	Hale Anderson, Jr.	. . . 1946–1959
Manning W. Heard	. . 1937–1939	Herbert P. Schoen .	. . . 1952–1959

Assistant Secretaries

George B. Butterfield .	. . 1939–1953	W. G. Falconer .	 1914–1920

John F. Wagner	1914–1915	Jere J. Flynn	1946–1958
J. Collins Lee	1915–1918	James F. Keating	1946–1950
	1919–1920	Robert D. Ewens	1950–1955
Francis T. Fenn	1930–1946	Donald Day	1950–1958
Edmund G. Armstrong	1934–1936	Henry G. Mildrum	1950–1958
W. R. Liedike	1934–1945	John F. Gilmore	1950–1956
Frank R. Aikin	1934–1948	Harold J. Graham	1950–
Robert V. Ahern	1936–1948	Arthur W. Gregory, Jr.	1950–1951
George B. Butterfield	1936–1939	W. K. Boger, Jr.	1955–
S. E. Williams	1936–1941	Arthur A. Hansen	1955–1958
R. H. Dexter	1936–1948	J. J. O'Loughlin	1956–
J. O. Lummis	1936–1944	William P. Ford	1956–
Ralph A. Ferson	1936–1941	Thomas M. Meredith	1957–
Edward L. Duncan	1936–1949	George C. Munterich	1957–
John L. Barter	1936–1939	Albert J. Hall	1958–
Frank C. McVicar	1936–1939	Orrin S. Burnside	1958–
A. W. Spaulding	1936–1939	Gerald T. Joyce	1958–
Joseph L. Broucek	1937–1940	Francis J. Hope	1958–
Charles J. Berlin	1937–1952	Alan D. Phillips	1958–
Francis P. Handley	1937–1948	Robert B. Dwyer	1958–
Barnard Flaxman	1938–1947	Gordon W. Shand	1958–1959
Ralph W. Mullen	1941–1951	Philip C. Loomis	1958–
Charles M. O'Dowd	1941–1948	Martin W. Davenport	1958–
C. W. Collier	1941–1958	Robert C. Hannah	1958–1960
Chester W. Collins	1941–1948	J. D. Cheney	1959–
Neil J. Brown	1941–		
E. A. Cowie	1944–1950	*Assistant Treasurers*	
A. P. Sigmans	1944–1950	Wilfrid Platt	1951–
R. V. Sinnott	1944–1950	Thomas A. Shannon	1960–
Donald C. Mackinnon	1945–1956	Edward F. Lindeman	1960–
H. V. Williams	1945–1950	A. Edmund Tuller	1960–
Philip S. Bonthron	1946–1951		

HARTFORD LIFE INSURANCE COMPANY
formerly
THE COLUMBIAN NATIONAL LIFE INSURANCE COMPANY

OFFICERS

Honorary Chairman of the Board
Francis P. Sears 1959–

Chairman of the Board
J. C. Hullett 1959–

President
Julian D. Anthony . . . 1959–

Vice President, Secretary and Counsel
Joseph A. Kelly 1959–

Vice Presidents
Charles F. Nettleship, Jr. . 1959–
Elliott C. Laidlaw . . . 1959–

Vice President and Director of Sales
Fred S. Sibley 1959–

Vice President and Manager of Group Department
Daniel H. Quigg . . . 1959–

Vice President and Actuary
James G. Bruce 1959–

Second Vice Presidents
Frank L. Shoring 1959–
Willett K. Boger, Jr. . . . 1959–

Second Vice President and Actuary
Henry A. Plimpton . . . 1959–

*Second Vice President and Manager—
Accident and Health Department*
Christopher F. Lee . . . 1959–

*Second Vice President and Medical
Director*
Frank L. Springer, M.D. . . . 1959–

Associate Counsel
Francis E. Hannon 1959–

Actuary
Gerard A. Vicino 1959–

Auditor
Elwood A. Mallett 1959–

Treasurers
Charles F. Nettleship, Jr. . 1959–1959
Raoul J. Grandpre 1959–

Assistant Treasurers
Marie L. Coleman 1959–1959
Woodrow C. Perry 1959–

Owen D. Murphy, Jr. . . . 1959–
(and Manager Mortgage Loans)
Charles E. Maltby 1959–
Francis E. Wilson 1959–1959

Assistant Counsel
William A. McMahon . . . 1959–

Assistant Directors of Sales
Frederick M. Smail . . . 1959–
John J. McDevitt 1959–
William T. Condon . . . 1959–1959
Russell E. Dexter 1959–

Assistant Secretaries
Charles P. Phillips 1959–
(and Assistant Auditor)
John F. Wulff 1959–
William A. McMahon . . . 1959–1959
Thomas G. Wrenn 1959–
Martin W. Davenport . . . 1959–

Assistant Auditor
Raoul J. Grandpre 1959–1959

Agency Secretary
Francis E. King 1959–

Assistant Medical Director
Ferris J. Siber, M.D. . . . 1959–

Associate Actuary
Gerard A. Vicino 1959–1959

Assistant Actuary
Allie V. Resony 1959–

HARTFORD LIVE STOCK INSURANCE COMPANY

OFFICERS

Chairmen of the Board
Charles E. Chase 1916–1932
Charles S. Kremer 1953–1956

*President and Chairman of Finance
Committee*
J. C. Hullett 1956–

Presidents
Richard M. Bissell 1916–1941
Charles S. Kremer 1941–1953
J. C. Hullett 1953–1956

*Assistant to the President, and Vice
President*
Roland H. Lange 1958–

Vice Presidents
Whitney Palache 1916–1920
James Wyper 1916–1945
Frederick C. White . . . 1921–1945
Wallace Stevens 1937–1955
James L. Thomson 1938–1953
Arthur L. Polley 1945–1960

Alfred W. Tyrol	1945–1950
J. C. Hullett	1946–1953
Philip S. Brown	1953–
Roland H. Lange . . .	1953–1958
M. R. Bigham	1959–

Financial Vice Presidents

W. A. Forrester, Jr. . . .	1949–1954
Barnard Flaxman	1953–

Vice President and General Counsel

Manning W. Heard . . .	1955–

Vice President, Secretary and Treasurer

R. E. Young	1956–

Vice President and Comptroller

Harry K. Haag	1958–

Vice Presidents and Secretaries

Brice M. Draper	1957–
Arthur W. Gregory, Jr. . .	1958–

Assistant Vice President

Charles F. Nettleship, Jr. .	1959–

Treasurers

D. J. Glazier	1917–1936
Clyde P. Smith	1936–1946
Francis T. Fenn	1946–1956

Secretaries

James L. D. Kearney . . .	1916–1937
Clyde P. Smith	1937–1946
Francis T. Fenn	1946–1956
Harold C. Grossman . . .	1953–
R. E. Young	1955–1956
James F. Keating . . .	1956–
J. Stewart Johnston . . .	1956–

Recording Secretary

D. J. Glazier	1917–1935

Assistant General Counsels

Hale Anderson, Jr. . . .	1959–
Herbert P. Schoen . . .	1959–

Financial Secretaries

Arthur W. Gregory, Jr. . .	1953–1958
James C. Parr	1956–

Assistant Secretaries

J. S. Briggs	1922–1928
Clyde P. Smith	1928–1937
Francis T. Fenn	1932–1946
Robert D. Morse	1937–1946
C. B. Edwards	1946–1953
Elin Malmquist	1946–1955
Gertrude M. Schroeder . .	1957–

Assistant Treasurers

Thomas A. Shannon . . .	1960–
A. E. Tuller	1960–
Edward F. Lindeman . . .	1960–

CITIZENS INSURANCE COMPANY OF NEW JERSEY

OFFICERS

Chairmen of the Board

Charles E. Chase	1929–1932
Charles S. Kremer	1953–1956

Presidents

Richard M. Bissell . . .	1929–1941
Charles S. Kremer . . .	1941–1953
J. C. Hullett	1953–

Assistant to the President, and Vice President

Roland H. Lange	1958–

Financial Vice President

W. A. Forrester, Jr. . . .	1949–1953

Vice Presidents

James Wyper	1929–1945
F. C. White	1929–1945
James L. Thomson	1934–1936
	1953–1959
Charles S. Kremer	1936–1941
Joy Lichtenstein	1937–1946
C. H. Smith	1944–1953
A. W. Tyrol	1944–1950

A. L. Polley 1944–1960
J. C. Hullett 1944–1953
Barnard Flaxman 1953–
Philip S. Brown 1953–
Roland H. Lange . . . 1954–1958
John L. Barter 1959–
Frank C. McVicar . . . 1959–
William H. Wallace . . . 1959–
M. R. Bigham 1959–

Marine Vice Presidents

C. S. Timberlake 1938–1945
J. S. Gilbertson 1946–1953

Vice Presidents, Secretaries and Treasurers

Francis T. Fenn 1953–1956
R. E. Young 1956–

Vice Presidents and Treasurers

D. J. Glazier 1929–1936
James L. Thomson . . . 1936–1953

Vice President and General Counsel

Manning W. Heard . . . 1955–

Vice President and Comptroller

Harry K. Haag 1958–

Vice Presidents and Secretaries

G. S. Atkinson 1953–
Burton B. Gracey . . . 1953–1960
W. S. Vanderbilt . . . 1953–
Roland H. Lange . . . 1953–1954
Sidney G. Behlmer . . . 1956–
Brice M. Draper . . . 1957–
Arthur W. Gregory, Jr. . 1958–
James F. Keating . . . 1959–
J. Stewart Johnston . . 1956–1960
James Wyper, Jr. . . . 1960–

Assistant Vice Presidents

Barnard Flaxman 1950–1953
Malcolm G. Wight . . . 1950–1952
G. S. Atkinson 1950–1953
Philip S. Brown 1950–1953
W. S. Vanderbilt . . . 1950–1953
Burton B. Gracey . . . 1950–1953
Arthur W. Gregory, Jr. . 1953–1958
James C. Parr 1957–
Charles F. Nettleship, Jr. . 1959–

Executive Secretary

Clyde P. Smith 1944–1947

Secretaries

Clyde P. Smith 1929–1944
C. S. Timberlake 1936–1937
John M. Holmes 1936–1946
A. W. Tyrol 1936–1944
Malcolm G. Wight . . . 1936–1950
Francis T. Fenn 1941–1944
                        1947–1953
George S. Atkinson . . . 1941–1950
Robert D. Morse 1941–1947
Philip S. Brown 1941–1950
Arthur L. Polley 1941–1944
W. S. Vanderbilt 1944–1950
Barnard Flaxman 1944–1950
Burton B. Gracey 1944–1950
R. C. Chapin 1944–1948
Roland H. Lange 1951–1954
Arthur W. Gregory, Jr. . 1951–1953
E. M. Kelley 1953–
Francis E. Mann 1953–
R. E. Young 1953–1956
Harry K. Haag 1954–1958
James F. Keating 1956–1959
James Wyper, Jr. 1956–1960
James F. Wyatt 1958–
John F. Gilmore 1959–
R. Channing Barlow . . . 1959–
Donald Day 1959–
Robert C. Hannah 1960–

Marine Secretaries

J. S. Gilbertson 1932–1946
C. L. Goldby 1932–1936

Secretary and Actuary

Harold C. Grossman . . . 1953–

Assistant General Counsels

Hale Anderson, Jr. . . . 1959–
Herbert P. Schoen 1959–

Assistant Secretaries

C. S. Timberlake 1929–1936
G. A. Russell 1929–1936
Charles S. Kremer . . . 1929–1936
John M. Holmes 1929–1936
A. W. Tyrol 1929–1936
Francis T. Fenn 1929–1941
W. S. Vanderbilt 1931–1941
Malcolm G. Wight . . . 1932–1936
George S. Atkinson . . . 1935–1941
Robert D. Morse 1935–1941

Philip S. Brown	. 1935–1941	Robert B. Dwyer 1958–
Arthur L. Polley . . .	. 1935–1941	Gordon W. Shand . . . 1958–1959
Elin Malmquist	. 1935–1955	Philip C. Loomis . . . 1958–
Barnard Flaxman . . .	. 1937–1944	Martin W. Davenport . . . 1958–
C. B. Edwards	. 1940–1952	George C. Munterich . . . 1959–
Burton B. Gracey . . .	. 1940–1944	J. Kenneth Cagney . . . 1959–
R. C. Chapin	. 1940–1944	Robert C. Hannah 1959–1960
C. F. C. Hutt	. 1940–1959	R. H. Kutteruf 1959–
G. A. Robinson	. 1940–1948	Thomas M. Meredith . . . 1959–
B. L. Whorf	. 1941–1942	B. T. E. Stoddart 1960–
W. T. Bissell	. 1942–1954	

Arthur W. Gregory, Jr. . . 1948–1951
Russell B. Barton . . . 1950–1954
Barton M. Douglas . . 1950–1958
E. M. Kelley 1950–1953
Francis E. Mann . . . 1950–1953
Harold Wilkinson . . . 1950–1960
R. E. Young 1950–1953
Harry K. Haag 1953–1954
James Wyper, Jr. . . . 1955–1956
Gertrude M. Schroeder . 1957–
Albert J. Hall 1958–
Alan D. Phillips . . . 1958–

Assistant Secretary and Actuary

Harold C. Grossman . . . 1951–1953

Assistant Treasurers

Wilfrid Platt 1951–
Thomas A. Shannon . . . 1960–
A. E. Tuller 1960–
Edward F. Lindeman . . . 1960–

Marine Assistant Secretary

Madoe M. Pease 1937–1944

NEW YORK UNDERWRITERS INSURANCE COMPANY

OFFICERS

Chairmen of the Board

Charles E. Chase 1925–1932
                 1933–1934
Charles S. Kremer 1953–1957

President and Chairman of Finance Committee

J. C. Hullett 1956–

Presidents

Richard M. Bissell . . . 1925–1941
Charles S. Kremer . . . 1941–1953
J. C. Hullett 1953–1956

Assistant to the President, and Vice President

Roland H. Lange 1958–

Financial Vice Presidents

W. A. Forrester, Jr. . . . 1949–1953
Barnard Flaxman 1953–

Executive Vice President

H. C. Davis 1953–

Vice Presidents

F. C. White 1925–1945
T. D. Richardson 1925–1937
R. M. Bennett 1925–1929
J. C. Stoddart 1929–1941
James L. Thomson . . . 1934–1959
R. L. Tanner 1937–1949
T. C. Taliaferro 1941–1949
R. S. Stoddart 1941–1956
J. C. Hullett 1945–1953
Harold C. Davis 1949–1953
Philip S. Brown 1954–
G. W. Owens 1956–
William H. Wallace . . . 1957–
John L. Barter 1959–
Addison C. Posey . . . 1959–
Frank C. McVicar . . . 1959–
M. R. Bigham 1959–

Vice President and General Counsel

Manning W. Heard . . . 1955–

Vice President, Secretary and Treasurer

R. E. Young 1956–

Vice President and Comptroller

Harry K. Haag 1958–

Vice Presidents and Secretaries

F. R. Scott 1949–1956
R. S. Stoddart 1956–
Brice M. Draper 1957–
Arthur W. Gregory, Jr. . . . 1958–

Assistant Vice President

Charles F. Nettleship, Jr. . 1959–

Assistant General Counsels

Hale Anderson, Jr. . . . 1959–
Herbert P. Schoen . . . 1959–

Secretaries

A. R. Stoddart 1925–1929
R. L. Tanner 1929–1937
Clyde P. Smith 1930–1947
T. C. Taliaferro 1937–1941
R. S. Stoddart 1937–1941
F. R. Scott 1937–1949
H. C. Davis 1941–1949
H. C. Klein 1941–1956
G. W. Owens 1942–1956
R. D. Morse 1945–1947
A. J. McDavid 1947–1957
Francis T. Fenn 1948–1956
Joseph Nelson 1954–1958
C. H. Avery 1954–1954
R. E. Young 1955–1956
James F. Keating 1956–
J. Stewart Johnston . . . 1956–
E. G. Bock 1956–
D. A. Kretschman 1956–
L. D. Ulrich 1957–1960
B. T. E. Stoddart 1957–
John F. Gilmore 1959–
Donald Day 1959–

Resident Secretary

C. E. Johnson 1957–

Secretary and Treasurer

D. J. Glazier 1925–1929

Treasurer

D. J. Glazier 1929–1936

Financial Secretaries

Arthur W. Gregory, Jr. . . . 1954–1958
James C. Parr 1956–

Secretary and Actuary

Harold C. Grossman . . . 1960–

Assistant Secretaries

R. L. Tanner 1926–1929
J. C. Stoddart 1926–1929
T. C. Taliaferro 1927–1937
F. R. Scott 1929–1937
R. S. Stoddart 1931–1937
Francis T. Fenn 1933–1948
Harold C. Davis 1935–1941
H. C. Klein 1936–1941
J. A. Reid 1936–1941
Barnard Flaxman 1938–1953
J. M. Holmes 1941–1946
R. D. Morse 1941–1945
J. O. Lummis 1941–1945
Joseph Nelson 1943–1954
C. H. Avery 1951–1954
E. G. Bock 1954–1956
D. A. Kretschman 1954–1956
B. T. E. Stoddart 1954–1957
L. D. Ulrich 1956–1957
Gertrude M. Schroeder . . 1957–
Dryden Small 1957–
Thomas Meredith 1959–

Assistant Treasurers

Thomas A. Shannon . . . 1960–
A. E. Tuller 1960–
Edward F. Lindeman . . . 1960–

TWIN CITY FIRE INSURANCE COMPANY

OFFICERS

Presidents

Richard M. Bissell . . . 1921–1941
Charles S. Kremer . . . 1941–1953
J. C. Hullett 1953–
  (and Chairman of Finance
  Committee 1960–

Assistant to the President, and Vice President

Roland H. Lange 1958–

Vice Presidents

Frederick C. White	1921–1945
John H. Griffin	1942–1944
C. W. Hall	1944–
J. C. Hullett	1945–1953
Roland H. Lange	1953–1958
Barnard Flaxman	1956–
Philip S. Brown	1960–
M. R. Bigham	1960–

Vice President and Manager

John H. Griffin	1927–1942

Vice President and General Counsel

Manning W. Heard	1960–

Vice President, Secretary and Treasurer

R. E. Young	1960–

Vice President and Comptroller

Harry K. Haag	1960–

Vice Presidents and Secretaries

Brice M. Draper	1958–
Arthur W. Gregory, Jr.	1960–

Vice Presidents and Treasurers

John H. Griffin	1921–1927
C. W. Hall	1933–1944

Assistant Vice Presidents

James C. Parr	1960–
Charles F. Nettleship, Jr.	1960–

Secretaries

William Walsh	1927–1928
William Collins	1928–1929
	1933–1934
L. B. Van de Wall	1934–1948
Michael Schweihs	1949–

Secretary and Underwriting Manager

William Walsh	1921–1927

Secretary and Treasurer

William Collins	1929–1933

Secretary and Actuary

Harold C. Grossman	1960–

Treasurers

William Collins	1927–1928
L. A. Lundquist	1946–1960

Treasurer and Assistant Secretary

Oscar J. Eastman	1944–1946

Assistant Secretaries

Benjamin Herberg	1921–1926
L. E. Larson	1926–1928
Oscar J. Eastman	1928–1944
L. B. Van de Wall	1928–1934
Clyde P. Smith	1931–1946
J. B. Berkvam	1933–1951
Frederic D. Weld	1945–
Francis T. Fenn	1946–1956
O. B. Jacobs	1946–1958
Neal E. Johnson	1948–1959
Roland H. Lange	1952–1954
R. E. Young	1956–1960
Kenneth J. Lilja	1958–

Assistant Secretary and Assistant Treasurer

C. W. Hall	1930–1933

Assistant Treasurers

A. W. Jones	1921–1928
J. B. Berkvam	1928–1933
L. A. Lundquist	1944–1946
W. J. Long	1951–

LONDON-CANADA INSURANCE COMPANY

OFFICERS

Presidents and Managing Directors

A. H. C. Carson	1921–1923
Peter A. McCallum	1923–1932
B. W. Ballard	1932–1950
H. Douglas Coo	1950–

Vice Presidents

F. D. Williams	1921–1923
B. W. Ballard	1924–1932
A. C. McMaster	1932–1933
A. R. Martin	1934–1954

Philip S. Brown	1954–

Financial Vice President

Barnard Flaxman	1957–

Secretaries

A. V. Stamper	1921–1951
G. G. Rivard	1951–1957
A. A. Milton	1958–

Assistant Manager

J. M. McFadyen	1956–

Financial Statements
of the Companies
As of The Sesquicentennial Year 1960

———•—•———

HARTFORD FIRE INSURANCE COMPANY
AND SUBSIDIARY COMPANIES
Consolidated Balance Sheet—December 31, 1959

ASSETS

Bonds	$ 579,109,272
Preferred and Guaranteed Stocks	59,138,771
Common Stocks	315,215,562
Cash, Real Estate and other assets	166,285,115
Total Assets	$1,119,748,720

LIABILITIES

Unearned Premiums	$ 291,273,505
Life Policies and Contracts	102,906,094
Losses and Loss Expense	278,417,618
Other Policyholders' Funds	779,541
Taxes	15,646,772
Other Liabilities	14,924,633
Dividends Payable to Stockholders	2,005,169
Security Valuation Reserve	2,392,567
Total Liabilities	$ 708,345,899
Minority Interest in Subsidiary Companies	$ 241,749
Capital	$ 26,735,590
Voluntary Reserve	155,000,000
Surplus	229,425,482
Policyholders' Surplus	$ 411,161,072
Total	$1,119,748,720

HARTFORD FIRE INSURANCE COMPANY

Balance Sheet—December 31, 1959

ASSETS

Bonds	$162,847,766
Preferred and Guaranteed Stocks	27,545,822
Common Stocks	378,503,722
Cash, Real Estate and other assets	51,951,936
Total Assets	$620,849,246

LIABILITIES

Unearned Premiums	$155,292,982
Losses and Loss Expense	36,016,201
Taxes	6,963,092
Other Liabilities	9,410,730
Dividends Payable	2,005,169
Total Liabilities	$209,688,174
Capital	$ 26,735,590
Voluntary Reserve	155,000,000
Surplus	229,425,482
Policyholders' Surplus	$411,161,072
Total	$620,849,246

HARTFORD ACCIDENT AND INDEMNITY COMPANY

Balance Sheet—December 31, 1959

ASSETS

Bonds	$320,462,597
Preferred and Guaranteed Stocks	24,979,659
Common Stocks	124,951,312
Cash, Real Estate and other assets	71,327,808
Total Assets	$541,721,376

LIABILITIES

Unearned Premiums	$124,762,873
Losses and Loss Expense	238,741,503
Taxes	7,330,592
Contingencies	1,000,000
Other Liabilities	3,694,499
Total Liabilities	$375,529,467
Capital	$ 10,000,000
Voluntary Reserve	57,000,000
Surplus	99,191,909
Policyholders' Surplus	$166,191,909
Total	$541,721,376

HARTFORD LIFE INSURANCE COMPANY
formerly
THE COLUMBIAN NATIONAL LIFE INSURANCE COMPANY
Balance Sheet—December 31, 1959

ASSETS

Bonds	$ 76,834,316
Preferred Stocks	2,456,560
Common Stocks	4,748,418
Mortgages	30,900,157
Cash, Real Estate and other assets	11,394,974
Total Assets	$126,334,425

LIABILITIES

Reserves

Policies	$ 95,287,429
Other Funds held for policyholders and beneficiaries	8,234,303
Policy Claims in process of settlement	940,693
Total Reserves	$104,462,425

Special Reserves

Company Retirement Plans	$ 1,225,967
Security Valuation Reserve	2,392,567
Total Special Reserves	$ 3,618,534
Total Other Liabilities	$ 1,623,158
Total Liabilities	$109,704,117
Additional Group Reserve	$ 415,659
Reserve for Contingencies	2,000,000
Capital	5,000,000
Unassigned Funds	9,214,649
Policyholders' Surplus	$ 16,630,308
Total	$126,334,425

HARTFORD LIVE STOCK INSURANCE COMPANY
Balance Sheet—December 31, 1959

ASSETS

Bonds	$1,732,128
Preferred and Guaranteed Stocks	897,210
Common Stocks	4,940,362
Cash, Real Estate and other assets	504,965
Total Assets	$8,074,665

LIABILITIES

Unearned Premiums	$ 548,994
Losses and Loss Expense	82,470
Taxes	144,000
Other Liabilities	13,436
Total Liabilities	$ 788,900
Capital	$ 500,000
Voluntary Reserve	2,400,000
Surplus	4,385,765
Policyholders' Surplus	$7,285,765
Total	$8,074,665

CITIZENS INSURANCE COMPANY OF NEW JERSEY

Balance Sheet—December 31, 1959

ASSETS

Bonds	$2,482,449
Preferred and Guaranteed Stocks	1,180,160
Common Stocks	4,976,225
Cash, Real Estate and other assets	219,903
Total Assets	$8,858,737

LIABILITIES

Unearned Premiums	$1,640,036
Losses and Loss Expense	374,881
Taxes	84,810
Other Liabilities	58,376
Total Liabilities	$2,158,103
Capital	$2,000,000
Voluntary Reserve	1,800,000
Surplus	2,900,634
Policyholders' Surplus	$6,700,634
Total	$8,858,737

NEW YORK UNDERWRITERS INSURANCE COMPANY

Balance Sheet—December 31, 1959

ASSETS

Bonds	$10,926,590
Preferred and Guaranteed Stocks	2,075,300
Common Stocks	11,433,708
Cash, Real Estate and other assets	660,935
Total Assets	$25,096,533

LIABILITIES

Unearned Premiums	$ 6,560,144
Losses and Loss Expense	1,499,526
Taxes	387,240
Other Liabilities	566,860
Total Liabilities	$ 9,013,770
Capital	$ 2,000,000
Voluntary Reserve	4,300,000
Surplus	9,782,763
Policyholders' Surplus	$16,082,763
Total	$25,096,533

TWIN CITY FIRE INSURANCE COMPANY

Balance Sheet—December 31, 1959

ASSETS

Bonds	$2,378,772
Preferred and Guaranteed Stocks	4,060
Common Stocks	4,368,837
Cash, Real Estate and other assets	376,235
Total Assets	$7,127,904

LIABILITIES

Unearned Premiums	$1,230,027
Losses and Loss Expense	281,160
Taxes	134,393
Other Liabilities	44,806
Total Liabilities	$1,690,386
Capital	$1,000,000
Voluntary Reserve	2,100,000
Surplus	2,337,518
Policyholders' Surplus	$5,437,518
Total	$7,127,904

LONDON-CANADA INSURANCE COMPANY

Balance Sheet—December 31, 1959

ASSETS

Bonds	$1,444,654
Common Stocks	295,800
Cash, Real Estate and other assets	308,305
Total Assets	$2,048,759

LIABILITIES

Unearned Premiums	$ 788,226
Losses and Loss Expense	319,719
Taxes	19,428
Other Liabilities	5,712
Total Liabilities	$1,133,085
Capital	$ 200,000
Surplus	715,674
Policyholders' Surplus	$ 915,674
Total	$2,048,759

INDEX